THE GUTFELD MONOLOGUES

CLASSIC RANTS FROM **THE FIVE**

GREG GUTFELD

Threshold Editions

NEW YORK   LONDON   TORONTO   SYDNEY   NEW DELHI

To Elena

Threshold Editions
An Imprint of Simon & Schuster, Inc.
1230 Avenue of the Americas
New York, NY 10020

First Threshold Editions hardcover edition July 2018

THRESHOLD EDITIONS and colophon are trademarks
of Simon & Schuster, Inc.

For information about special discounts for bulk purchases,
please contact Simon & Schuster Special Sales at 1-866-506-1949
or business@simonandschuster.com.

The Simon & Schuster Speakers Bureau can bring authors to your
live event. For more information, or to book an event, contact the
Simon & Schuster Speakers Bureau at 1-866-248-3049
or visit our website at www.simonspeakers.com.

Interior design by Paul Dippolito

Manufactured in the United States of America

1   3   5   7   9   10   8   6   4   2

Library of Congress Cataloging-in-Publication Data is available.

ISBN 978-1-5011-9072-8
ISBN 978-1-5011-9074-2 (ebook)

CONTENTS

PREFACE

The Mystery Behind My Failure

I've told this story before, but it's worth retelling on the printed page, because it's funny, revealing, and most important—it makes me look stupid.

It's election night, 2016—and I'm at work. It was supposed to be an easy lift. Donald Trump would concede the election around 9 p.m., I'd be home by 9:30, drinking wine, and would be drunk by midnight. You know, the average Tuesday.

That would not be the case. I was asked to do a second episode of *The Five* at eleven. (Can't remember the exact hour: It was a very foggy time.)

Around 4:30 or so I checked the *New York Times* election tracker, this neat little online gizmo that told us what chance Hillary had at winning. I think it was around 90 percent.

I checked that thing regularly, and it looked like things would only get worse for Trump.

When the first episode of *The Five* ended that day, I went to a nearby bar to eat and have *one* drink.

This bar had a doorman, a black immigrant who knew my face, but we had never met. As I made it past him, he asked me how the election looked. Quickly and robotically, I said, "Hillary's got it in the bag." I showed him the addictive little *New York Times* gizmo on my phone as proof.

To my surprise, his face changed. He appeared devastated. I am not exaggerating. The effect on him was *physical.*

"There is no hope for America," he said.

I was shocked. I hadn't expected that. It hit me that my own biases likely played a role in my reaction. I saw a person of color and assumed he'd be relieved by the news. I mean, how could an immigrant—a black one, no less—be this upset that Trump was going to lose?

I wasn't even close. He went on an angry diatribe about how awful the Clintons were (all crooks), and that America was blowing its last chance to save itself, and the world. He seemed inconsolable.

I went inside and ordered some overpriced appetizers. And *one* wine. (And believe me, I wanted more than one, at that point.)

Then weird stuff started to happen. I checked the election tracker, and it moved. But not in the direction I was expecting. Not a lot, mind you, but the likelihood of Hillary's victory was now around 80 percent (again my recollections are not exact, but I'm trying).

Then it dipped to the mid-70s. This couldn't be.

I went outside to vape.

The doorman asked me if I'd heard anything more, and I showed him the tracker that was still around the 70s, but moving south, little by little. I told him Hillary still had the win in her pocket.

Just then a pair of British tourists, a man and a woman, happened toward us. They were in their midfifties, but dressed like kids at a water theme park—long, wide shorts to ensure no chafing, fanny packs and backpacks, and folded touristy brochures.

The election was such a momentous event that strangers were talking to each other, so these Brits came up to us and asked us both who was going to win.

I said, "Looks like Hillary."

In a supreme gesture of virtue signaling, they jumped in the air, did a sloppy high five, and made audible whooping noises. Once they calmed down, they looked to the doorman as if expecting his approval at their glee. He only stared ahead with an expression as stony as those on Mount Rushmore. The couple seemed lost, then approached the menu on the bar's window.

The British dude ran his eyes down the list and looked up at the doorman and asked, "How's the food?"

Without missing a beat, he said, "Try Times Square," and pointed them down the road.

Their virtue signal had been rejected, and they left, miffed and certainly confused.

Now, I could mock them, but really I had just made that same mistake an hour or so ago, with the same guy.

And days ago; weeks ago, months, even.

Frankly, I can't remember how many times I dismissed benign, curious friends and strangers when they asked about Trump's chances. Cab and livery drivers, medical personnel, bouncers all asked me about Trump's chances, and I said, "none." And I assumed they would be relieved.

They never were. Most would go silent, then pitch a follow-up question, to see if I really knew what I was talking about. I continued to dismiss them.

A restaurant owner I knew would constantly intone, "Don't count him out," as if he knew something I didn't.

He did.

Some of these folks would go silent after hearing me, but one woman—an Eastern European immigrant performing a chest scan on me—proceeded to lecture me on how President Trump was the only chance America had. Again, I nodded, then ignored her.

Like the doorman.

I returned to the bar, and the election tracker had moved again. It was now maybe around 50 percent. The election could go either way. I felt unsettled. I hadn't expected this.

I emailed two coworkers (you don't know them).

Both told me the same thing: "This is normal, the rural areas who voted for Trump get counted early, but once they tabulate the city vote, Hillary will destroy him," or something to that effect.

They were talking to me the way I had talked to the doorman.

And it certainly *wasn't looking* like they were right. The tracker was now at 80 percent FOR Trump!!

Holy crap. This can't be real. What the hell is happening???? I thought. *If this is truly happening, we are in for a world of cognitive dissonance that might last four years.*

I got up from the bar, and walked outside and handed my iPhone to the doorman. "Looks like I spoke too soon," I said.

His countenance changed to relief. To joy. He then said he would pray for Mr. Trump.

I paid my bill, and headed to the office (after having only *one* wine).

By the time I was at HQ, those folks who had been so sure Hillary had it in the bag were in a daze. I include myself in this group.

I ran into an analyst who had told me Brexit was *not* a sign of the "silent voter," a variable that I had thought could predict Trump's win. Turns out he was wrong, and I was more wrong for believing him. (More on that later.)

So, what was I missing? And what was I missing on purpose?

What was the mystery behind my cluelessness? What had brought on my own failure to read the world correctly?

Well, I was primed to see the world incorrectly. My emotions tricked me—anger and glee, together.

First, my negative emotions clouded my judgment. I was angry at times (often incorrectly) at Trump's quips. His jokes became my triggers. I'll get into this later in the book, but I was damning Trump for some of the same things I do every day. Make jokes.

Second, there were online Trump fans (and bots) who harassed me and my friends for having criticized Trump. I also got regular grief on blogs where I would write—the comments sections became a teeming stew of invective. This made me more resolute in my anti-Trumpism.

Third, there were also Trump supporters I knew whom I couldn't bear. The more they slathered Trump with accolades, the more critical of the candidate I became. This was emotional, to me, and it influenced how I framed the election battle.

Now to the delusional effects of my positive emotions: I noticed that other people from the other side of the political spectrum were grateful for my criticism. This influences you, trust me. It made me feel good. I was getting rewarded for once by my ideological adversaries.

I became a victim of something I regularly mocked: the "strange new respect" syndrome (this was coined by the American Spectator decades ago). This occurs when you gain fans among the people who previously hated you—it's addictive: just a taste makes you want more because it's novel, hence "strange." To use a rough metaphor, your old political allies become your boring spouse, and the new fans are the alluring seducer.

So my view was emotionally tainted by strange new respect and a deep dislike for Trumpian online mobbery. This was no place for a person to make logical rational decisions, but there I was. And not alone.

Now (it's June 2018). I realize that I cannot let this kind of pernicious influence happen again. I vow never to let emotion cloud my judgment, and instead I promise to listen to everyone. And be willing to be wrong, any, or all of the time. Including now!

I've learned to be more skeptical than ever. Because if the *New*

York Times had an honest "Russia collusion" needle like that election tracker, it wouldn't have been at 90 six months ago, and perhaps at 20 as I write this. Who knows where it could be as you hold this book in your hands.

But seriously, I could be dead wrong right now. And you'll have to buy the next book for me to tell you that story.

INTRODUCTION

Now and Then, and
All the Crap in Between

It's a humbling experience to have written a book called *How to be Right*, and to then begin a new book by explaining how I got something wrong.

That something was, more precisely, the election of Donald Trump.

Granted, nearly every other living breathing human being got the 2016 election wrong. Hell, even Donald Trump himself wasn't planning on winning, according to some sources. But I assumed Hillary had it wrapped up—as did Hillary herself, judging by her lethargic behavior. Instead of hitting the places that mattered, she chose to nosh with the most elite, out-of-touch person of them all, Gwyneth Paltrow—which is the equivalent of making out with fruit bats during a rabies outbreak.

But yes, I was wrong on the election.

But oddly right about it, too. How is that possible?

First, because I'm the one writing the book here. When you write a book—it's absolutely amazing how right you can be, after the fact, about everything!

Note to young writers: The key to becoming a bestselling author is to never write something BEFORE something happens; always after. Good example: the Bible.

Second, I was exactly right on the issues that set the table for the most dramatic, surprising political story since Tracy Flick beat Paul Metzler by one vote at George Washington Carver High School in 1997. (Look it up.) For the past five to six years, on the hit television show *The Five*, I would deliver a monologue on the issue that I found most important on that particular day. In that monologue, I'd address why that issue was important, break it down, and offer, if not a solution, at least a new way to look at it—which is a solution in itself!

On rare occasions, I might have been wrong—but, like I said ten words ago—it was rare. Of course, hindsight is 20/20, a phrase I coined in the early 1970s.

My batting average was high, when you observe the repudiation of the previous eight years of governance before 2016. That repudiation was a reflection of the issues that I perceived as troubling during that period. I knew what was getting on the average American's nerves (besides me), and it was stuff that the rest of the media ignored. That was mainly due to the fact that I know what gets on people's nerves (for the most part, it's me).

Donald Trump watched Fox News—so he had a firsthand look at the same stuff I was yakking about. I'm not saying he cribbed from me—I'm saying we were both on the same page on a lot of stuff. Not on all stuff—but on some of the big stuff.

Now, some of this introduction is going to feel a little like déjà vu, especially since Trump's election may be the most revisited topic since the (alleged) moon landing.

But forgive me if we revisit it yet again.

Donald Trump's election was made possible by the willing disregard for the basic but important concerns of Americans.

And the points that I hit home from that corner seat in studio D (and later, studio F) were all the kinds of things Trump understood completely—which some of the other candidates gave a passing glance, or didn't hit hard enough. Stuff like terror, police, borders—these were issues that fell under the vision of "a return to law and order," and it was that vision Trump embraced and espoused like a Fox News guest host in waiting (a cross between Lou Dobbs and a Creamsicle). It was that vision that made it easy for voters to overlook his numerous flaws. As long as he was big on the big stuff, you forgave him the small stuff.

It also helped that he never claimed to be a role model. In fact, I think at some point he actually said, "I'm not a role model." Which gave him immunity when Playmates started appearing like Ghosts of Hotel Rooms Past, after he had already become president. Who cared at that point? He won. And he's a cad. Call me when you have something that might shock me (Trump sleeping with a porn star is as shocking as Mike Pence *not* sleeping with a porn star). Little-known fact: In New York City, it's actually *against* the law if a billionaire doesn't sleep with a porn star.

Law and order: the explanation for Trump's win. I know, I know—he's the "drain the swamp" guy! Well, not really. He was first and foremost the "aren't our cops the greatest" guy, followed by the "let's kill the terrorists and their families" guy, and of course, the very sloppy "send those rapists and murderers back" guy.

The biggest appeal of his candidacy—a return to appreciating law and order—played on three different levels.

- It delivered on the aspirations of a population who want a safer environment for their kids and their kids' kids.
- It echoed the fear that the country was headed in a direction of divisiveness and soon lawlessness, then anarchy. Fear always works, especially if there's a truth to it (and there still is).
- It delivered on a memory of the past—when you felt safer (even if you might not have been). And as a bonus, all the

cops and soldiers voted for him—which is always a clue about something vital that the chattering chuckleheads on CNN are missing.

These concerns were all but ignored by, and often mocked by, the media, liberal politicians, and their enablers in entertainment and academia. And it was the marginalization of such concerns by these groups that made the concerns grow larger. They were driven by these things:

A previous (but at the time current) president's weird aloofness over radical Islam (or was it aloof weirdness?—you be the judge, and get back to me).

The media's obsessive condemnation of law enforcement—an incident of brutality was no longer portrayed as a bug in the system, but as the system itself.

An academic elite and coddled, shrill activists perpetuating the "oppressor vs. oppressed" bunk at every opportunity.

An entertainment industry that harassed its dwindling audience by portraying anyone who wasn't a liberal as a bigot.

Inside this ideological bubble (which Trump helped burst), the media trampled around—happily unaware that its ideas were wearing out their welcome, like a hospital visit from Joy Behar. No one was buying their bullshit anymore—it just needed a loud voice to say so. I was saying it every day on *The Five*—but I wasn't running for president (that's for 2024, folks . . . and not the U.S. I'm thinking seriously about Vanuatu. Those folks really *get* me).

In nearly every instance, our country is at fault for everything bad that actually happens to our country. For example, when our cops got shot in Dallas, the media did its due genuflection, but always steered the story back to an intolerant police state that contributed to the shooting. Sure, illegal immigration is bad—but that's our fault for demanding a border and being so mean to Dreamers. North Korea says it wants to blow us to bits? Well, that's our fault for calling their leader a silly (but highly sticky) name.

This is a pattern—open your eyes and you'll see it: Instead of calling out all forms of evil (from terrorists to violent felons), we use our past sins to absolve them of everything wrong they have done.

Over time this malignant idea expanded and bloated (like Harvey Weinstein in his Caverject period), casting a shadow over our country—just waiting for someone to come along and pop it. Like it or not, the guy with the pin was Trump.

The pin was a vision based on common observations about the world that rational people could all agree with:

- That law enforcement was getting a bad rap, and without them we'd be nowhere.
- That Islamic terror is an actual thing, and if you can't name it, you're sunk.
- That our military is overworked and undervalued and requires our very best care.
- That a porous border reflects a shrinking appreciation of the definition of American citizenry.
- That the Clintons should just go away. They'd become that piss-stained old frat buddy who just won't stop doing shots, even into his depressing thirties. Believe me, I know these people. Actually, I've worked with these people. Hillary is the patch of stale carpeting in the basement that absorbed all the spills around it, and yet it never actually gets dumped—it just gets moved around to another part of the room. She is the worst hire you ever made, and one you cannot fire because

she's a friend of the family. She's the Democratic Party's ex—the ex who won't let you move on, because she has nowhere to move on to, either.

Now when average citizens (I count myself as three-fourths of one) hear this, they like what they hear.

I presented these topics daily. Because I liked hearing myself say it, too! But there weren't a lot of people voicing this stuff—just me, and a few others who were slightly taller than me, if not as charming. I can count them on a three-fingered hand. Then came Trump, who took the topics of a cable news show and made them into a visionary plank that carried him to the White House.

Now when leftists and the media (one and the same usually, but they'll deny it) saw this powerful message coming at them, their instinct was to place it in historical context. "Yep, we've seen this before!" they would scream, pointing to past racists who ran on similar concepts (studiously avoiding all the racist Democrats, naturally). They fashioned a filter of intolerance—claiming that everything Trump said was a "dog whistle," a secret noise that only bigots could hear, and nodding at each other in glee. But the irony is that the only ones who heard these dog whistles were leftists and Trump critics. They could identify the racism, alerted by the secret whistles. Which raises the question: How aren't *you* the racist, if you hear the whistle and we can't? Why is it that only the antiracists who accuse people of being racist can hear the racist clarion call?

(Interestingly, I can hear A-ha's "Take on Me" when no one else can—but what does that prove? That I am mentally ill.)

Trump critics weren't just on the left, of course—there were many on the right, precisely because we had so many candidates in the running. I counted myself as one of those critics. Although I knew Trump and liked him, he was not my first, second, or third choice because I foolishly thought he had no chance. A man who took too many verbal risks would end up falling flat on his face, sooner or later—and it would just take too much effort trying to explain to everyone that he was just kidding. I didn't want that role—I wanted a president who explained my aspirations, not the reverse. I liked Rubio—he seems pretty sharp and articulate, and wouldn't mess up in major ways. Though the Clinton camp expected Jeb would be their opponent, they seemed to think Rubio was their biggest challenge. He scared them the most (I believe it was the dreamy eyes and that he also owned a boat), so that was going to be my guy. I was wrong. But more than wrong, I was also a hypocrite.

Trump was a challenge to people like me who required the "liberal vs. conservative" construct to see life clearly, and to also benefit our lives, and careers. I identify as a conservative libertarian (or a conservatarian, if you wish an exact label)—which was nearly impossible to square with Trump's positions on trade and immigration. I'm for free trade and believe healthy immigration is good for a growing economy. But what I noticed was that Trump wasn't so much setting policy as he was setting the table for policy. He was taking strong, extreme positions, so down the line, more moderate positions could be negotiated and embraced.

I also noticed that his positions weren't jarring just the right, but also the left. They were looking at what Trump was saying and liked what they saw. I met a (mercifully) few Sanders supporters who favored Trump over Hillary (probably on the stands I liked least about Trump).

It slowly dawned on me that it was no longer about left or right, but about who could win. Still, I assumed anyone could do better, but looking back, I'm not so sure.

The bull (Trump) in the china shop (traditional ideological boundaries) made it impossible for anyone to get solid footing anymore. It was his overarching message that reached Americans beyond any ideology. No one cared about the litmus test anymore. We were all slipping around, grasping at straws, as the ground sank beneath us. The upside: We survived, Kathy Griffin didn't. This election broke people, but it also broke the lightweights who placed more emphasis on emotionalism than on fact. You saw them wilt, scream, and implode all around. At certain times, I was definitely one of them.

Trump was a strange orange meteor that hit Earth and only took out those who couldn't take a joke.

How weird is it that so many of his victims were comedians!

This brings me to my Sherlock Holmes Infuriation Trump Theory (or SHITT). You remember Sherlock and his work wife, Dr. Watson? Whenever they came across a startling event, Dr. Watson was always expressing anger, glee, passion, or frustration. He was an emotional mess. Then Sherlock waltzed in and crapped all over Watson, with pure rational analysis. Watson would say, "Sherlock, I'm in love with the most perfect woman alive! I think I shall propose!" And Sherlock would respond, "My dear Watson, that lass you are smitten with is no woman at all, but a store mannequin in the front window of Aunt Elena's bridal shop. She is nothing but a collection of woven straw and plaster."

Watson would say, "My God, Sherlock, how did I miss this?"

And Sherlock would respond, "It is what you wanted to see, my dear, perverted Watson. It's what we call, in scientific circles, confirmation bias."

A lot of good books have been written about the rational gifts of Sherlock. He's the slow-thinking tabulator of reason, and Watson is the emotive chap who feels stupid after Sherlock smacks him harshly with facts.

So what's my theory? Oh yeah.

My theory: Our media, when it comes to Trump, are *all* Dr. Watsons. There isn't a Sherlock among them. All reactionary, impulsive, emotional, and rash. Whenever he does anything, they react with shock and surprise—as if they've never experienced someone who likes to screw with you.

Except for me. I'm a Holmes. At least, now I am. If you remember me during the primaries I was very much a Watson—repeatedly saying, "Oh my God, I can't believe Trump said that! Holy crap, did he really do that??? Jesus, I can't believe he ate that!"

I wasn't the only one. But every day I was "Dr. Watsoning" everything (I'm sure a few of you were doing the same thing, too). During the debates, I used to yell at the TV, "He's our only choice for president!" Then *on* TV I'd scream, "He can't be our only choice for president!" I was a total mess.

But then, I stopped. I pulled a Rachel Dolezal and changed my identity from a Watson to a Holmes. So how did I move from the emotional to the rational?

First, I cut Trump a break. I stepped back, rationally, and assessed, slowly, the entire context of his life.

First, he's a billionaire, and a seventy-year-old man. Meaning, he doesn't give a rat's ass anymore about anything other than what matters. He's lived a wild life already—so he doesn't care who his casual comments offend. When he makes a joke it's like when a baby farts. It's nothing personal, the baby's forgotten it, while everyone is choking out in the room.

But the baby doesn't care.

I also had to admit that he's never been in public office, so he doesn't know how to be that particular kind of phony. I mean the phony that we all accept—which I call the "mandatory fake." The mandatory fake is the married news anchor who condemns unseemly sexual behavior while banging Dalmatians in a nearby hotel.

Being an old rich uncle who's never been in politics, Trump has no familiarity with mandatory fake. There is, however, a different kind of fakery in Trump's world of real estate fibbery. But such lies—salesman's lies—are deliberately obvious by their excess.

You know a salesman is lying when he tells you the car you're buying from him was only driven by a little old lady once a week to church, which is great because she lives in the attic above the church! A salesman's lie is done with a wink and an exaggeration ("This is the biggest crowd ever!"). A politician's lie is a promise that could very well be true, but never is ("Read my lips, no new taxes"). You see the difference? Trump's lies are common and do not insult us, because he assumes we're all in on the joke. Politicians are daring you to go against your own innate skepticism (which is always a mistake). Am I "Trump-splaining"? Yes, I am. For now that he's our president and up against so much, it's no longer fealty to do so. It's actually fairness.

Anyway, as a Holmes, I've since reevaluated some positions that I've taken for granted. I've looked at the research on illegal immigration and its effects on unemployment. I've also looked harder at crime numbers, legal vs. illegal offenders. I've pretty much stuck to my original precepts, but I realize that ideology ultimately helps no one in that debate.

What helps is an ability to talk about all things, an ability to be flexible, to adhere to a greater vision that is centered on security—security from criminals, terrorism, suffering in general.

That vision won.

Pot, Kettle, Black

Yes, I was a hypocrite—and I will point this out in many parts of the book, later on. My hypocrisy lies in the assumption that as a TV host I can make silly jokes and petty asides in speeches, insult the looks of adversaries, and in general stir up shit—but a presidential candidate cannot!

This is inherently wrong, I realized, after some thorough self-examination. I asked myself a simple question: If I had run for president myself, would I have changed the way I express myself? Would I have stopped making jokes and delivering insults? Of course not. I would have done pretty much the same thing as Trump. I would have said outlandish things—joking, of course—which the media then would recast as something said in all seriousness, as immoral, as the product of an evil mind. (Mind you, this is something I noticed among many talking heads: After Trump ran, they all wondered if they should have, too. One such host even said to me with a hint of hurt in his voice, "I should have run. Why didn't I?" Sorry, Lou Dobbs. You would've been a *fine* president.)

Now there are some things I would not have done—such as mock a reporter's disability. But as it turns out, Donald Trump didn't do that either—it only *looked* that way. I assumed initially that Trump was a heartless prick, but then I saw a segment by the great John Stossel on his FBN show. Stossel—no fan of Trump by any stretch—showed other examples of Trump using the same body language when mocking a critic or competitor (one of them being Ted Cruz, who has no visible disability). The conclusion: Trump was mocking a reporter, but not the reporter's disability. And yeah, it was juvenile, but was it hopelessly cruel, as we the media had originally thought? No. It just goes to show you that Trump can be a dick to everyone: He's blind to race, creed, or disability. In a weird way, he might be the most egalitarian politician around, because he'll tease a three-legged dog, if given the chance. Because he *doesn't see* the three-legged dog.

He just sees a dog.

As you can see, it takes a lot to defend Trump. And it raises the question: Given the mountain to climb, why should you? That's a lot of work. And that was my point about Trump. It takes a lot of sweat to explain the guy—so he makes it hard on you. And the rewards might not be commensurate to the effort put into it. I mean, he could lose!!! Defending Trump is, in many ways, a long drive for a short day at the beach. And during that drive, people are pelting you with hot coals.

Having to parse exactly how your guy was using a gesture to mock the meltdown of an adversary is a big burden. And with Trump, a swamp-draining bare-knuckled bowl of sherbet with a colorful past, such burdens are an everyday thing. When you're in a situation where you have to say, "No, he was just imitating a convulsion, not a disabled reporter," you're losing.

And yet, he still won.

I remember complaining to Ric Grenell—a top Republican analyst at the time, now he's ambassador to Germany—speaking about having to always assess and defend a candidate's flubs. His response was simply: "Go ahead, then, Gutfeld, you run. If you're the better candidate, then do it. Fact is, everyone needs explaining. Everyone."

It struck me: He's probably right. Even if I ran—perfect little me—my supporters would have to explain a lot of crap about me, too.

But Trump was tops on the big picture, so the other stuff was forgiven. It's like Paul McCartney. He wrote "Yesterday" and "Hey Jude." So who can hold "The Girl Is Mine" against him? Or that his hair is now actually more orange than Donald's?

One such thing I really couldn't forgive—until I recalibrated the context—was Trump's joke about John McCain's military service. If you remember, he joked that McCain, a POW for many years, wasn't a war hero—because heroes don't get caught. It was an absurd, idiotic comment—if you're taking it seriously. But as a joke, well, it's pretty funny in a "not supposed to be funny" sort of way. Larry David made a career out of this (check out the episodes when he refuses to say "Thank you for your service" to a veteran, or "*Namaste*" after yoga class).

I realized that most of Trump's performances are performances. He's like a rock band doing the classics. "Build the wall" is his "Free Bird," and "Lock her up" is his "Stairway to Heaven"—and they are fashioned less for debates and press conferences, and more for Friars Club roasts. So my view of these comments changed. I imagined Trump making that joke at a roast for John McCain. Shocking, blunt, and absurd—maybe even McCain would have laughed. Trump's jokes operate on the absurdity of their, well, absurdity!

However, I probably wouldn't have made that joke. (And it turns out that Chris Rock made the same joke years before!) Because I don't want to take the heat. And as for Trump—is there any heat that he can't take? He can't be fired.

But I would also have judged the venue and the crowd. Which Trump seems to have little time for. But then again, I wonder—have I ever done worse? And I think maybe in speeches I have made jokes about people that were crude and sometimes cruel. I once told Dana Perino that I would eat her dog Jasper. It gets no crueler than that.

So, by making this observation, am I lowering the bar for becoming president? No, I am removing the bar altogether.

Trump is able to get 60-plus-million people to overlook his unseemly comments, his taunts and impulsiveness, because he was exactly right on the big picture. Sure, he colored outside the circle at times, but at least he picked the right circle.

Whenever I'm confused over my feelings about Trump, I think of two people: my mom, who died four years ago, and Andrew Breitbart, who died six years ago.

They're the only people I can reliably hear in my head, without having them present. I know for a fact that . . .

Both of them would KNOW exactly what Trump is. He's a mercurial, brawling bastard.

But after all their complaints, they would find him absolutely hilarious. If both were alive today, we'd be on the phone every afternoon recounting the day's events amid heaving bouts of laughter.

If Trump is making my mom laugh right now, and making Andrew smile, then frankly he's okay with me. Their memories have reminded me how to take Donald Trump: with a grain of glorious, hilarious salt.

Where Are We Now?

The funny thing is, for a while I thought Trump was going to win. Then I made the terrible error of talking to an "expert," an analyst. My gut told me that the success of Brexit predicted a Trump victory. I told this to a polling "expert" (again, I misuse quotes) who said, condescendingly, "Greg, referendums are not elections." Well, pumpkinhead, thanks for clearing that up. When I then asked, roughly, "Aren't they similar in that polls may not reveal a voter's intentions, if their vote is roundly criticized by the media? And since they remained quiet about their true voting choice, the other side saw no need to show up." The analyst said, and I quote, "Shut up already about Brexit!" And you know what? I did shut up.

My personal response to Trump—at home, among friends, watching debates—was "*This* was the *man*." But at work, it became "He has no chance."

And it was because I foolishly let an expert tell me my gut was wrong. I regret that foolishness to this day.

But now let's jump ahead. . . .

It's May 2018, and cable channels are gorging on Stormy Daniels, Mueller, and collusion. Meanwhile, what's missing from the news feed? ISIS videos. Remember those? They scarred our retinas weekly. They are *gone* (for now). Remember the North Korean nuclear holocaust? Just months ago, we were going to die! C'mon, remember the false alarm in Hawaii! *GONE.* So, what were previously considered existential concerns have vanished under Trump. And the media response? Porn and Russia.

They've turned a distraction into a disaster, because they had no other options in reporting on Trump. They were simply unprepared to report on a successful presidency. It was not in their bitter, infantile tool kit. What was in that bag of junk: rumors, gossip, porn stars, collusion. Their careers are now predicated on squalid distractions that serve only to undermine a president.

And it's a president in the midst of a good—no, great—run. It's my warning to Dems and the media: If your goal is impeachment, history and the public will not be kind to you. Both will view your actions as an emotionally driven exercise done to unseat a president as he solves a major world crisis. My gut tells me: The more desperate they get, the better Trump does.

It's crazy and absurd that as major, earth-changing events are occurring with a major existential nuclear threat—North Korea—networks are devoting a majority of airtime to a tryst with a porn star that happened years ago. (This obsession from a group of enlightened individuals who never thought sex was a big deal when their guy did it.) They overlook the possibility that if you asked the world if you'd be okay with a cad if he solves world peace, the world would say "Cool." And that only someone as "out of the box" as Trump could have opened the door for this majestic development. It's still too soon to tell where this is going, but give the guy some credit—please—for something no one else has done.

So What the Hell Is This Book For?

Since I started my steady, profoundly bizarre TV career at FNC eleven years ago, the only real thing that people know me for, besides my delightful blue eyes, is my prickly, persuasive monologues. Wherever I go—shopping, commuting, windsurfing nude—I am hit repeatedly by the same question: What's Kimberly Guilfoyle's address—and where can I read your monologues? I've tried to find them myself, and frankly the world is too vast, confusing, and chaotic for even me to look up my most awesome crap. Also, I'm no good with technology. These kids and their computers! I tell the cops: The video with the donkey came with the phone when I bought it!

So that's where the idea of this book came from: loads of people telling me to do this damn book.

How can I track down all these monologues? After all, I'm a busy guy with lots of hobbies (basically I sit home in a bathtub and read Dilbert). Then I came up with an answer! Hire someone to do it for me! One of these millennial thingies everyone is talking about. Then when "Sean" finds all my monologues, I'll go through them and pick my favorites!

But this book will be more than your usual run-of-the-mill anthology. Because unlike most anthologies, for this one I've found the original work and feverishly improved on it. I've updated, edited, and updated some more. The monologues are still there, but now they're steroidal. (Note: I didn't change any monologue to make a wrong prediction appear correct in retrospect—that would be an immoral act, and I don't need more of those in my life. But I did cut out any stuff that appeared garbled in transcription.)

My monologues are designed to do one thing: tackle one subject clearly and concisely. Whereas most essays take their time, mine cut in line and grab you by the scruff and say, "You must hear this now!"

Like me, they are short, straight, and usually done in under eighty-five seconds.

They don't mess about. They tackle a subject—whether it be Trump, Obama, drugs, guns, crime, race, terrorism, feminism, progressivism, or pandas—in under a few hundred words, and they do it in a way that makes sense of the world, so you don't have to.

My goal is to do the thoughtful thinking early in the morning, and deliver it to you like a philosophical Domino's—so you can get on to other important things (like buying my books or sending me pastries shaped like a unicorn's head).

When I write monologues, my goal is to make politics bite-size and delicious. I think of Mitch McConnell and Nancy Pelosi as Milk Duds. And Steve Bannon is a Circus Peanut left out in the sun on a minivan dashboard.

It's not enough to complain about how bad something is, you've got to make it fun, smart, and persuasive. One thing I've learned in my tumultuous life: The left is great at selling bad ideas; the right is awful at selling good ideas. My monologues are an attempt to help the right have a fighting chance in the battle-field of ideas. (Yes, that's a bit Napoleonic—but heightwise, I am sort of qualified, no?)

My goal in these monologues is to be funny and clear—not angry and bitter. Mad, after all, is short for "madness." So I look for ways to deal with a topic that I might try to articulate at a bar, to a friend (were I to have one). I want it to be memorable—and the only way to do that, in my mind, is to make it relatable.

Hence, this awesome book.

If you're a regular viewer of *The Five* and *The Greg Gutfeld Show*, these should sound wonderfully familiar. However, they should also sound amazingly new, for I've drenched the monologues in additional material and personal afterthoughts—marinating them in my toasty brain pan and augmenting the original material with stuff I wish I had said, or explanatory material that's necessary now that the monologues are without all those lovely accompanying television visuals. It's like discovering your favorite album remixed by someone who might be on mushrooms.

On *The Five*, I took aim at progressive politics, as well as the members of the left-wing media, academia, and entertainment industry who push such inane politics. My recurring themes?

- Obama catered to the antipolice sentiment.
- The Democrats champion bureaucracy over the individual— a bureaucracy could therefore be well armed and protected; not so much the individual.
- The Dems, including Hillary, championed the group over the individual—identity over the kind of rugged individualism that made us ALL Americans.
- Obama championed issues du jour of his fellow liberals (such as climate change) while belittling the fear of terror (he might tell you that you're more likely to get struck by lightning— leaving out the fact that lightning does not plan night and day to kill you—the way al Qaeda, ISIS, and tequila do).

So after many requests, I finally decided to gather up the best monologues and put them together in this fat, glorious book. However, I realized this job isn't as easy as I expected it to be. In fact, it was brutally hard. First, out of a thousand-plus monologues, I had to pick the very best two hundred—which is like choosing your favorite two hundred children from a thousand (I imagine this is how Genghis Khan and Kirk Douglas must have felt).

But beyond even that, I was faced with some scary propositions! What if the monologues didn't hold up over time? What if times have changed so abruptly and monumentally that today makes a fool of yesterday's perspective? (Right now I am deleting all the monologues on what a great president Martin O'Malley would be.)

What if people I harshly criticize are now dead? Would it be fair or right to include those?

Well, yes and no.

See, I needed a solution that went beyond packaging these monologues willy-nilly (an underused word, if you ask me). I needed to point out where my monologues proved prescient or idiotic. (So far that ratio is about 75/25.)

So, I'm not going to make it easy on myself. In fact, this kind of book is actually way harder than simply writing a fresh book about the current political landscape. Instead, I'm reading a book and writing one at the same time—marking my words as an editor might. I am you, trying to make sense of me—a job I wouldn't wish on anyone.

So, that's the book. I've broken down the topics into their own chapters and put the monologues in chronological order. I'm trying to make it as easy as possible to follow, even as I make it as confusing as possible to read.

But in doing so, I've stumbled back into a realization I made during the 2016 election season. And it's one that should be a topic for my next book—that the confusion, anger, and disbelief from the last five years are the result of the death of ideology. The conservative vs. liberal paradigm crumbled—seemingly on both sides. Trump's entrance helped create this dissolution. His past of floating above both political parties—switching allegiances, playing off the expectations and greed of both sides—led to a present candidate who had little time for the old game of ideology. He just wanted to win. He's the guy who didn't get the memo. There was no right, left, Republican or Democrat. You could be anything, at any time, as long as you were persuasive, brutal, and funny. Only a creature like this could be so audacious to think he could destroy ISIS *and* solve North Korea. No typical politician could be this crazy . . . and this savvy. Or so willing to try anything.

So, in short, this is not your grandmother's anthology. Hell, it's not even your step-great-uncle-who-sells-meth-under-a-bridge anthology.

This is the first anthology in which the writer picks apart his own work, and admits when it works and when it sucks.

But this was a weird process. The transcriptions culled for these monologues were sometimes muddled. At some point, I couldn't make heads or tails of the things I was purported to have said. There's a section where the transcript claims I say, near the end of a monologue, that "it sucks balls." If I truly said that, I would have been sent home for a month without pay (now, it could be that I was, and I don't remember!). So forgive me, I used a little artistic license when cobbling these "Gregalogues" together. Sometimes it's impossible to get anything word for word. I either smoothed something over that seemed confusing or eliminated some car crash of words that made my head hurt every time I tried to type it out on these pages.

So, with that, I say good luck and enjoy!

CHAPTER ONE

IDENTITY POLITICS

If there's one issue that sank the Democratic Party, it was identity politics. It permeated everything they did—the idea that the person matters less than the group. Even as I write this now, identity politics is still spreading its venom all over the world. Wherever there is fun, identity politics shows up to ruin it. It's an antifun fire hose. It's cancer of the funny bone.

Consider how identity politics destroyed all the traditional fun to be had at an NFL game.

Colin Kaepernick taking a knee during the National Anthem may be textbook identity politics—driven by a desire to achieve a temporary sugar rush of progressive respect from the virtue-signaling vultures in the media. By injecting identity politics into what normally would be a Sunday afternoon three-hour scoop of fun, he poisoned the entire sport with a divisive toxin one normally experiences on noisy campus quads. And that led to a massive backlash that Trump capitalized on. If Colin really was pissed about the cops (especially those who protect him daily), he could have just picketed a police station. But that never would have gotten him prime real estate on the cover of *GQ*. I'll paraphrase what I said on *The Five*—turning on football to find a political statement would be like turning on *The Five* and finding us playing badminton.

Identity politics didn't infect only sports. Look at what it did to the entertainment industry. You can't watch award shows without being lectured by Hollywood on gender and race. Meanwhile, as they lecture you, they turn a blind eye to assorted sex pests in their midst—or standing at the lectern with them. Yes, the #MeToo movement has finally made them look inward, to a degree, but only because they were finally forced to. And imagine this irony: If Hillary had become president, do you think we would have heard about her greatest supporter, Harvey Weinstein? Fact is, the only reason Hollywood started publicly paying penance for its perversion is because finally the spotlight was on it. You become noble once the options for alternatives disappear.

Look at any college campus: Identity politics has irreparably damaged academia. If you're not part of the aggrieved group of the month, chances are you're going to be made uncomfortable at least three times a day. If you do not apologize for being born who you are, God help you.

If you're invited to speak at a college, and you're not a vetted social justice warrior, good luck getting a word in edgewise, as mobs of misery merchants will chant for your silence, likely on their mommy and daddy's (and the taxpayer's) dime. Worse, they will advocate violence in order to silence. Speeches by Ben Shapiro (a fairly polite kid, if you ask me) now require hundreds of thousands of dollars' worth of security to maintain his safety.

College used to be an education soaked in beer; now it's indoctrination drenched in fear. The cult is identity politics, and it's bloomed into a full-time religion, complete with sins, indulgences, high priestesses, and punishments.

No one is safe from identity politics—including those who push it themselves. See the Democratic Party as it devours its own. Meanwhile, Hillary ran on identity and little else.

Hence, she lost. She treated everyone else the way she treated the help, and depended on her chromosomal makeup to carry the day. It didn't. Now her party reviles her. They detest her. She rigged the damn thing, then she lost. As I used to say when I played Monopoly in juvenile detention (up until 2015, actually), if you're going to cheat, you better win. She couldn't even do that. What a ferocious loser. She screwed her party the way her husband screwed the intern—without a local path of egress. And now her party is devouring her, like an idiot cannibal gnawing on his own gangrenous foot.

Identity politics, like water, flows in the path of least resistance. Which is why, if you don't fight back, you'll likely drown.

> **Note to Readers: This is where the Monologues start. Forgive me if I interrupt here and there. I get as bored as you do.**

January 13, 2014

In a new essay, Hillary Clinton claims that America doesn't do enough for women. Translation, America doesn't do enough for Hillary. And you can fix that by electing her. It's a smart but predictable move.

In 2007, she was the most qualified Democrat for president, and she got tossed aside for a little-known grad student with a résumé thinner than Kate Moss's septum.

> **I take back that "smart" part.**

So, why was she dumped like an aging first wife for a younger model?

> **In the spirit of equality, I would like to replace that metaphor with "Brian Stelter's hair."**

Well, in the highly competitive world of identity politics, black trumps female. Voting for Obama became historical instead of hysterical.

So, Hillary realizes for her to win now, what was once about color must now be about chromosomes. A vote for her is a vote for all women. And even better, criticism of Hillary will now be viewed as sexist, the way criticism of Obama was seen as racist.

> Maybe Hillary should've claimed to be part Cherokee, too? The car, not the nation.

But if she claims America doesn't help women, then what country does?

Holy crap—did I call this one or what? Let's review this. I stated that:

- Hillary would run primarily—or rather, only, as a woman.
- If you denied her the right to be president, you denied her this on the basis of gender.
- Therefore she really didn't have to try to win your vote. Instead you had to win immunity against accusations of sexism by voting for her.
- That's how you got Trump! Sure, a lot of women voted for Hillary, but a lot of women voted for Trump, too— women who had previously voted for Obama—and in places that mattered more.

October 28, 2014

Right now, America is a barroom brawl, populated by exhausted drunks, tearing each other to pieces. Why are they fighting? All we know is the bar is trashed and it's time to stop, shake hands, and clean the damn place up. That's the endpoint of identity politics, an emotionally charged, bitterly driven ideology that operates solely on anger and retribution. For if one identity must be pursued, another must be accused. But what has this pernicious behavior brought?

A torn, distracted, angry country. We are that ruined bar, with our enemies outside laughing at our internal turmoil. Strange that it's Bill Clinton echoing this sentiment, at the human rights campaign dinner on Saturday. Behold his majesty. . . . "I believe in ways large and small, peaceful and sometimes violent, that the biggest threat to our future children and grandchildren is the poison of identity politics that preaches that our differences are far more important than our common humanity."

> He really said this! If Hillary hadn't hated him already . . .

That is amazing—and from a member of the party that mastered identity warfare. This is their sport.

I suppose the good news is that in a world besieged by division, even some liberals are tapped out. Perhaps they realize that obsession with race and gender has made this country more obsessed with race and gender.

Identity, once reflected by achievement, has now assumed cultish malice.

The result: misconduct, masked as empowerment.

Now, perhaps Bill is saying all this stuff for the benefit of Hillary.

> Meaning, he gets to be the bad cop, the sober adult in the face of juvenile rantings of identity finger-pointing that Hillary indulges, but really doesn't mean.

It's clever that he's condemning a practice still extolled by Sharpton, Holder, and Jarrett, all White House darlings. But I don't care, I'm so desperate for a new patriotism, a happier union based on the American idea, that I don't care who's with me, even Bill.

Although I'm not touching the cigars.

Yes, a cheap joke at Bill's expense—but I'm allowed this, since I spent the previous paragraphs praising him. And also, if the Clintons won't go away, Bill's "indiscretions" remain fair game. By the way, "Indiscretions" should be the name of his boat, if he ever chooses to have one. And he should. Something about the idea of having Bill adrift in international waters surrounded by jaded supermodels puts me at ease.

October 29, 2014

In the *Washington Post*, a dad explains why he isn't paying for his kids' college. He says it's better to teach them the value of work, which then teaches them about money while also pointing them toward professions that they might like. It makes sense: College doesn't corner the market in education.

Did I learn anything there? I'm not sure. I was drunk.

It's true. I don't remember much from Berkeley, other than how little I remember. I'm not even sure I went to college. Actually, that's a copout. I remember college. And I remember how I really missed out on an opportunity to actually learn stuff. Remember that line by Oscar Wilde—that "youth is wasted on the young"? I'm beginning to think education is wasted on the young. Or at least, a young me.

That's my point. You should help your kid figure out what he loves, because all college teaches him to love, is college. Four years of fooling around, stumbling home drunk—what's not to love? I loved it so much, I did it until I was forty.

Worse: College teaches you to love yourself. Take the current novelty of identity as achievement, which values "being" instead of "doing." A shtick on the self—college becomes therapy that champions internal infatuation. The result: self-righteousness that's inversely proportional to one's own naïveté.

No longer an incubator of ideas, the classroom becomes an impenetrable bubble where only the mold of grievance grows. Real-life experience, which brings you into contact with actual real people, matters not at all.

> The same thing happens when a young actor becomes politically relevant in Hollywood. The self-righteousness masks his ignorance.

But we know that real work leads to true independence, not this phony rebellion advocated by pierced TAs. We used to call it the school of hard knocks. It is the lost art of self-reliance. If we bring that back, we might rescue this country from the incubated elite currently in charge.

We better do it fast: Their diapers are full.

> That was written nearly four years ago. Has it gotten worse? I can safely say, yes it has. Fact is, who would have predicted that speaking your mind is now considered hate speech on a college campus? Well, I guess I did. I guess my honorary PhD from Berkeley is lost in the mail? At least I still have my BA degree, although I think I left it somewhere in a bar along with my pants.

March 20, 2015

Gender, race, and climate, behold, the three horsemen of the liberal apocalypse, designed not to start a national conversation, but to stop a real one.

> I always wonder—do we really want a "national conversation"? Perhaps we actually prefer to have a nonconversation, as a way to express our opinions without having the headache of defending them. We used to go to the corner bar and unload on the stranger next to us. Now we can just find people just like us, who will nod in agreement. This is happening on both sides. And, of course, my side is right.

With race, if you don't agree that we are a racist country then you are a bigot, and therefore, you are evil.

With gender, if you don't see the patriarchal victimization of all women, you are a sexist and likely evil.

If you question faulty climate models, you are a denier, a smear that puts you on par with Holocaust deniers. This crud persists due to an endless supply of enablers churning out tripe from their purchase in the media, teachers' lounges, and soundstages.

The good news is that the evil arts of division are imploding into parody as America mocks campus shirkers and race-baiting charlatans. The joke is on the left when all that is left is identity politics. So how do you kill off horsemen once and for all?

> Okay, kids, this is where the big suggestion comes in, and what likely became the winning message in 2016. Drumroll, please . . . or not—I hate drumrolls (I prefer that my rolls be cinnamon).

A call for unity might work. When race comes up, point out that a scab won't heal if you keep picking at it.

And, isn't it sexist to expect women to care only about gender? What about foreign policy, unemployment, immigration . . . or is that just man stuff? And yes, climate does change, but the climate pause should give us all pause. So hopefully, years from now, we will look back at this time as if we were in a bad dream where a sense of self and country was turned inside out. We used to be one country. We can be one again. Let's hope it's not Greece.

> The call for unity is the fiery orange unicorn Trump rode in on: We aren't a mix of warring factions, but simply, and clearly, Americans. Sadly, that message was regurgitated in the media as xenophobia. Or "nationalism." Patriotism is now racist. Donald Trump still won, but make no mistake: We saw how many in media viewed this strategy as hate-mongering, when it was really just a return to proclaiming love for country. Here's a question for you smartasses: Why is America the only country not allowed to be patriotic? Or to have borders? Even Greece gets those! Pericles or someone set them up, as I recall. I think I read it in *Beowulf*. Or in CliffsNotes. Who really reads *Beowulf* in its entirety? Even Beowulf put it down after three pages, and it was about him! One day we all must admit that Old English or medieval English sucks—the west Saxon dialect went extinct for a reason. It takes forever when texting.

June 16, 2015

This monologue covers that weird news story about Rachel Dolezal—that troubled white leftist who self-identified as black. She's either nuts, savvy, or inspirational: nuts if she actually believes she's black; savvy in realizing that she'll get sympathy and fame from the left; inspirational in that I might now start self-identifying as a unicorn—or as Rachel Dolezal.

On MSNBC, whatever that is, Michael Eric Dyson said Rachel Dolezal is blacker than Clarence Thomas. Roll it, Francine.

MICHAEL ERIC DYSON: You know those of us who talk about race as a social construct, that it is more complicated. It means that, she may be not African-American, but she certainly could be black in a cultural sense. She's taken on the ideas, the identities, the struggles, she's identified with them. I bet a lot more black people would support Rachel Dolezal than . . . Clarence Thomas.

> Note, Francine is a fictitious person, just like Rachel!

> Or that you can choose your own color? How fun is that?

Awesome. He just admitted that ideology is a skin color. To him a white communist is blacker than a black business owner. By this logic, Dyson is whiter than Vanilla Ice. He wants you to accept "identity cross-dressing." We could all play along, even Kareem Abdul-Jabbar said, let Rachel be black, never mind that she once sued a black college for discrimination because she was white, or that she was always the victim of alleged hate crimes. If she lies about race, is she lying about that?

And if she got her job and schooling due to race-based affirmative action, doesn't that mean that an actual black person got passed over because of her? So why not have all of us identify as black and really level the playing field without having to actually do the work of ending discrimination? Just hire white girls who say they're black!? Not sure Dyson would go for that.

Funny thing: A few years ago I wrote a screenplay about a white guy [my age] who wakes up and decides he's a black lesbian, and demands that everyone around him buy into his delusion. I never finished it. Reality beat me to it.

But I thank Rachel. By exposing the limits of identity politics, she reveals the absurdity of those who cling to it. "I think, therefore, I am" does not apply to pigment. For one cannot claim experiences one never had.

> Unlike Steve Martin in *The Jerk*.

Rachel didn't grow up as a black child.

Rachel pulled a racial Rosie Ruiz.

Ruiz is the woman who hopped in at the last mile to win the Boston Marathon. Rachel simply cut to the finish line of the identity marathon. She hoped to illicitly gain from a lifetime as a black woman, which is the ultimate left-wing sin: cultural appropriation.

Wear an Indian headdress at a concert. Have burritos at a college exchange. Activists will call you racist for incorporating other cultures. If so, then Rachel's black persona must be the worst form of white privilege. I say that as a snake charmer from the Telugu community of Sri Lanka.

Yes, I have no idea what that joke means at the end. I just enjoy saying the word "Telugu." But the point is clear: The same people who condemn a white female child for dressing up as her Disney heroine Moana—a Polynesian princess—on Halloween will champion a white woman who adopts an entire false racial identity. It's the ultimate in mindless illogical hypocrisy. Radical identity politics merchants announced that it was morally wrong for children to wear a costume for one day—yet, by all means, pretend you're black if you're a middle-aged lady with braids!

Then again, expecting some sort of intellectual consistency among race-obsessed ideologues is like expecting legal objectivity from the North Korean Supreme Court— or the U.S. Ninth Circuit. Which I hear share notes and makeup tips.

June 24, 2015

So the Treasury has announced that it's putting a woman on the ten-dollar bill. Originally, there was talk of putting a female on the twenty, but now it's ten. Once again, women end up making half as much as men.

Alexander Hamilton has been on it for a long time. He had a good run. I wish him well, but truth be told, not a lot of people even remember who he is. Was he the guy with the tan? I don't know.

LOL

A shout-out to George Hamilton, who was fantastic in *Love at First Bite*—which, if you haven't seen, I urge you to rush to Netflix and continue not to see it. His wife follows me on Twitter—not sure which wife, but I know it's a wife.

Put a woman on the ten? I'm all for it. We've done it before. Remember Susan B. Anthony? That really took off.

But who cares, honestly? I'm beginning to sense that shared histories are, like, old—as the age of identity puts feelings above everything else. The result is an ambivalence toward the past. They don't really care. Could you build the

We put her on coins—coins no one uses.

Lincoln Memorial or the Washington Monument now? Hell, no. The debate would crumble into a war over white maleness and white privilege, and we'd scrap both for an empty field commemorating shame for our past.

Wow, someone called the monument brouhaha, didn't he? That someone is me. But also, probably a thousand others, too. I just happen to be writing a book! Don't you wish you could turn off these comments?

But it seems we decided to make it a woman without deciding who that woman should be. My suggestion for the ten, obviously: Caitlyn Jenner.

For, ultimately, the best solution is a beloved modern symbol that resists the endless condemnation that always erupts later from activist professors and whiny students. With Jenner, you get a foolproof icon that no one dare question. Talk about getting change for a ten.

Or how about Bo Derek, the perfect ten. Or be totally literal and have just ten bucks. You know, ten deer. By the way, there is no way the media would allow putting Caitlyn Jenner on a bill. Remember that before Bruce became Cait, he was a conservative Republican. And still is. A transgendered conservative? How do identity politics merchants deal with that? They can't. That's like finding out Mother Teresa's a drug dealer—a male drug dealer. Anyway, Dana Perino met with Jenner at an event, and she said she was a fan of mine. Which means I see a reality show in our future.

December 20, 2016

Welcome back to "We're All Racists." MTV released a video that offers New Year's resolutions for white guys. It's so bad that it's bad. Here are clips from the video:

UNIDENTIFIED FEMALE: First off, try to recognize that America was never "great" for anyone who wasn't a white guy.

Sorry, gotta interrupt here. . . . Okay, it wasn't always so "great" for the vast majority of white guys either, Tinker Bell. They were too busy fighting wars and working themselves to death so you could make videos in college. Life sucked for so many people that I consider myself lucky that I'm living now—not then. Okay, sorry, carry on.

UNIDENTIFIED FEMALE: Can we all just agree that "black lives matter" isn't the opposite of "all lives matter"? Black lives just matter. There's no reason to overcomplicate it.

Sorry, back again—and sorry to confuse you, child, but we can't all just agree—and it is rather complicated.

UNIDENTIFIED MALE: Also, "blue lives matter" isn't a thing.

Sorry, so you're telling us that cops' lives don't matter? Would love to see how that attitude changes when this paid actor gets his iPhone stolen on the L train.

UNIDENTIFIED FEMALE: Learn what mansplaining is, and then stop doing it.

UNIDENTIFIED MALE: Oh, and if you're a judge, don't prioritize the well-being of an Ivy League athlete over the woman he assaulted.

Sorry, as in the Duke case, genius?

UNIDENTIFIED MALE: We all love Beyoncé. And yes, she's black, so of course she cares about black issues. I'm talking to you, Fox News.

Isn't it hilarious when losers with no pedigree of achievement are lecturing YOU on how to act? Do any of these actors have anything on their résumé besides "nonspeaking waiter" role on *Two Broke Girls*?

Now, I'd call that a pile of crap, but why insult crap? This slick video is straight from the social justice warrior canon. Campus babble spooned like strained carrots into the mouths of the mentally infantile, disguised as thought, but really just moronic mantras repeated by smug goons whose idea of intellectual achievement is retweeting Katy Perry while they sniff their puffy fingers.

Their goal must be to elect Donald Trump. By smearing whites as dumb aggressors, trashing cops, and mocking interracial friendships, they make leftists seem more noxious than ever.

> **Look, I was wrong a lot on a lot of stuff, but here is where I saw that glimmer of the pendulum swing toward Trump, resulting from the left demonizing decent Americans. Entitled media elitists lecturing you about how awful you are and how awful your country is could only lead to a powerful rebound. The country got sick of it, and registered its sickness at the voting booth.**

So wait, maybe I loved this video.

In the quest for PC obedience, MTV has found a group of people whose smarmy repulsiveness transcends all identity. I didn't see black, white, straight, or gay in that video. I just saw "loser." And the more they talk, the more they lose.

But perhaps that's the goal: creating a new victim group, the loser class.

Their goal: to demand special preference for those who just aren't very good. As failures who see excuses instead of opportunities, the loser class are victims of your success, because they just can't keep up.

So congrats to the stars of this video. You're the poster children for deadbeats.

Can MTV please air an update of this video? Preferably of these same actors on election night? Because their lines were part of the very attitude that got Trump elected. Congrats, brats—mission accomplished! But how can you ever show your face at Burning Man again? The shame! You delivered Ohio!

Where Are We Now?

You'd think after their debacle in 2016, the Democrats would run screaming from any remaining shard of identity politics. Instead, their most vocal faction—the people you see on TV, at marches, and showing up screaming at Trump properties—seem to be tripling down on this divisive, pernicious twaddle. If they continue on this march to madness, they will do all the work needed in staying out of power. I hope the country resists the desire to elevate identity over achievement, but I'm not entirely optimistic. For so many people, it just feels better to shout "It's your fault," instead of "We're in this thing together."

And I'm guilty of this, too. Or, at least I was, when I was younger. Fact is, when you stumble into an ideology or belief that offers you something bigger, you become instinctively tribal. The key is to notice when it's happening. Tribes are helpful in that they create comfort and order—a protection against chaos. But they also prevent you from interacting with people who hold different opinions, and can lead ultimately to conflict and death.

On an up note, more and more of my liberal friends are seeing the toxicity of identity politics and the weird hyperintolerant, vaguely violent direction of virtue signaling.

Virtue signaling, in short, is defined as an obvious display to others that you are obedient and subservient to any prevailing

Something of this nature actually was tweeted—but I'm summarizing here.

identity demand. For example, tweeting, "As a white woman, I will not go see the film *Black Panther*, because I don't want to upset the audience members who are black and who do not wish to see me and pollute their experience." That's pure virtue signaling. Where does it ultimately lead?

If you do not amp up your allegiance to the dogma of postmodern identity tribalism, daily, then even falling behind on the accepted genuflections can make you the enemy. At some point virtue signaling might result in your own self-flagellation in the town square. You might not go for that. (Me, on the other hand . . . it's kind of a dream!)

CHAPTER TWO

LAW AND ORDER

So, after eight years of being told that law enforcement is the problem, what would you expect the American public might be thirsty for? A communist? An Occupy Wall Streeter? An adorable wallaby dressed in overalls that answers only to the name Captain Wuffles?

No, it was someone to tell you that it was all bullshit. And that, in fact, if it weren't for law enforcement doing all the shit we refuse to do, we wouldn't have a country. We would have anarchy in the streets; pain and suffering everywhere. Like Raqqa, but with beer summits.

Bottom line: The police are the first people there, on the scene, when the scene ain't good. As for those protesters who show up later? Well, say, during a generic bungled robbery when a poor cop is forced to make a hair-trigger decision, these activists were on their respective couches tweeting about how racist hotel shampoo is. (This actually happened. Please google it.)

If you want to discover another reason America elected Donald Trump, it was the braying club who sought to demean those who protect and serve. These monologues chronicle this toxic mindset—for a reason. Because I think we all knew that if this psychological, media-driven abuse were to continue unfettered, we wouldn't have a country left.

Sure, we were dealing in "boutique" protests—a hysterical group of activists shouting here, a confluence of students weeping there—but it was building, mainly because it went unchallenged in the media. And ultimately, the protests created a deleterious result: The cops walked away, or were told to walk away, from the danger zones—what became known as "the Ferguson effect." The theory is that the increased scrutiny of police that came after the 2014 shooting of Michael Brown in Ferguson is purported to have led to a jump in murder rates in major U.S. cities.

What you saw was more crime—more shootings, more murder—in places like Chicago, especially. The activists claim to be protecting minorities from police brutality; instead they made such communities vulnerable to those who preyed upon them— the criminals. The entire police force became unfairly accused of actions performed by a tiny minority, and when scrutinized further, even these actions at times seemed like unfortunate, tragic outcomes that occur during chaotic events.

My monologues record the nonsense.

September 20, 2013

Last night, thirteen people were shot in a Chicago park, including a three-year-old boy hit in the head. This is not rare . . . there. Yet the same people who scream about gun control after a horrible mass shooting are always AWOL in these cases.

Both kinds of atrocity suck. The one gets a spotlight and the other, crickets. There are way more victims of daily gang shootings, but they are forgotten by the media and political classes, because it's easier to condemn a rifle than gangs, for you escape uncomfortable truths about besieged communities plagued by thuggery and government cowardice.

By ignoring the terrible numbers in Chicago, we turn communities into animals, and by animals, I mean sitting ducks— targets at a fairground that's anything but fair.

You just know the left was hoping that when I said "animals" I was referring to criminals. Which would then be cast as dog-whistle racism. I tricked them—I'm tricky like that.

Is it a statistical coincidence that since the stop-and-frisk law was ruled unconstitutional in New York, shootings rose 13 percent as gun seizures dropped 17 percent? Weird. Perhaps the police reduced frisking for fear of legal hassles, which emboldened prisoners to pack heat.

And who are the victims? Look at communities where stop and frisk was used. It's the minorities who get hurt. So, if you think about it, ending stop and frisk is a racist's dream.

Meanwhile, New York has appointed professors to review police behavior, which is like hiring me to write a book on height.

I doubt they see the numbers, too. Although stats speak louder than words, it's doubtful anyone will listen. If there's no microphone nearby that can boost their career, then why bother?

Bottom line: Demonize police in neighborhoods full of minorities, and it's the minorities who suffer.

Now, I admit the stop-and-frisk debate is ongoing, and there's plenty of ammo on both sides to defend or condemn it. But what's definitely unfair is assuming it targets minorities, rather than protecting minorities. Most of the communities besieged by criminals are low-income, minority neighborhoods. I don't see stop and frisk in high-end 'burbs of Atlanta or Chicago, where wealthy blacks live. There goes your racial narrative.

But, as I write this, New York City had another dramatic reduction in murders, in the year 2017. Does that refute the "we need stop and frisk" debate, or is it a sign of something else? I think it's a testament to the NYPD, a force made up of minorities, doing such a great job under the biggest boob of a mayor—one who is so incompetent he brings out the best in everyone. But also, there is more targeted enforcement, better technology, and really at the thirty-thousand-foot level, you've got momentum. Safety breeds safety. As unsafe neighborhoods were rendered newly safe, people moved in and performed the evil of all evils: gentrification! Yes, the mortal sin of white privilege!

The "broken windows" theory maintains that disorder [broken windows and other visible bad stuff] is linked to occurrences of more serious crime. So, as whole ZIP codes gentrify, people just behave better. Which drives the crime level even lower. It happens on a microcosmic level in my own bedroom. When my wife enters the room, I immediately stop breaking wind. I call that the "breaking wind" theory.

March 5, 2014

So, a nomination vote failed in the Senate today. The loser, a staunch defender of a cop killer named Debo Adegbile, was going to head the Justice Department's civil rights division despite obsessively defending Mumia Abu-Jamal, who had denied the civil rights of a police officer by killing him back in 1982.

Fortunately, the vote failed, but it's not over. Harry Reid actually voted against it just so he could bring it up again. Creep.

Interesting side nonsense: According to Wikipedia, Debo also was a child actor on *Sesame Street* during the 1970s, playing the character Debo for nine years. I knew there was something about him that rubbed me the wrong way. I was more of an *Electric Company* guy. Everyone had jobs, there.

Meanwhile, Maureen Faulkner, the wife of the slain officer, Daniel, wasn't allowed to testify. That's how it works. If only she were a victim of oppression, had dreadlocks, and belonged to a death cult, then she would be the cherished radical and documentaries would be made about her instead.

Instead, being widowed by a racist militant doesn't rate, and the White House now fumes that their guy lost.

For Eric Holder's balkanized America, race must always win the race, and killers earn respect just by living longer. Gray hair makes the truth less black-and-white.

Look, we get it—every perp gets represented. That's how it's done, but this lawyer crusaded, revealing a bitter bias. Worse, his nomination speaks to an administration steeped in its own bias. After all, isn't the defense of Mumia kind of racist? You think if Mumia was white, he'd be a hero, or if the dead officer was black, would Holder even know Mumia's fake name? I doubt it.

You can't build a career on black-on-black crime.

The great story here is Maureen Faulkner, Daniel's widow, God bless her. She called a lot of senators who were on the fence, got them persuaded.

Her husband would be very proud of her. Even if the media ignores her.

And then the president responded.

He called it a travesty based on wildly unfair character attacks against a good and qualified public servant.

Whatever.

> I summarized Obama's quote here, because the transcription seemed muddled.
>
> Even now, it's pretty amazing that the widow of a police officer had to make the calls to stop this nomination from being approved. If anything caused the Democratic Party to implode, it's this ghoulish blind spot that allowed thuggery a sickening lionization, while those who protect us get smeared with the brush of bigotry. People remember this stuff in the voting booth; they just don't talk about it. Well, I do, it's my job.
>
> And it never ends . . . see below, my friends.

November 25, 2014

> This monologue pertains to the Ferguson riots, a key moment in the growing crisis over our country's sense of unity, as well as a targeted trust in our nation's laws, and those committed to enforcing them.

When buildings burn, any sympathy you have left for protesters goes up in smoke, as you hear so many bragging about the attention they get, taunting the police, or deciding which building to burn. I realized that it wasn't really about injustice, instead it was a conduit for destruction, a time to break things that aren't yours, and take things that aren't yours. Racial conflict became an excuse for the purge. A free-for-all of looting, vandalism, and fun.

You've got to love creeps who scream for justice after torching a car. And any tool wearing a Guy Fawkes mask is almost always a white male in his late thirties who still air-guitars to Rage Against the Machine. Chances are he didn't have to get up for work the next morning, because he doesn't work.

> **Theory: This is why liberal protests outnumber conservative ones by ten to one—a stat I made up. Conservatives are invariably too busy trying to earn a living. You know, the whole "employment" thing. If you don't have to get up early to go to work, then it's just easier for you to go out the night before to trash everything around you. And everything you trash belongs to those poor saps who have to get up the next morning to go work.**

But if you burn businesses to the ground in your community, what does that say about your investment in that community? No person who loves Ferguson would burn Ferguson. Of course they are outsiders, but outsiders are simply those out for themselves. It wasn't their Walgreens that burned, and there is no value if it doesn't cost you. Looting is redistribution on meth.

> **I don't really think "protesters" think that deeply about this stuff. It's just fun to destroy shit and get away with it. That's the real unspeakable truth: People like to loot and vandalize because, well, it's fun.**

But what of the other outsiders? The press who flocked to Ferguson, hoping to capture the story in one stark image? That's their job. But it's an ugly game we perpetuate: We go and they perform. And when all that's left are cinders, we can return to our cities. Our stores and our cafés will be fine. But Ferguson is done. It's dead, and you can't blame the cops for that.

This monologue was a response to the media's role in encouraging conflict, by casting criminality as a form of protest.

Not only were we seeing people commit crimes in the name of injustice, we actually had a media manufacturing excuses for it.

The network's complicity here bordered on a form of co-conspiracy. If the media had worried about the stores being destroyed, that's one thing. But instead, they portrayed rioting and looting as political expression, paving the way for that pendulum swing in 2016. Millions of people realized a simple fact: If there's a group of people in the media who think it's okay to destroy property, then we, the public, must stop this at the voting booth. And the solution wasn't going to be "vote for a Democrat."

But it must be worth noting again and again: The looting was all opportunistic crime performed not by the citizenry but by their oppressors. No neighbor torches another neighbor's home or business. But the media chose to portray it as a community, enraged. No, the community had no interest in such nonsense.

Also, this idea that violence is an acceptable form of protest didn't occur only in these instances, but also on campuses when certain ideas that were presented were deemed offensive, too. The idea of dialogue became an inferior path for the modern leftist. It's why so many smart liberal professors are finding sanctuary in the welcoming arms of conservatives.

November 26, 2014

In this monologue, I do my best to address both sides of the police brutality controversy. I think I do a pretty decent job, describing this frenetic game of political Ping-Pong. I'm not sure if I accomplished much.

Here are both sides of the Ferguson debate in ninety seconds.

- It's open season on black youths by cops.
- Actually, no, it's open season on black youths by black youths, it's the cops trying to stop it.
- Well, a black youth didn't shoot that teen, a cop did.
- While the cop felt threatened, the teen was aggressive and high.
- Well, you don't kill a kid because he's high.
- Well, he was violent and he attacked the cop.
- Whatever, you're just going to side with whitey, because the justice system is rigged in this racist society.
- And you say that about everything. What if it were a black cop?
- Well, find me a black cop in Ferguson.
- Well, whose fault is that? The police? Or a culture that advocates hating cops?
- Well, you try being black in a white cop world.
- Well then, why not become a cop and change things?
- Well, why would we want to be part of a corrupt system that's stacked against blacks?
- That's a circular argument. You don't want to change a corrupt system because the system is corrupt. Not being a cop is your copout? Anyway, can we agree on one thing?

- Sure.
- That Darlena Cunha is a big moron?
- Who's that?
- In *Time* magazine, she defends rioting as part of the American experience, necessary for the evolution of society. Lucky for her, as a hack for this irrelevant rag, her office was never in danger of being torched by those she defends.
- Yeah, you're right, she is a moron.
- Well, at least we can agree on one thing. Thanks, Darlena, your stupidity is so vast, it could unite all of America.

Now, I haven't checked back with Darlena, but I'm assuming she is still a moron, wherever she is. And *Time* has become a parody of a newsmagazine. Are interns from Riverdale High writing that thing? Or is that an insult to interns from Riverdale High?

But let me digress on a purely hypothetical question: What if a defender of rioting suddenly sees a rock fly through his window? And everything he owns is taken by a laughing mob? Rioting and looting can only be romanticized in the abstract, a delightful place all leftists tend to inhabit. The opposite of the abstract—what I call reality—is just too dangerous a place to hold idiotic ideas that might get you killed. So, you can hold those ideas. You just can't let them be practiced near you.

December 4, 2014

> This monologue examines the death of Eric Garner, but focuses not on the rift between cop and criminal, but on the laws that create this tragic conflict. Garner should not have died—if the laws made sense, he would be alive right now, one predicts. The poor guy was selling loose cigarettes. Why should that be illegal? And why should a cop be forced to arrest him? That's the real problem, and that problem led to a man's death. Remember, again: This case began with cops having to deal with a guy selling loose cigarettes on the street, which for some idiotic reason is illegal. Don't forget it.

Adding the Eric Garner tragedy to other recent incidents is an understandable thing to do, but it's off. The factors leading to his death are different.

Still, for many people this decision was a shocker. It doesn't make sense.

We saw the video. But if you look closer, it's really not about cops versus blacks, but government versus citizens, the nanny state crushing the individual. The grand jury might have screwed up, the tape paints a grim picture—but who knows.

But the cop wouldn't have approached Garner if the law didn't make him. I don't believe for a moment that any man, even a cop, wants to wrestle a 350-pound man over a single damn cigarette.

But let's face it, most of what cops must do, they'd rather avoid. Policing is a series of tough spots requiring sensitive and constant assessment. So why make it worse with idiotic, stupid laws? I get it, store owners complain about people selling single smokes and the black market in cigarettes is huge because of the crazy taxes. It's an old story. I used to buy loosies when I was young and broke. But the only way to gain justice from this mess is to cling to the truth.

Tying this to centuries of racism as a way to indict society may work for some, but for people who truly care about the city and not their own rising status, remember this one fact—you can buy one beer but not one smoke. Garner provided for those who didn't have the fifteen dollars that a pack of twenty required. Unnecessary laws have consequences, and in this case that consequence was death.

> Maybe this is one of the helpful tenets of libertarianism. The fewer laws we have, the fewer ridiculous laws we have. And the fewer ridiculous laws we have, the less likely some poor cop will have to enforce them and some even poorer dude will die during such enforcement.
>
> At this point I would like to recommend a book, which I rarely do in one of my own books. It's called *The Impact of Regulatory Law on American Criminal Justice*, by Vincent Del Castillo. The book reveals all the ugly consequences of regulatory laws—most important the lack of resources needed to enforce such violations of the law.

I wrote this next monologue after two police officers were murdered in NYC, while they were sitting in their patrol car in Brooklyn. They were shot, point-blank, on a Saturday, by a fiend who traveled from out of state, bent on killing officers. The officers were Wenjian Liu and Rafael Ramos. Don't ever forget them. I'd mention the name of the killer, who committed suicide afterward—but why bother. Right after it happened, I left my apartment, angry and probably tipsy, to see if there were any protests downtown. All I found were the typical milling tourists, and some isolated clumps of devastated, angry cops. I talked to them, but realized they needed no commiseration from me. They had had enough. I returned home to finish my remaining bottle of wine, wondering if this war on cops would ever end.

So Santa came early for cop haters.

Of course, we will be told that there's no connection between protesters chanting the desire for dead cops in recent city marches and cop killing. Sorry, a bat could see that connection.

I'm referring here to videos of NYC protesters chanting "What do we want? Dead cops. When do we want it? Now," among other things, like "Pigs in a blanket—fry 'em like bacon."

Seriously, what do you expect after months of demonizing the police? Murderers are not a power structure, but chanting death to cops suggests there's a fan base. The unbridled protest implied official support—a left-wing version of a half marathon.

God bless the cops for not cracking, because I would.

Saturday night I took a walk to City Hall, it was dead quiet.

I realized that the city only supports the outraged when it's sanctioned by the left. It would be nice to see a large city with unbelievably low crime support those who have made their lives safer.

But police are victims of their own success. None of these activists realize that cops have done more to save their minority lives than Al Sharpton ever could. After all, those murdered cops were protecting citizens in a high-crime area. It's heartbreaking how loud Twitter was this weekend and how quiet New York was, on the streets. Maybe it's time to change that.

> This is sooo important. Where is the damn gratitude?

A fact lost in this case: Both the dead cops were "minorities," which of course shouldn't matter, but with the narrative the media has constructed, it does. The names of these officers, once again, are Wenjian Liu and Rafael Ramos. But in the entertainment/media/academic complex, every cop is assumed to be a white bucket of muscular, tattooed privilege. In fact, however, they're the picture of diversity—an amazing sign of progress in an increasingly tribal world. If you put a recent class photo of NYPD graduates up against the yearbook roster of any liberal network, where would you find more color? If you live in any major city, you know the answer—it's the men and women in blue. To claim otherwise is a smear that ends, ultimately, in violence.

December 23, 2014

This is pretty amazing: After the cold-blooded murder of those two police officers, a poll of the press revealed what they believe is the top story of the year: police killing blacks. I wonder if they could see any cause and effect in their overblown reporting that might have led to the deaths of these minority officers. I'm probably overstating it, in that question—I don't know. I just remember the endless coverage that portrayed law enforcement as evil and lawless. Could that have had unforeseen consequences? I remain, as always, wondering.

An AP poll of the U.S. press asks for their top story of the year. They chose police killings of blacks. Not Ebola, not ISIS, not a missing airplane and its 227 people. *The police killings of blacks.* I call that bad timing, but it's also the media completing its self-fulfilling premise. This is how it works. You take something awful and claim it reflects an epidemic; when the facts refute, you resist, because you dig the excitement of antagonism.

Then comes the looting, the assaults, and now murder. Who built that? Such incidents are stories, but the media shaped them into an indictment creating an exaggerated narrative that endangered cops.

Is it any wonder the press is currently about as trusted and respected in this country as a Russian hedge fund? Their approval numbers are hovering somewhere near scurvy. Scurvy is bad, right?

And now that cops are making fewer arrests to protect their own lives, CNN asked if crime could spike.

What are you talking about?

Isn't that what you wanted—a stunted police?

> This kills me: You have a network that has played the police brutality song over and over, and now acts shocked and worried that the police are skittish about doing their job.

Now that's what you have. The media also wonders if the killings would derail protests. Shut up. The cop killings derail something far nobler—the cops' lives.

See, for the media, protest is their pal, for it allows them to slam law enforcement as a proxy for America itself—it's the leftover habit from college.

Fact is, the police save more minority lives every year, and the communities value their presence. You remember the Public Enemy song "911 Is a Joke"?

About how cops wouldn't come to black neighborhoods?

Now they do.

And they're despised for that as well. Funny how the left created the term "hate speech," yet they're the ones who mastered it.

> This makes me wonder: What is "hate speech," really? The left sees it as speech that hurts people, I guess. But what about language that encourages violence against a group of people? By that definition, the media's treatment of law enforcement is textbook hate speech—for it contributed to a climate that led to the deaths of young officers—minority officers—just doing their job.

April 21, 2015

This monologue focuses on reformers trying to get the New York City police to swear less, tell fewer jokes—as if this is our biggest problem. Sorry, if you're not swearing and telling crude jokes, I don't think you qualify as a New Yorker. I get it—bigotry has no place in the force—but have they seen the force? It's more diverse than the cast of *This Is Us*, or the staff of any newspaper or left-wing cable network that criticizes them.

The feds overseeing police reforms have this advice for New York cops—don't be racist, don't be sexist, don't be jerks.

Finally, now crime will vanish!

So another bureaucracy lectures a group of men and women who have saved more life than airbags have—and I include Al Sharpton in that. These guys have risked their lives daily and they are told now to watch their language.

That's like going up to a nurse in the ER and saying, "You know, darling, you should get your hair done."

By the way, have you seen the police force lately? Minority is the majority. It's a well-armed Benetton ad.

> I need a new description besides "Benetton Ad." Does Benetton even exist?

So we have marches for every color but blue. The only time you see some appreciation is at the cop's funeral. Strange that it's only the police force where a few bad apples are cast as the norm.

Have the feds ever lectured the Crips on manners? What about extremist imams?

Now this new advice comes after a story emerged this morning in the papers, about a creep who raped a woman in a New York City bar. The rapist still roams free, and the feds are busy chasing mean jokes.

The fact is, most slime arrested for such crimes would be in jail much longer if it weren't for a court system that has more cases than it can handle, mainly due to arrests for regulatory crimes.

So instead of solving those crimes, the feds prefer to slam the decorum of the world's best and most integrated police force.

But it's not about words. It's about cops forced to chase smokers and taillights, instead of rapists. If I were a cop, I'd be swearing, too.

> In retrospect, I can't even believe this was a thing. What a perfect distillation of an administration's elevation of feelings over results, of regulation over reality. It's a miracle there's anything left for the adults to build on.

April 30, 2015

> The short-term effect of demonizing the police: The police stop policing. The rebound effect: The public wonders what the hell happened to law and order. How Hillary did not see this as an opportunity to distance herself from the far left is beyond me—wasn't she supposed to be a canny political thinker? Instead, Trump had that turf all to himself, which underlines a core theme: If the police favor a candidate more than another, you want to be *that* candidate. If the cliché is that people vote with their pocketbooks, it stands to reason they vote the safety of those pocketbooks, too.

On Monday we watched as Baltimore police retreated from the rioters, making stores bull's-eyes for bandits. Then, a baseball game was played to no one, so no one would get hurt.

Here is the mayor of Baltimore explaining why a game was played to no fans.

STEPHANIE RAWLINGS-BLAKE, MAYOR OF BALTIMORE: I think in the heat of a state of emergency, every decision that's made is going to be scrutinized. The Orioles wanted to make sure that they were able to continue to play. We had to make sure that we protected our police resources, so the best decision based on what was available was made.

Those empty stands were an empty stand.

For such appeasement energizes those who pretend to champion the underclass when, in fact, they seek destruction. This is not about race, but radicals. Forget facts; they want friction. Radical idiocy abounds. You can't call a thug a thug, but you can call the police an occupying force.

This leads to imitators in New York blocking tunnels and traffic. Who does this hurt really? The man? Please, you're only hurting people trying to get home from work. But activists don't care. They're in this for themselves.

Sure, a Baltimore CVS burns, but if you get your pills at a Brooklyn store, who really cares? They claim the protest was in solidarity, but with whom? The folks whose buildings burned? The people who lost the senior center? The stadium vendors who lost business?

The solidarity was with other cretins who treat black suffering as a nighttime hobby. Shouting at cops is their aerobic anthem, recorded for ego-stroking playback in their comfy, well-lit dorm.

> Protest is, for the left, their most effective group therapy.

Fanning the destruction—just to say they were there, these are the casual collaborators of minority pain. They don't suffer the outcome. Their buildings don't burn, but they get a neat story to tell their friends back home.

> You wanna hear a funny story about how TV works when the narrative doesn't? I had a close friend appear on Larry Wilmore's show—when he had one on Comedy Central—and one of the topics was about how street gangs banded together to protect stores from being looted during the rioting. It was a feel-good story for the myopic liberal. During the segment, when Wilmore mentioned how great it was that gangs got along better than our own political parties, my good friend pointed out that the story wasn't nearly that wholesome. The gangs did indeed dissuade looters from looting black stores—by pointing the criminals instead toward destroying other businesses, owned by other races. Which they did. That entire section was excised from the show.

May 8, 2015

> As I read these monologues, now, three years later, I can't believe how we tolerate the media bias against cops to unfold. We had a media/academic/entertainment complex all but sanctioning the hatred of police. And then the killings start, and they go silent. Or worse, defend the killers!

Today is the funeral for New York police officer Brian Moore, who was shot dead last week. On Monday, this Monday, National Police Week starts to show appreciation for all of our fallen officers. It's needed now more than ever because, unlike cop activists, cop supporters have jobs.

So we must try harder to thank the police, because they won't be asking for it. It was just months ago that ghouls demanded dead cops.

UNIDENTIFIED MALE: What do we want?

UNIDENTIFIED MALE/FEMALE: Dead cops.

UNIDENTIFIED MALE: When do we want them?

UNIDENTIFIED MALE/FEMALE: Now.

> Here we play the video of a group chanting.

Mission accomplished, you dirtbags. What is happening to police is what happened to businesses decades ago, activists smearing entire enterprises with isolated events—car companies, drug companies. You can't think of the oil industry without thinking of oil spills. This tactic is now applied to police.

> **The point: The police are now targeted like all the other so-called evil monolithic goliaths that compose the greatest country in history. It's all part of the same attack. The barfbags who demonize the military or "big business" are the same ones who apply the smear to law enforcement. It's an ideological strategy to dismantle a country. (Until, of course, they have to call the cops when someone steals their backpack.)**

Fact, in New York City, the number of people fatally shot by police has dropped 90 percent since the 1970s. But yet, they are the bad guys. No spotlight on gangs, or their black victims. To point that out would be racist. Condemning crime is condemning a lifestyle. Even with Baltimore's police mug shots, both black and white, the dukes of division make it about race. For this is really about subversion. Forget big business now. If you bring down the cops, you bring down society. That's the goal of the agitator, who has an edge over you. For while you go to work, the agitator has no such commitment. This is all that they do.

This is an important point: Does no one in the media ever wonder why a demonstration by "activists" is so well attended on a Wednesday afternoon?

So how do we stop that? Why not give them what they want? I call it the police exemption pass. If you hate cops, then ask for a pass that says, "Under no circumstances will the police ever assist you." It's a "do not resuscitate" for radicals. Getting them to live by their actual words. I mean, why would you want to be saved by the people you want dead? The cops have a duty to protect you, but do you have the guts to refuse it?

This is one of my absurd ideas. And sadly, no one took me up on it. Is there a way to disconnect the 911 system for the Antifa members and the media elite who love them? How about for all of Hollywood and NY's Upper West Side? I know that's a terrible idea, but if you can't posit terrible ideas in books written while drinking, where else can you posit them? And can we please ban the word "posit"? I don't even know how I started using it. It sounds like the perfect name for an acne medication.

May 14, 2015

> I love stories that have a happy ending. My version of a happy ending is the ventilation of a creep, of course!

For the last few days a sick creep has roamed New York City attacking women with a hammer. Yesterday, he assaulted a female cop, and her partner filled him with lead. *Nice.* Here's Police Chief Bratton.

BILL BRATTON, NYPD COMMISSIONER: These officers had no chance to call for assistance. . . . The whole incident that you will see took about three seconds from start to finish. During that, the officer O'Rourke was attempting to call on her radio as she was being struck and fell to the ground, her partner officer, making a literally split-second decision to save her life, shot the suspect, seriously wounding him. Again, I want to commend both officers for their alertness and their behavior during the performance of this incident.

So why are we covering this? Well, FNC must balance the other networks' obsession with police misconduct. After all, who stopped this fiend? Not a student activist stinking of bong water, or a CNN hack in fake glasses full of faux concern. Two beat cops did, and they didn't hesitate for fear of outrage. Do you think Sharpton or your typical social justice screamer would have stopped this guy? Those cops did more in three seconds than they will do in a lifetime. It reveals who stands between you and the world's worst threats. Could you ever handle that job, Mayor de Blasio? No, you're busy staining the country on a self-promoting tour, touting history's failures as new ideas.

Here's tape of the jackass:

BILL DE BLASIO, NEW YORK CITY MAYOR: We pledge to reach out all over the country to hundreds and hundreds of our fellow progressives and start a movement that would reach all the way here to Washington, D.C., and make an impact, so we could finally address income inequality.

He's worse than Mayor McCheese. If he only knew the thin blue line separates us from the horribles.

> **They say everything is bigger in Texas, but New York has the biggest boob, and it's this guy.**

Speaking of, the attacker was a schizophrenic with many violent arrests, a pile of weapons, and a public passion for blood-dripping hammers.

He was allowed to roam the streets like a lion loose in a playground.

Until we rebuild our institutions for the mentally ill, such attacks will repeat and the only people who will stop them are the cops maligned for their fearlessness. That's true bravery, which in the face of easy criticism and outright insanity might be called senseless.

> To counterbalance all the negative press cops were getting in 2015, you'd need a twenty-four-hour cable channel just reporting incidents like these. Something tells me that sort of thing would be a hit.
>
> But again—not in Hollywood or in New York's tonier neighborhoods. In fact, not in any neighborhood dominated by Pilates addicts who go to book clubs in their yoga pants. That line was in no way directed at a specific person . . . who may or may not be on *The Five*.

September 10, 2015

> This is an amazing story. God, I love doing this book! It reminds me of how vile and stupid so many in the media are.

BuzzFeed, the website devoted to lists about which bean you look like, decided to address the sensitive issues of policing with a video called "Men Try on a Police Uniform," where thoughtful beta bros dress up as cops, then comment on their feelings. It will make your brain puke. Here's a sample from the video:

> Note: The unidentified males are actors in the video. I don't differentiate them, because they're essentially all the same monotonous bozos who I hope are still unemployed and eating canned soup in a shared bathroom. So when you read these quotes below, remember, they are wearing police uniforms and telling you how they feel as they see themselves in a mirror. Enjoy.

UNIDENTIFIED MALE: Honestly, I see jerk before I see hero. And that sucks.

UNIDENTIFIED MALE: The fashion sensibility of being a police officer seems like it would be sort of a weird burden to deal with. You know, how do you carry yourself like a cop? What does a cop stand like?

> Seriously, eff this guy.

> Not like you, you douchebag.

UNIDENTIFIED MALE: We could look at this police officer and feel safer, but I look at myself now, it makes me a little uncomfortable and skittish, if anything. Especially because it's me.

> You should simply jump off a cliff.

UNIDENTIFIED MALE: Seeing this reflection of myself, I want to turn away from myself.

> I would, too, if I were you, you pointless piece of emasculated shit.

UNIDENTIFIED MALE: To see myself in this uniform feels like a joke. And you realize that there's guys who get up and look in a mirror like this every single morning, and it's not a joke.

> You're the joke. I hope no police officer ever helps you in your time of need. But they will.

UNIDENTIFIED MALE: I feel like I understand why people run away from these guys.

UNIDENTIFIED MALE: We can resolve our problems without resorting to this.

> Christ, were these idiots raised by plankton?

> How much you wanna bet these jerkwads call the police when they find a spider in their futon? I don't think I could hate any person more than whoever wrote this shit.

> These creeps make Barney Fife sound like the Terminator. No wonder the Chinese are militarizing. These idiots will make good house servants someday, if they can master Mandarin!

What a stinking pile of rotting garbage. You know why these guys felt bad about wearing the uniforms? Because they lack the guts. To them it's like dressing up as an astronaut on Halloween. Donning the apparel was amusing, precisely because it disconnected from their nonexistent skill set.

For these tools, dressing up is easier than showing up. They couldn't even wear a cop uniform as strippers at a bachelorette party. The girls wouldn't buy it, because they're not men but boys withering under the heft of responsibility.

It's not really us versus the police, but cops versus pampered, coddled, clueless media hacks with no concept of how the world works.

Seriously, the police should start taping their own videos of weak male bloggers when they come crying for help after their iPhone or man purse gets stolen on the subway. The next time they report a mugging, just say, "Wow, I feel like such a jerk helping you out. Seeing this reflection of myself, I want to turn away."

Finally, I wonder, would BuzzFeed ever have these goofs dress up as Bloods and Crips and then mock them? No, they're cowards, too. Cops are just easier targets. Literally.

> I wonder—do the people who filmed this stunt ever look back at this and feel a deep sense of shame and embarrassment? My guess is, they've already moved on to other stupid, hacky stunts, performed in well-deserved obscurity, between their shifts as children's birthday clowns in Paramus, New Jersey. Also: still waiting, Buzzfeed, to have your hired hands dress up as other occupations, or "types." But I guess only certain types of cultural appropriation are acceptable. Douchebags.

October 21, 2015

So when you read these monologues one after another, how clear is it—this growing sense of persecution against law enforcement? Does it not piss the hell out of you?

Last night, police officer Randolph Holder was shot and killed chasing a gunman during a gang battle in Harlem, New York. This five-year veteran displayed the usual sacrifice seen from law enforcement, running at trouble, not away. And chances are, whoever's being approached isn't an honor student with a bright future.

> . . . which is how every suspect is portrayed shortly after being arrested . . .

The officers' response is always under fire. Figuratively in the media, but literally in the street. You can thank gangs that always get a pass from our loudest outrage merchants. Recipients of tolerance welfare, gangs are viewed as cultural, not criminal.

> They're like a book club, but with more tattoos and guns. Oh, and yeah, no books.

Holder's killer had been arrested fifteen times and was on the street due to a program made to shrink the prison population. Keep that in mind when you hear of overcrowding. The solution isn't catch and release. It's build, catch, then keep.

Whoever called 911 was likely a law-abiding terrified minority member. Holder, a minority member, died in a place where his job mattered most, Harlem.

> Every lib who claims prisons are overcrowded should offer to take one inmate as a boarder in their home.

He was the fourth city officer killed in the last eleven months. Nationwide, 101 officers have been killed this year, a 50 percent jump from last year.

> **An amazing statistic, one you cannot deny has a connection to the tone and tenor of the anti–law enforcement drivel spewed by activists, media, political dipshits, and assorted gas-hats in movies and TV.**

True, we do live in safer times, yet we cannot deny an atmospheric change. As a subversive crusade against law enforcement rages, the callow media trains new generations to hate those who die to protect us.

Finally, Holder was an immigrant who took a tough job confronting thugs lucky enough to be born here. Countries often send us their best, only to deal with our worst.

> **While I say that we live in safer times, I mean for civilians and not so much for cops.**

> **That point makes me the sickest. This guy came here for a better life and put the time and effort in to do that. And who took his life? A person who had no desire for the same.**
>
> **And as always, forget that half the NYPD is nonwhite, which activists conveniently do. If black lives didn't matter to cops, why in God's name does their presence save black lives? The stats speak for themselves. As murder rates drop, it's clear black lives matter. They may mean more to the cops than anyone else.**

October 26, 2015

Wanna know where a lot of the anticop bias comes from? The very same people who rely on the police when they tie up your streets shooting their hypderviolent films.

Case in point: One sanctimonious twit in the media/ Hollywood complex who spewed such nonsense was Quentin Tarantino, a mouthy critic of cops, as well as a onetime mouthy defender of child-drugger-and-seducer Roman Polanski.

Director Quentin Tarantino graced an antipolice protest in New York just days after our own Randolph Holder was killed by the kind of dirtbag Tarantino usually embraces in his flicks.

Here's QT talking BS:

QUENTIN TARANTINO, FILM DIRECTOR: I'm a human being with a conscience, and when I see murder, I cannot stand by, and I have to call the murdered the murdered, and I have to call the murderers the murderers.

> And yet, he never called Harvey Weinstein on his serial raping— but why bite the slimy hand that feeds you.

What an ass. Once again, we see marches against cops, but rarely for—and led by pop culture parrots who make millions off violence. For it's easy to glam up thuggery in the fantasy land when the violence can't touch you, and when cops in real life protect you.

Driving by one protest, I must say there's nothing like seeing white leftists shouting at black cops. There's the racial divide Tarantino must ignore, so his false assumptions remain intact. New York's a minority force, manned by blacks, Latinos, gays.

Holder was from Guyana. But in Quentin's world, they're all

just white bigots who torture blacks in basements, just like in *Pulp Fiction.*

See, Quentin is just a film nerd who wants the left to love him. So he cultivates this outsider thing, but he knows absolutely nothing about crime. His movies are comic books from the fifties.

> He's about as authentic as an Elvis impersonator—a guy who gets all his references from other films, not real life. This is what happens when video store nerds actually score the director's chair.

Remember *Reservoir Dogs*, that long scene where the cop gets mutilated to the sounds of Steeler's Wheel? To Quentin that's cool. To a cop, it's torture porn.

The police union now urges a film boycott, but in this era of sanctuary cities, why not invite Quentin to set up a police-free community, where people like him can live and work without the benefit of cops. Carve out a small corner of Chicago where we can then place bets. In that cop-free world, will it be Quentin's film or himself that gets shot first?

> I actually like a few of his films, but his recent foray into social justice has pretty much peed in the pool of that experience. Every time I see one of his flicks on TV, I just think, "What a putz." Then I turn the channel and watch reruns of *The Brady Bunch*, where the wisdom lives. Fact is, his life experience cannot sustain any wisdom or truth in his movies. For a movie to offer any kind of real meaning, it needs to come from an adult who's lived a life.

May 16, 2016

> Again, the end result of all this anticop blather? Law enforcement pulling back, because they fear doing their job will land them in the sights of idiotic leftists bent on destroying their lives.

In more than twenty major U.S. cities, homicide spiked in the first months of this year, causing the media to search for explanations while denying their own role in this body count. So far they blame heroin, gangs, and economic factors, but one person isn't fleeing from the truth. FBI Director James Comey believes scrutiny aimed at police has changed the way it deals with citizens, creating a reticence that increases homicides mainly among minorities. Odd that the media says minorities are often victims of the police, yet more die when the cops back off.

> Remember when Comey was a logical, sensible chap? Those were the days. He was pretty good when he stuck to preventing real crime.

So is this a coincidence? When you prevent the police from doing their jobs, murders go up? No, that's a scientific method, a consequence of an experiment. The experiment, hold back; the consequence, death.

Now, liberals will bend over backward to say they are troubled by this, but they will resist any commonsense answers. More petty

> This is what's known as "cause and effect." Or to a leftist: "racism."

crime, assaults, and robberies occur when perps know the police aren't respected, and crime becomes more tolerated.

Witness the wild jump in shoplifting in California since a bill reduced penalties. Looting is now shopping!

Fact is, reality implicates those scrambling for excuses—politicians, activists, and media who undermine the men and women in blue, as gangs occupied by immigrant and out-of-work young men savage cities from Long Beach to Chicago. You might wonder, where are the police? They're looking out for themselves. Someone has to.

July 8, 2016

This monologue focuses on the shooting of five police offers in Dallas, Texas. To remind the reader: The Next Generation Action Network organized a protest after the killing of two men by cops in Minnesota and Louisiana. At the protest, where cops were actually protecting the activists there to protest them, a creep named Micah Xavier John ambushed the police, killing five officers and wounding nine others.

So after the Texas massacre, President Obama brought up guns.

BARACK OBAMA, U.S. PRESIDENT: We also know that when people are armed with powerful weapons, unfortunately it makes attacks like these more deadly and more tragic. And in the days ahead we're going to have to consider those realities as well.

It's the familiar refrain from Orlando to Dallas. But gun control doesn't address the acts, be they of terror or ambushes of police.

We don't hear the same response with vehicular homicide or arson. Here's Obama again on the shootings in St. Paul and Baton Rouge.

OBAMA: These are not isolated incidents. They're symptomatic of a broader set of racial disparities that exist in our criminal justice system.

> Ugh—there's the catchphrase of the progressive nincompoop: "symptomatic." Where are the statistics that prove that these actions are "symptomatic"? Apparently you don't need them when you traffic in bullshit "oppressor vs. oppressed" ideology. Funny how dead cops were never "symptomatic" to the White House.

Maybe so—but the tendency to group local, separate incidents into one greater national phenomenon often doesn't reveal real truth. It only serves to obscure specifics in each case. The Dallas police had no connection at all to those incidents, but they took bullets because of them. They suffered for a media narrative.

Fact is, today's police get more training, are subject to internal affairs and citizen review boards. They face more rules and procedures than ever. They've gotten better. But have we? We obsessed over Islamophobia, condemning negative portrayals of Islam—but we afford no such sensitivity to police.

So the idea that law enforcement is just racist whites killing blacks continues, even though we know it's absurd.

I could recite the facts showing how more whites die from police than blacks or that black and Hispanic cops are more likely to fire a gun at blacks than white cops, but why would I do that? You can't change minds that refuse to change, that rely on emotional conclusions, formed well before the facts are ever known.

So put on your outrage helmets. The road is about to get bumpy once again, and protest, if you wish, and be happy you're safe and protected by some of the greatest people on earth.

> A point worth reiterating, because I totally forgot I made it: We obsess over Islamophobia, but not Policeophobia. Police are afforded no such protections against abuse— even when they bend over backward to do the right thing. Maybe they should all convert to Islam! BTW, in NYC, there are roughly three to four hundred Muslim cops, and they do an awesome job.

July 11, 2016

> After the massacre of those police officers in Texas, the media took their usual tack: wondering about the back- lash, not the bodies of those dead men.

So the Sunday *New York Times* just whined how sniper fire halted the strides of Black Lives Matter. Sorry, it halted the strides of five policemen permanently. The paper also added that BLM, not the police or our country, faces its biggest crisis yet.

That's their default response. Grievance always trumps grieving.

It must have been hard then for the paper to report on a new study that finds absolutely no racial bias in police shootings, which undermines the whole narrative.

But facts lose to feelings, for identity politics always culminate in emotional tribalism because such division always guarantees attention.

But the *Times* shouldn't fret. The victories of victimhood remain intact. The media slobbers over a photo of one lone woman standing against the evil militarized police. So, even after five good men are murdered, the stereotype must be maintained: the brutal force against the bravely peaceful—how touching, how fake.

> And satisfies your reader base, which really is what this is all about.

Seriously, what happened to the rage? When the issue was police brutality, it was no justice, no peace. Now the issue's murdered police and it's let's sing "Kumbaya."

No thanks.

In 1989 Ice Cube's band N.W.A did a song called "Fuck tha Police." Recently, he got paid millions to play a police officer in *Ride Along*. In 1992, Ice-T's band Body Count did a song called "Cop Killer." He's been playing a cop on *Law and Order: Special Victims Unit* for sixteen years. So maybe targeting and trashing the police, truly, is a movement—careerwise, anyway.

> Why is this only a one-way street? If rappers can play cops, can cops play rappers?

> I do realize these monologues have started to take a more serious turn as the chapter goes on. It all weighs on you, which, given the topic, is no surprise. Can't make jokes about unicorns and Alec Baldwin here.

July 18, 2016

This monologue ties it all together—how antipolice movements and proterror groups meld into one force that seeks to destroy society. And it's this monologue that predicts a president.

It's day one of the convention, and the topic is security. Recent months have been a game of Ping-Pong between Islamism and attacks on police. One week it's Orlando, another it's Dallas, then France, then Baton Rouge.

Terror and attacks on police share a common desire: to dismantle civilization. For the Islamists, it's about ending the world because the next one is going to be so much better for them. For the haters of police, it's about creating warring tribes to rot a country from within. We face external and internal threats. How can America survive that?

The next president must be able to nail that question. He or she must prioritize threats, knowing that fossil fuels are way nicer than ISIS, and that transgendered bathrooms must take a back seat to killing jihadists. This leader must understand that terror changes, more so than climate, as technology creates new avenues at a breathless pace. It won't be just trucks and guns— add drones, phones, and bioagents. And safety won't be achieved through the coddling of identity hucksters demanding protection from the loathsome behavior they encourage. So as we focus on safety, ask yourself this: Who among our choices exhibits the temperament, drive, and attention span need to focus on security? And who will listen to those who know the threat? Because more of the same is not an option and, frankly, one of our options could be really worse.

That's "How to Beat Hillary" in three easy sentences, folks. I basically stumble through life like anyone else, but that last graph makes me feel like Nostradamus. A short, slightly overweight one, but a Nostradamus nonetheless.

Actually, I'm not too sure I was specifically talking about Trump here—I might have been. But one thing's for sure. As the campaign wore on, it became clear that Trump was the only candidate breaking through on these issues. Proof of that was November 8, 2016, when ten thousand revelers at the Javits Center on Manhattan's West Side found themselves chowing down on history's biggest reality sandwich, instead of hugging each other while shouting "I'm with her!"

Where Are We Now?

Since Donald Trump became president, we've definitely seen a more vocal defense of law enforcement. But we've also seen an equally vocal reaction to his reaction. Colin Kaepernick's protest in kneeling before the National Anthem garnered way more press than it deserved, perhaps because it flew in the face of Trump's powerful support of the police. But it's also a testament to the protest itself. It worked! Colin ended up on magazine covers and transformed himself from a fading athlete to a revolutionary figure. I gotta hand it to the guy—at the very least, it worked out for him (as for the country, that's another story). But his protest succeeded, because it was a perfect recipe for a media hungry for such narratives. It ticked all the boxes: Another American institution is cast as the oppressor, and race is the primary factor. The problem with the protest, however, is that it made the target not simply the police, but the country itself. By taking that knee during the National Anthem, at a normally apolitical event where people go to get away from such crap, we all became the bad guys.

Was Colin protesting the police, or the entire system? I say the latter—and here's why. If you look at his other political statements and activist endeavors, you'll see that it's all part of the "oppressor vs. oppressed" story line—a narrative where the only happy ending is to topple the evil, oppressive system. He drank the radical leftist Kool-Aid, and the media, as always, cheered him on. Meanwhile, the NFL's ratings took a hit, but cable TV didn't. Colin supplied so much fodder for so many segments, and will continue to do so if and when he decides to run for president!

As I finish this chapter, the NFL just announced new rules to put an end to the kneeling controversy, which involves fining players. Some people—even usually on-the-ball libertarians— saw this as infringing on one's right to freedom of speech.

They are *wrong*. The First Amendment is a right held by every citizen—*against the government*. But a private entity like the NFL? They own it—they make the rules. As long as there is no discrimination, the NFL can mandate that all players wear tutus and the referees speak Esperanto. It's their ball, they can take it and go home. And the players can protest, but they will be penalized if they try it during the game. Penalized, not *JAILED*. Only the government can jail you. See the difference? It's a shame the media can't.

And if any still call this discriminatory, tell them that the rule applies to everyone who disrespects the anthem *for any reason*. The NFL is killing a trend before we see others kneeling about guns, abortion, climate change—or, God forbid—any cause the media finds not left-wing enough for their virtue-signaling tastes.

CHAPTER THREE

HOLLYWOOD

It's too easy: going after movie and pop stars over their political pronouncements. It's like going after a clam for being clammy. But you know what?

They deserve it.

If you have an opportunity to (figuratively) smack one for their stupid, pretentious opinions, don't pass it by. Because they'd never let an opportunity pass to do the same to you. They hate you.

They also assume that their wealth and popularity are substitutes for thoughtfulness, grace, and wisdom, when in reality it is usually a mix of cheekbones and nepotism that got them where they are. They assume that they know more than you because perhaps a half-million girls between the ages of nine and fourteen downloaded a song in a fit of irrational hysteria that wore off once they discovered real life.

And now, after the Weinstein scandal, we can rest comfortably knowing we will never have to take a single suggestion on how to live our lives from a movie star again—about what to drive, how to eat, or how to think. Every time a star engages in a new bout of moral preening, simply remind yourself that they never stood up to Harvey, never condemned Roman Polanski, and always looked the other way when the casting couch extended into full-blown assault. Screw 'em.

So, when I can't find anything new to write about, I always know a celebrity will be there for me to provide new easy fodder.

They're as reliable as a champagne hangover. And it's this very fodder, once publicly outlined and mocked, that helped reduce sentimental leftist beliefs to uproarious parody.

That made it easier for Trump, in my opinion, to come out and say what we've been saying all along: that we aren't crazy for loving this country, for appreciating law enforcement, for believing that national security matters. These were the very topics that the entertainment industry felt compelled to mock on a daily basis. The same people who play cops and soldiers on-screen can't wait to denigrate them in real life. This is known in psychology circles as "an inferiority complex" or by its more colloquial term, "being a dick."

So Trump was a brash antidote to their pretension, a walking middle finger to the haciendas of the Hollywood Hills. And yeah, he loved movie stars and celebrities—but it seems, at least to me, that he got over that when he got older. It's like he realized he didn't need them. And he was right.

And then you heard so many hacks claiming they were gonna move to Canada over Trump. But does anyone anywhere know someone who's actually moved to Canada? And was not then drafted by the Maple Leafs?

Maybe celebrities should try something even more foreign—say, move to an Alabama church town (I think all of them are church towns). If they did, I'd bet my life they'd be treated respectfully as a fellow American by all those Trump-loving Nazis.

Of course, celebrity causes don't help. Which is why so many of us took great pleasure in the idiot parade that was 2016. Could anything be more delicious than the resumption of the Keystone pipeline, after Leo DiCaprio, Julia Louis-Dreyfus, and Mark Ruffalo made such a stink over it? For me, it's like a deep-fried Oreo smothered in barbecue sauce. (And because of increased fracking, which celebs hate, we're now less dependent on the Middle East for oil.)

Anyway, Hollywood is in a pickle. They're now exposed for

the behavior that we always knew was there. If they did a film on Roman Polanski's crimes, they would change a thirteen-year-old girl to thirteen-year-old scotch! But, after Hurricane Harvey (W.), it's too late. America is alive, and Hollywood is dying.

But I can hear a criticism coming:

Greg, aren't you a hypocrite for bashing celebs for their political musings, yet you embraced Kanye's positive tweets about Trump?

The answer: HELL NO. Kanye's different. What he did was a risk. He didn't back climate change, gun control, or any other liberal pet cause. He chose Trump. Which could cost him capital, fans, and album sales. And he took that risk knowing the consequences. He did so as an example to others that it's possible. Who does that remind you of? Kanye 2024!

December 7, 2011

> The Baldwin family is the most interesting dynamic you can find in a family: On one end, you have Stephen, who is sweet, playful, and decent . . . and then there's Alec, who's the opposite. And then there's Billy, who's as dumb as a stump.

So, what kind of man in his fifties throws a tantrum over a toy? Alec Baldwin, of course. He got *kicked off a plane* when told he couldn't play an electronic game.

So, he slammed the restroom door so loud it spooked the pilot. But look, it's just too easy to rip Baldwin over this.

Except that Alec thinks it's funny.

But everyone in the plane had to wait for him to move his big fat rump.

> I believe Alec was using a plane bathroom, which is actually grounds for an emergency landing.

But when you think about it? Isn't Baldwin the real hero here?

See, there are two sets of rules in America—one for us and then one for the truly vulnerable: celebrities. And someone has to stand up for the self-absorbed stars who are so often bullied by the little people.

Sure, Baldwin's tantrum delayed everyone's departure, but in the movie that is Baldwin's life, those folks are just bit players. Who cares about them?

And I condemn those who say the behavior reeks of hypocrisy. Sure, he is pro-union, but slurs the working-class flight attendant. And yes, he's a greenie, but flies cross-country constantly.

But in celebrity life, hypocrisy doesn't exist, because being a phony bleeding heart allows you to be a real-life jerk, which is why I'm starting a new charity called "Buy Alec a Drone" or BAAD. Send me your donations, and together we'll buy an unmanned plane operated from a salt flat in Utah to take Alec wherever he wants.

That way, no crew must deal with this insufferable jerk, and he can play his games alone in the sky like a giant man-baby in an oversized diaper.

> I ran into Alec about a year ago in my neighborhood. We chatted and he pretended he didn't know who I was. Which is funny, since he blocked me on Twitter, which I take as a badge of honor. I've also been blocked by Sarah Silverman and Lena Dunham, who both exercised this cowardly move after initiating a spat with me! I ask you: Is there anything lower than throwing a rock, then running and hiding? But to be blocked by Alec, Sarah, and Lena? I can't think of a better achievement. I might put that fact on my tombstone. "Here lies Greg Gutfeld. Blocked by three miserable celebrity cranks since 2011." Or I might just get cremated. (I think I'd look pretty sexy in an urn.)

February 24, 2012

As the Oscars approach like some diseased clown, a new study claims the Academy voters are way less diverse than the movie-going public. Oscar voters are 94 percent white and 77 percent male. So, an industry that sees America as racist is as diverse as a David Duke rally.

Worse, the median age is sixty-two, which means their hair is white, so their follicles are as bigoted as their feelings. If I were a cow, they'd make me sick in every one of my four stomachs. I actually have two stomachs, one just for Fiddle Faddle.

> I feel like Hollywood was listening when I said this. By 2018, the Oscars became a full-blown college brochure—depicting as much diversity per square inch as possible.

But relax, minorities aren't the only outsiders. Here are some folks you *never* see in the movies:

> What in God's name was I smoking when I wrote that paragraph? Please tell me—because I want more of it. Also, please tell me: What is Fiddle Faddle?

- An American soldier who is not a psycho.
- A Christian not portrayed as a wild-eyed nut.
- A corporate head who isn't corrupt.
- An Italian who is not a mobster.
- A community activist who is really just a protester living off the government.
- A journalist who is a lefty propagandist, and an academic who's the same.

All of these represent reality far more than movies—because they're not defined by fake edginess and how cleverly you can diss America.

This matters. Hollywood is how America talks to the world.

Why put this bunch of coddled geezers in charge of that? Thanks to their relentless drone since the sixties about the state of our nation, it's no wonder the world hates us.

If America really reflected what's in our movies, wouldn't you?

These films don't reflect us at all. They reflect an America existing in the Viagra-addled minds of Starbucks socialists who hate our country, its values, and themselves.

Which is why my favorite movie of the year is the one I made in Mexico with an ostrich. It's still up on YouTube despite the complaints.

It used to bug me that it took a while for part of *The Five* viewing audience to understand me. When I read that last paragraph, I totally understand why it took a while. I purposely made it difficult, bringing up "art" films I might have made in another country. You might wonder, why would I do that? Because it was a sort of code I used for fans. If that line made you smile, then I knew and you know that you were "one of us," the weird legion of *Red Eye* fans who understood that introducing deviancy now and then was important to make sure you're listening— and to make sure you knew I cared enough to take stupid risks and not say the same old crap.

Where was I? Oh yeah—the Oscars ceremony is one national ritual America needs to get over. Once a year the American tribe turns its eyes to Hollywood, our own Mount Olympus, to watch the golden ones tell us the meaning of our lives. There is only one problem: They're almost all a mess. Look, let's be honest: Any dope can act. Even great actors will tell you that. I mean, O.J. Simpson had a screen career. Why so many of these moral twerps have been anointed, or rather have anointed themselves the moral compass of the nation, I just can't fathom. Hitchcock had it right: They're talking props. And they talk too damn much. I can't wait until CGI is good enough to make movies without any real actors. Let's see how "woke" Mark Ruffalo is when he's scrubbing hubcaps for a living.

Then again, I *love* the Oscars, because they remind me to hate the Oscars. And it's important to be reminded of the things you hate. Hate provides helpful focus, and reminds you that unless you hate things that deserve hating, they get away with stuff that ends up hurting you. So I hope the Oscars never go away, for there's nothing that bothers me more, and obviously nothing I like to talk about more. Besides Fiddle Faddle.

March 12, 2012

So, I didn't see the movie *Game Change*. I've been on vacation and the nude rodeo camp didn't have cable. It's about us and how dumb the film and TV industry thinks we really are.

We're dumb, they think, because we don't bend to their lazy assumptions about life—that America is evil, the left is always compassionate, and Republicans eat babies.

By the way, Colin Quinn told me once at the gym to stop saying "Republicans eat babies" because it's a "hack joke." I told him that he probably eats Republican babies, but yeah, he's usually right about these things. He coached me for my appearance on *The Daily Show* and made me way more nervous than if he hadn't coached me. I think he did it on purpose. He also told me *The Greg Gutfeld Show* needed a live audience, which I initially ignored. Turned out he was

right. Once we added an audience, about six months after
we premiered, the whole vibe changed. We knew what was
funny, and what wasn't. The jokes we made didn't die in
weird silence anymore. And bam—our ratings jumped by
100 percent, thanks to the energy provided by 160 clapping
hands. So I guess I owe Colin a beer, but he doesn't drink.

But what do you expect? Asking Hollywood to rip the left is
like asking a Van Halen tribute band to make fun of Van Halen.

You can't skewer those you idolize.

See, Hollywood is nothing more than a tribute band for the
left, banging out hit after hit on the right, when they're not sleeping with dopey starlets in PETA shirts.

But whose fault is that?

Look, if there is a restaurant that serves bad food, it's bad. You
avoid it. But if every restaurant serves bad food, then you got to
make your own.

So, it's time for conservatives to stop complaining and start
doing. We need a new generation of right-thinking chefs with a
mission to make the food you want to eat. Our kids need to write,
they need to go to film school. They need to invade pop culture,
or the joke will always be on us.

Until then, movies will be oh so predictable and so will our
complaints. It may take decades to complete this mission, but it's
the only way to make a game change for real.

That monologue is directly descended from Andrew Breitbart's famous claim that politics is downstream from
culture, a point proved correct by the first pop culture

president in history to be elected, Donald Trump. Trump won not because he was a movie or TV star, but because he knew their terrain and refused to be boxed in by them. I have a feeling he's not going to be the last in the line of nonpolitical pop cultural personalities running for office. I predict by 2100 every offshoot of the Kardashian family will have been president [of California]. I'm only slightly joking: I maintain that if Oprah decides to run and has no devastating skeletons in her closet [is Steadman actually a space alien she's kept captive?], then she could out-trump Trump. (Note: I wrote this months before the Kanye West seismic event. You know he'll be in Trump's 2020 cabinet.)

As for the point that we need more right-thinking perspectives in the entertainment industry—be okay with the fact that it may never happen. For two reasons:

- Right-wingers and libertarian types often don't think politically in business, so even if they were in movies, they wouldn't let it influence their decisions in films. It's not like a right-wing Tom Hanks would suddenly do a "Corporations are Awesome!" movie. But, on the other hand, there might be fewer screeds directed at flyover country.

- Nonliberals might just be hardwired to do other stuff than acting, singing, and dancing. Wishing there were more conservatives in film might be like wishing there were more leftists in mixed martial arts. It's just not part of the makeup of either crowd. True, there are exceptions—which is why they stand out, or do their best not to.

April 9, 2012

So Matt Damon is making an antifracking movie. Yay! John Krasinski will star in it, no doubt, also an expert on this cruel practice that extracts natural gas from the ground.

I hope he makes goofy faces like he does in *The Office*.

> God, did that get old—instead of getting an audience to laugh at a joke, they just threw to Krasinski's "look how dumb they are and how smart I am" face. I'm sure he's a nice guy in real life, but by season three I wanted to hit him with a blunt object—like maybe Matt Damon.

But like every film these days, it's just a remake, harkening back to *The China Syndrome*—that shrill antinuke script from the seventies. If you think culture doesn't change politics, remember nuclear power is still recovering from that celebrity-driven smear, which means you can blame Hollywood for our dependence on oil right now.

> Yes, the nuclear technology America pioneered could have likely freed us from the tyranny of fossil fuels, if not for actress/aerobic star/war criminal Jane Fonda. And a concert given by someone named Jackson Browne, who tried to save us from energy independence when not terrifying Daryl Hannah.

So, why hate fracking? Isn't it just a horizontal windmill, shattering rocks instead of birds?

Come on—it's true! Fracking is really a horizontal wind-mill . . . that works!! And doesn't kill innocent bald eagles. Seriously—why are greenies up in arms over drilling in the Arctic National Wildlife Refuge and upsetting some caribou, but don't give a flying toss over the zillions of birds chopped to bits by windmills? I'll tell you why: because they're silly people. That's why I'm here: to point that out, in case you miss it.

Well, the greenies hate it because it works. Yes, a funny thing happened on the way to Solyndra. Fracking cut a path toward energy independence, making similar green efforts look kind of silly. And Matt knows we can't have that; then America wouldn't be the bad guy anymore. This one fact alone would eliminate the only major villain in today's movies.

True, with drilling, there can be environmental side effects. But there are environmental side effects to everything, including filmmaking.

Research has shown that the film industry pollutes like mad, thanks to the idling trucks, special effects, and set construction. But that's Hollywood. So never mind. Anyway, I think someone must have pumped sand and water through Damon's head, because he certainly exudes enough natural gas to power a small city.

I live in New York, where there's a movie shot on every street almost every day. The trucks idle there for hours; the caterers create garbage bag after garbage bag of trash. And that's just to feed Seth Rogen. If it weren't for the hard work of millions of folks in the oil industry, these dopes would be depending on the oral tradition to tell their vacuous stories. Which I wouldn't mind—the oral tradition is the only way I get my legends—anally is just too painful.

Anyway, here's a pop quiz for all the present-day anti-pipeliners:

- How does the U.S. currently transport oil?
- Is that method actually safer or cheaper than your alternative?
- Does more expensive transport hurt the poor consumer more than the wealthy?
- Is there the remotest possibility that renewables can power the nation even enough to install renewables?
- In fact, do you know one basic fact about the subject that you're opining about?

April 20, 2012

So, George Clooney will host a $6 million fundraising dinner for Barack Obama at his L.A. home. And people can donate three bucks to win a spot at the table. I wonder if they're serving free-range terrier.

Ah yes, a dog joke. In case you forgot, around this time we learned about Obama's sampling of dog as part of his diet when growing up wherever. Yeah, he ate a dog. The media found it exotic and adventurous. Of course when Mitt Romney DIDN'T eat a dog, but only had a live pet in a box on the roof of his car, he was SATAN. Satan with

> amazing hair, by the way. Can we agree that Mitt Romney
> was the best-looking presidential candidate we ever had?
> (Maybe I should quit writing him those letters.) Obama
> could put Romney himself on the roof of his car and drive
> cross-country and not get half the shit Mitt had thrown
> at him.

Yes, it sounds like a presidential kissing booth. But what's weird, only three dollars? That's what Dana pays her intern for a day's work. Sad story—Dana's intern came to America to chase a dream, and now, all he does is wax spelling bee trophies from 1989. I guess his quiet sobs are music to someone's ears.

But three bucks? I guess four would be too much to hear Obama say, "Wow, these organically grown fair trade green beans are delish. Hey, Biden, would you eat with your mouth closed, please?"

Here's the point of this "win a date with a 1 percent" event: A bunch of Hollywood zillionaires invite unwashed slobs to Clooney's place . . . and the Republicans are elitist? I guarantee you they'll be eating with silver spoons.

> This reminds me of the scene in *The Elephant Man* when
> the socialists had poor John Merrick to dinner. It's as if the
> Democrats can't believe such a thing as a blue-collar Republican exists. After the Trump win, they better believe it now.

And celebs like Clooney are so special they can't even live in America. It's so small a playing field and doesn't make them special enough to their countrymen. Patriotism is so red state.

But this fits perfectly with Barack's philosophy of American unexceptionalism. So, now, some lucky winner can sit at the table with these wealthy internationalists and hear lines like "Wow, I would say this is exceptional chicken. But if it's American grown, I say it's no better than anyone else's chicken."

If that doesn't make you a Republican, you're hopeless.

> I especially like that dig at Dana over spelling bee trophies. I once asked her if she had any regrets in life and—and I'm not kidding—she said, "I wish I had taken harder courses in college." What kind of regret is that? It's a Dana Perino Regret. A Dana Perino Regret is not a regret over a shameful act, but a desire to have done something better that was already done great. My typical regret involves some sorry combination of tequila and a lonely long-haul trucker. But a typical Dana Perino Regret: "I wish I had four different cheese dips for the nachos, not just three. Do you think anyone will notice?"

August 6, 2012

Legendary actor Clint Eastwood—you remember him from *Die Hard*—endorsed Mitt Romney for president.

> Yes, I know Clint wasn't in *Die Hard*—I just do that to rile up viewers. When they write in to correct me, then I know they're listening. After all, everyone knows the star of *Die Hard* was Bob Saget.

Now, a friend of mine laughs when I get excited over stuff like this. After all, I often wish that lefty celebrities would stay out of politics. So he thinks my excitement over Clint makes me a hypocrite. Not really. See, righty celebrities are different. If you meet a politically active celebrity, nine times out of ten they are to the left of Hugo Chávez. And if you meet an apolitical celebrity, nine times out of ten they will just parrot the liberal line. That's because when asked about a cause, they just can't shrug, they must play the role or end up losing roles later.

So that leaves a tiny group of gutsy types who are not afraid of losing work by expressing views that are branded evil in Hollywood. So my excitement over righty stars is really a recognition of guts. And yes, I realize Clint's political outspokenness came much later in his career. Knowing that actors lose work over things they say, perhaps Clint realizes he has got less to lose at this point.

> This is why Kanye's pro-Trump tweets are vital—he did that at age forty, at the height of his powers, when he has most to lose. And it looks like he could lose a lot for his bravery. But he gained his freedom.

But lefty stars risk nothing, ever—in fact they gain from their political views, jobwise. So the next time some young star lies about how fracking causes breast cancer, realize it's only for his career. Because the lefty ladder has now replaced the casting couch, which means they can now screw the whole country at once.

> I should note that not every Hollywood star is a bleeding-heart leftist—there's actually a strong cohort of righties in there, but they're smart enough to keep a low profile. Being a conservative in Hollywood is like being a belt in Michael Moore's house—rare, and despised, for it's a reminder of long-lost standards. I get into that next!

September 28, 2012

Nothing says presidential leadership like decisive action.

And that's what we saw last night as the producer of the anti-Islam film was arrested for violating probation.

Yes, this arrest has nothing to do with the film that Obama and crew idiotically pinned on the Middle East mob!

No, this is just a coincidence, it's all about probation!

Yeah—and I'm five-foot-ten.

> This was the same guy who was blamed for the terrorist attack on our Benghazi outpost that left four Americans dead . . .

Anyway, this filmmaker gets no bail because he is dangerous. He makes scary films, films that kill people. It's like *The Ring* but without the creepy Japanese girl.

> Okay, okay, I admit it—I'm five-eleven.

So, where the hell is Hollywood? Shouldn't this scare the diapers off Alec Baldwin? Matthew Modine, where's the march for freedom of expression?

A guy gets arrested over a film?? And Hollywood is dead silent.

> If anyone should be arrested for a film, it should be whoever made *Love Actually*.

Streisand, Depp and Clooney, Julia Louis-Dreyfus, where the hell are you people? Hiding under Harvey Weinstein? I know that it's physically possible.

> Yes, a fat joke about Harvey Weinstein. I would say it's "too soon," except I made that joke BEFORE the scandal broke. Little did I know that he used his heft when climbing all over actresses. Now it just doesn't seem funny anymore.

October 25, 2012

> Looking back, it's amazing how Harvey Weinstein really played a role in keeping liberals in power. They really do owe him a lot. No wonder they kept their mouths shut when he roamed the Hollywood Hills like a rutting, rabid boar.

So you know that TV movie about killing bin Laden, which airs two days before the election? It's now being reedited to make the president's role more prominent. According to the *New York Times*, Obama backer Harvey Weinstein, who owns the rights to the film, personally stepped in to help recut it to strengthen Mr. Obama's role.

Weinstein and director John Stockwell deny the changes are politically motivated.

I called myself for a response, which was: "Ha, ha, ha, ha, ha!"

So, with Obama in trouble, Weinstein reedits to give Obama more credit. Just a coincidence? Yes. So is getting wet in the rain.

Look, we already know Mitt Romney is running not just against Obama, but against the Hollywood arm of his own publicity machine.

But it raises questions, like why can you politicize bin Laden and not Benghazi? Obama takes credit for one, and avoids responsibility for the other.

What happens if this films triggers mob violence? This administration blamed Benghazi on a film that inspired Islamic outrage. Will Weinstein be arrested if this happens with his flick? It's a good question, since he's been silent on the subject of free expression, while the anti-Muslim filmmaker blamed for Benghazi sweats in jail.

Perhaps Harvey could keep him company. Heck, they could watch the movie together.

> Who knew I was predicting Harvey's downfall for an entirely different reason!
>
> As usual, Hollywood treats history as toilet paper. This film was a break with fact of Oliver Stone proportions. But dammit, it's not political! So I guess the "Reagan saves the West from the brutal scourge of global communism" movie will be out any day now?

March 6, 2013

On March 5, we saw misty-eyed left-wing hacks pay tribute to a dead tyrant. Sean Penn, Oliver Stone, Jimmy Carter, Joe Kennedy, all shower Hugo Chávez with wreaths of blithering babble.

But the winner in the Chávez dribble Olympics is the nobody at the *Nation* who wrote this: "The biggest problem Venezuela faced during his rule was not that Chávez was authoritarian, but that he wasn't authoritarian enough." Tell that to the dead.

While it's rude to bag on the dead man, it's more off-putting to lionize a bad man. The default cliché that infects all lefties is that Hugo was David to our Goliath. Even though this Dave stole billions of dollars fostering a murder rate that dwarfs Chicago's.

When Oliver Stone and Sean Penn weep over a man who demonizes America, their message is simple: We agree with him.

What perverted minds these celebrities have. It's like women who fall in love with killers on death row. In the end, it's all about the desperately low opinion they have of themselves—an opinion we all share.

The equation seems to be, "I'm a piece of crap, so I have to fall in love with someone who also sees me as a piece of crap."

The fact is, Hugo was the least popular Hugo since the Yugoslavian national vehicle. Maybe all these Hollywood ghouls should be forced to drive them just to remind themselves what amazing tools they truly are.

Funny—Penn, Stone, or any of the other Chávistas who lionized this low-rent despot never loved the man so much that they actually moved there. They apparently preferred the living hell of America under Bush, Obama, and now Trump. Go figure.

Hugo's legacy still lives on, as Venezuela is in a slow-motion descent into hell. Citizens can't afford toilet paper—as their currency is actually worth less than the paper used to wipe asses. Due to rationing of food, citizens have resorted to eating their pets, as their president happily eats a meat pie DURING an actual live televised address. This is the epitome of true socialism: Cling to an idea as the world around you crumbles. Because as long as you're at the top, you'll never go hungry. This is a truth conveniently ignored by Hollywood [maybe because their own means of survival is so similar]. They choose to embrace the romanticized notion of the revolutionary, while overlooking the pile of victims left behind.

March 26, 2013

This monologue is a response to a putrid antigun music video Jim Carrey made, in which he mocked the late Charlton Heston for his work with the NRA. The big joke that the video showcased was that Heston liked guns to make up for his manhood. I know—brilliant. But I get it—knocking Carrey for unoriginality is like knocking shit for stinking.

So yesterday, I nailed has-been Jim Carrey for a skit attacking rural Americans and Charlton Heston, a man who cannot respond because he's dead. It was vile stuff—mocking a dead man—and it vainly tried to be disguised as edgy, implying that gun owners compensate for the lack of manhood with guns.

So I guess our Navy SEALs are all neutered?

Now, I don't expect depth from a roiling bucket of sewage. Gun rights were never a core issue for me, but Carrey and tools like him made it one. This is Hollywood with its slip showing.

Carrey's video shows what they really think of flyover America. They hate you. To them, you're all white rednecks. When he mocks a dead and decent man . . . Dude,

What are the chances Carrey would ever say any of this brave stuff to a Navy SEAL? Or a SWAT cop? You think his face is all twisted now . . .

I get that you are a clown, but at least hit someone who can hit back, you simpering tool.

I think even a dead Charlton Heston may be more than a match for this mugging maggot, who seems incapable of picking on anyone who can stand up to him.

And Hollywood, where the hell are you? If you worked with Heston or respected his work in civil rights, *say something*. How can you let this odious twerp defile Heston's memory? You should regurgitate Carrey like a cat upchucking a crusted fur ball.

Carrey has not made a good film in years, which is why he is a marionette trying to please his liberal puppeteers. He's desperate.

But forget your thoughts on guns. His cruelty reveals how cloistered Hollywood is. Carrey thought his crap would be welcome. Beneath Jim's phony New Age persona, he is as hateful as the KKK, and his self-esteem is so low he cannot go a moment without feeding it, which is why, when he is called out, he hides. And he hides behind a gun. He has armed security, which by his own logic means he has tiny genitals.

Carrey's reputation and career have steadily declined—proof that the public likes a clown only if the clown isn't an asshole. What he did to Heston was unforgivable—especially coming from a toad who couldn't act his way out of bed. It is pretty funny: Heston's been dead for a while, but he has a brighter future in films than Carrey.

But here's one reason I love social media: It exposes jerks like Jim, who posts his noxious twaddle for all to see. Twitter exposes the soft simplemindedness of the celebrities. They undo everything their publicists try to mask. The mysterious is replaced by the moronic. The publicity machine used to be able to hide the asshole that lurked behind the poster-boy persona. Now it's virtually impossible—because there are now too many avenues for jackasses to expose themselves [I'm going to leave that comment without an obvious punch line].

We hear a lot about bullying—it's the go-to issue for celebrities who want to appear to care. On one hand, they'll tell you how to live your life, and on the other, crap all over the dead, and, of course, gun-toting Middle America.

Now, I am going to go out on a limb and say I'm against bullying. But I'm also going to go out on a shorter limb and call b.s. on all the antibullying campaigns featuring well-off stars and starlets who keep their mouths shut when there's far worse crap going on in their own industry. I also LOVE how celebrities always portray themselves in interviews as the "geek" or "ugly duckling" in high school. You know, that's true maybe 5 percent of the time.

I have no science to back that up, just my gut, which is 98 percent more accurate than science. I also have no science to back up that stat either, but now that it's published in a book, it's as good as gold.

April 12, 2013

So Jane Fonda is playing First Lady Nancy Reagan in an upcoming film called *The Butler*. And some veterans are ticked off, given that Fonda's most famous picture isn't a moving one, but a single photo of her seated on an antiaircraft battery aimed at us. She claims she's going to play Nancy Reagan fairly, with no cheap shots. Yes, and dogs know Esperanto.

> I try to work in a reference to Esperanto whenever I can. I actually speak it. But because no one else alive actually can, you'll never know if that's true or not.

A navy veteran has started to boycott the movie. But Jane had a mocking message for him. Quote, "Get a life," unquote.

That's exactly what she said. When asked about it by the *Hollywood Reporter*, she added, "If it creates hoopla, it will cause more people to see the movie."

> You could likely argue the opposite. Who wants to see a movie by an asshole! I'm sure many Vietnam vets would love to "get a life"—especially the ones killed by the enemy Jane cheered on. Both her responses—telling a vet to "get a life" after he put his on the line for jackasses like Jane Fonda, as well as saying "bad publicity is better than no publicity"—reveal the depth of Fonda's thinking. There isn't any.

The film is distributed by the Weinstein brothers, who are about as respectful of conservatives as some rappers are of women.

> I could rewrite this sentence to "The film is distributed by the Weinstein brothers, who are about as respectful of conservatives as some Weinsteins are of women." In a way, I owe an apology to rappers for including them in the same sentence as the Weinsteins.

Which is why John Cusack, a lefty, is playing Nixon, and Robin Williams plays Dwight Eisenhower. I'm surprised they didn't get Roseanne to play Kissinger.

It's all done on purpose to generate publicity by upsetting the right people, i.e., the right. The movie gains mojo by satisfying the smirking left.

So, let them—who cares about these fools?

Look, we know this is a casting stunt meant to create an uproar. But telling a man who served his country to get a life when his angry response is exactly what you wanted makes you a jerk.

But it's Jane Fonda. She's had forty years of practice. Expecting her to change now is like expecting opera from a toad.

I could tell I was probably hungover when I wrote this—that last line is very hackneyed: "That's like expecting X from a Y," in which "Y" is incapable of actually delivering "X." When I don't feel like thinking too hard about something, I end up falling back on that construction, and I am not proud of it. It's my version of a 7-Eleven burrito. Yeah, you could get something better, but you're there, and they're cheap and easy, so . . .

MORE IMPORTANT: If you combine the full effects of Southeast Asian communism—from the Viet Cong to the utter madness of Pol Pot in Cambodia—Jane Fonda's support was the historical equivalent of supporting malaria. I can't even joke about this woman. She was Typhoid Jane in aerobics tights.

August 23, 2013

Ben Affleck is playing Batman.

Batman, as you know, is a rich man who fights evil, which sounds kind of Republican to me. I mean, imagine if Batman were the hero our media wanted him to be—he'd be a grad student, a leader of drum circles who pickets fracking sites while vandalizing Monsanto labs. His Robin would be his tapeworm, his daddy's trust fund acting as Batmobile.

Or perhaps he'd be a sexually confused whistle-blower leaking key info to our enemies. The evil he fights would be the U.S. because it always is, for those who mock the war on terror. Instead, we get a rich white guy, Mr. Affleck, playing a rich white guy who stops bad guys, because it sells.

Hollywood may deny the existence of real evil in the world—other than other rich white guys—but it knows that on-screen morality makes financial sense, even if they laugh at it privately. No one wants a superhero who frets over gray areas. We want exceptional men who kill. But the problem with Batman isn't Batman at all. Each film depends on a new evil, a villain beyond shocking who justifies our repulsion.

The problem is, real evil now outstrips movie evil. When boys kill an Australian ballplayer for fun, when boys kill a war hero for fun, when scum rape and mutilate a young couple, or when a young girl is shot dead for fun, when a young man is rewarded with a *Rolling Stone* cover for blowing up children, you get pretty jaded.

> I am referencing some of the more grisly real-life crimes that occurred around the time the film came out.

I mean, who does Batman fight now when what we are fighting right now seems so much worse?

So basically, in my head, if you read the synopsis above, Affleck is playing Donald Trump. HA! I mean, when you think about it, isn't Donald Trump basically a crude version of Bruce Wayne? Bruce Wayne, a rich guy in a time of trouble, became Batman to save the city. Trump, a rich guy, in a time of trouble, became president to save the country. So who does that make the villains?

The Joker = Hillary [the laugh is identical].

The Riddler = Chuck Schumer [the resemblance is uncanny].

The Penguin = Harvey Weinstein.

Catwoman = Nancy Pelosi.

I dare you to refute this amazing analogy! Simply write your argument on a large sheet of paper and mail it to Greg Gutfeld c/o Go Screw Yourself. Eat Me, Colorado, 10021.

This is one of my favorite monologues. It's something I think about a lot—that what Hollywood deems heroic in real life is far different from what they promote in movies. How we see heroism—a fearless, freedom-loving badass Navy SEAL—is exactly how Hollywood portrays heroism . . . when it wants to make money. But in real life—in their rich, secluded, existences behind armed security and iron gates—their version of heroism is something different. It could be a traitor who leaks defense secrets. It could be a cop killer on the run in Cuba. It could be a radical bomb maker who's now a professor in your local college. The average Hollywood industry hack can live in two worlds—the one they sell you, which they hate, and the one they believe, which is a lie. And you just know that when they're selling you the brand of heroism you believe to be true, they're laughing at you all the way to their therapist [isn't it weird that the psychiatry industry is concentrated on the coasts?]. They only do THOSE movies to fund the other smaller movies that make fun of you.

Note: I realize these are sweeping generalizations, but that's what Hollywood does to us every day. And it's not hard to find the evidence that backs up such generalizations. They churn it out daily in films and television. It's not a generalization: It's just overwhelmingly true. And while there are genuinely honest diamonds in the rough—real, rebellious television and brave moviemaking—they are overshadowed by the dreck that ticks every cynical assumption about American life.

Last but not least, I realize that since 9/11, I have stopped watching zombie films, and horror films in general. They do nothing for me, or to me. They don't raise my pulse, they don't make me sweat. The only reason I can think for this change: Such villainy just doesn't match what we're facing in real life. Is the postmodern Joker really as bad as the everyday ISIS decapitator? Not even close.

October 30, 2013

Sean Penn was on a local cable access program recently, interviewed by a mangy kitten, where he said that the Tea Party were rubes and Ted Cruz should be institutionalized. Behold the vile.

SEAN PENN, ACTOR: Let's go to the Tea Party influence on Congress. I think they have—there's a mental health problem in Congress. This would be solved by committing them by executive order, I think, because these are American brothers and sisters. We shouldn't be criticizing them, attacking them. This is a cry for help.

PIERS MORGAN, CNN: Literally commit people like Ted Cruz?

PENN: He's my American brother. We should take care of him. He's in trouble.

MORGAN: Actually have him committed?

PENN: I think it's a good idea.

> **Note: he had a chance to walk it back—Piers followed up on the comment. But this commie progeny [look it up] advocates the forced incarceration of people who disagree with him politically. I would dismiss it as a joke, until this . . .**

But moments later, this furious self-tanner admonishes Americans for saying nasty things about each other.

PENN: Between an uneducated people and the solipsism of people like Ted Cruz and their party, it's a poisonous thing. Here's this country where we have it all. We have it all to make it great and we find ways of self-destructing. And by saying nasty things about each other and being crazy.

> **You see? We're crazy—not the guy who just *completely* forgot what he said moments earlier. Anyway, talk about complete blindness. Saying nasty things about each other! AFTER he says nasty things about each other! The "solipsism" is profound!**

Wow, that's either amnesia or great cocaine. I put money on the coke.

But he's kidding. And this is humor among the left. The Tea Party, they're so stupid. The takeaway is how desperate Penn has become to maintain his cool cred in Hollywood.

Remember, Penn has always fashioned himself a rebel, yet his pronouncements are mundane, so lockstep that he shares DNA with sheep. Ribbing on the Tea Party is just lame dialogue, cut from a bad Woody Allen flick. It's so hopelessly boring.

How hilarious is it that the Tea Party is edgier than Sean Penn? They're fighting the man. He's just spooning him.

> Boy, that creates an ugly image. It's kind of sad that Penn's peak was pretty much his first movie, when he played Jeff Spicoli in *Fast Times at Ridgemont High*. After that, it was all downhill for this self-serious, pretentious twaddlemuffin.

And it reeks of distress from an aging bad boy who's just gone bad in a spoiled-lettuce sort of way. No wonder he ODed on bronzer.

What do you expect? Hollywood is home to fake rebels who bash Americans to preserve their status with a dollop of phony concern to mask their lack of depth.

> Ugh, another tanning joke. Damn—even I get tired of my own insults.

The urge to limit intrusive government is considered insane—and amassing crippling debt isn't. That's more a sign of insanity than anything. But I'd never suggest Penn be committed, for he already lives in Hollywood.

> The thing about Penn: He's likely a talented person, I think—or at least once was a talented person. So his obvious lameness in this interview reflects not simply intellect or personality, but what happens when one's assumptions are never challenged. He's gone from a vibrant young

actor to a monumental, catastrophic bore. When he talks, nothing shocks you. What he finds funny is on par with a comment left on the *Huffington Post* by a gender studies TA. He reminds me of the guy who used to be in a band, and now just works tuning guitars. He's got all the same mannerisms, but nothing else. Go home, Sean, you could use a good sleep. Because that's what you're inducing in us.

So, I have a theory about celebrities who get deep into liberal politics—the latest example being Jimmy Kimmel. Here's how it works.

Individuals who come to politics later in life possess a false confidence that's inversely proportional to their knowledge of issues. This happens on both the left and right. A person like, say, Kimmel, is only sure of his stance because he hasn't yet graduated from that adolescent emotional platform of belief onto a mature, fact-based position of thought. I've been there—the only difference was that I was twenty-two at the time. Pick any celebrity—from Penn to Kimmel to that angry lady from *Will and Grace*—the tribalism they express is born from being new to their political tribe.

Celebrities also cultivate liberal agendas because they're often safe-spaced in comfortable settings for such endeavors—and met with accolades by people with lower status who don't want to upset them at film shoots and press conferences. In Hollywood, everyone who isn't a star is that star's fearful fanboy.

And another note: Last week (March something, 2018) Sean Penn released a novel of such immense badness that even his lefty sympathizers in the media disowned it. This supports my earlier point: Come to something later in life, be it politics or writing, and your confidence is inversely proportional to skill. The book was so bad precisely because you could tell that as Sean wrote it, he thought it was sooooooo good. . . . He used a thesaurus the way a terrible cook uses salt—to cover up the lousy meat. Without that crutch, you realize that Sean Penn is as dumb as a post (not the wooden kind, the Huffington kind).

November 12, 2013

According to a new study, gun violence in PG-13 movies has tripled over the last twenty years, going from under one gunfight per hour to three per hour. Modern PG films now blast more guns than R-rated films from way back then—which goes to show you how much Hollywood loves their guns.

Unless . . . they belong to you, and you use them for protection and not pictures.

I bet if Matt Damon had to fire a real gun, he'd shoot himself in the butt, where his head currently resides.

Still, gun crime is way down, as movie crime increases. So, I'm not sure you can blame Hollywood for gun violence.

So, how about all violence? To me, one fact rears its ghoulish heads in most heinous crimes: resentment . . . which brews in the world of unrealistic luxury and unquenchable desire for infamy. Violence is now a performance for a worldwide audience, from shooting up a school to savagely punching innocent pedestrians, to hacking a harmless family to death. The weapons are all different, but the need is ever-present: "Look at me. Look at what I have done."

We call the perps insane, but it is way worse than that. Beneath it all is a pattern of entitled recognition, the desire to be known forever. Where does that come from?

As families and communities decline, recognition finds another route.

If you can't be famous for giving, you can live forever by taking away.

I basically touch too lightly on the following points:

First: Hollywood loves its guns as long as those guns do two things—make them money at the box office, and protect them at the premiere. You—the average obscure schmuck—can't have guns, but they can have them in every room. The typical Hollywood male loves a good firearm. It gives him even more power than the drugs make him think he has. It's the worst combination you can think of: an entitled celebrity, a gun, and a medicine cabinet. The only thing a Hollywood celebrity likes more than a gun is a bodyguard with a gun.

A lot of the violence perpetrated by mass shooters and terrorists alike isn't done by madmen. It is done by sane, bitter boys who see the fame around them and feel insignificant. Why is that movie star famous, and I am not? He shoots fake guns. I will shoot real ones. Violence—especially the kind that culminates in a horrifying spectacle [the recent Vegas or Florida attack]—can take someone from obscurity and exponentially make him infamous. You want to blame the NRA for that? No. Blame Hollywood, and us [cable news]—which has made fame the only currency that matters, and violence the magical way forward to immortality. Hollywood is a religion predicated on the idea that anything you do to get to Mount Olympus will be forgiven—and forgotten. But whatever you do—don't shoot inside the tent [see Weinstein, Harvey].

And finally, this concept of insignificance is new. It didn't exist before television. Before fame of a worldwide magnitude existed, you could live a life of importance in your hometown or village. If a hundred people knew you, that was enough, and your behavior mattered to THOSE people. Because they were the people you saw every day. You had meaning—you had family.

But TV- and film-based fame changed that. Now, you can afford to alienate yourself from local society if you believe you deserve greater notoriety. This is driven by an underlying cause: the emptiness of your own obscurity. The more you see of the world—on TV, Twitter, or Instagram, with instantly famous and vacuous models—the more you believe you're owed something greater than simply your neighbors' knowing your name. And when you don't get that expected fame, and feel that insignificance, you settle for infamy. You shoot up a school, or a concert. Until we learn to reconnect with the people around us, reject superficial desires for greater recognition, and stop reporting breathlessly on every garish crime [which elevates dead ghouls to a seemingly immortal status], such horrible crimes will continue to occur.

The opinions above coincide, I believe, with a lot of what noted professor Jordan Peterson has been saying about mass shooters. Peterson doesn't believe the Columbine killers were insane at all—they knew exactly what they wanted to do. They wanted to bring the world down. And that impulse is born from a nihilism that permeates current society. If we don't have a purpose in life, then what is life for? Hanging around until we die. We are now replacing the idea of purpose with the notion of exposure. More "likes," more retweets, more followers—desire for attention has replaced the need for belonging to a community, or living for a greater goal. It's not about guns, but the minds that see them as tools toward achievement in a world where nothing seems to matter. In sum, a totally connected world of social networks reveals the status inequalities that drive the worst kind of envy: the envy that doesn't seek but also destroys. And it reveals a path to infamy that the media breathlessly covers: violence.

February 19, 2014

As the debate over income equality blossoms like a flower of failure, how come no one ever targets Hollywood? A left-wing actor might make $20 million a flick as the on-set caterer makes only a hundred bucks a day.

Shouldn't Obama and his envoy of envy focus their punitive pupils on that? Of course not, because those are O's buds and they're famous, cool, and rich.

As Gregory Mankiw in the *New York Times* reports, in 2012, Robert Downey Jr. raked in $50 million, ten times what the top 1 percent of the top 1 percent make.

Yet, no outrage from class warriors in the White House. Why is that? Afraid to lose the votes? Or the famous friends?

Mankiw says actors like Downey do more than act. They pay millions in taxes, which fund schools, police, and military, and they employ a lot of people. Even if their motivation is money, the by-product helps everyone. It's the opposite of socialism—where the motivation is to help but the by-product is misery.

> I agree completely on this point. What bugs me is that this defense is never applied to other rich folks who aren't liberals, Democrats, or Hollywood stars.

It's something the left, rarely, if ever understands. There's nothing more helpful than making, and nothing less altruistic than taking. One should never attack Downey or anyone for their success. If the market can bear it, only the losers will whine.

Which is why I ask the White House to respect others who aren't as glamorous but just as hardworking. After all, Downey plays a maverick CEO. Why pamper the famous who pretend to be achievers, while punishing the real achievers themselves?

Maybe that's what President Obama really wants, to play the president instead of being one.

> I wish the *New York Times* would write articles like this about me—I do pretty much the same thing as Downey [on a smaller scale], employing a lot of people in various occupations. I spend almost all my money in my community—mostly in bars and restaurants and on handymen who fix all the crap I can't fix after I break things when I miss *Final Jeopardy*. I have supported more struggling actors and actresses with my drinking habit than all the fine arts scholarships you can name. After all, in New York, whoever waits on you is playing Fortinbras somewhere . . . even if it's in their own head.
>
> The bottom line: Superrich people are really awesome only if they're movie stars. But if you make your money any other way, you're a greedy monster. Downey makes a shitload more money than most CEOs—but he makes it "the fun way"! He entertains us! Which is way more important than figuring out how to pay for experimental vaccines. Yes, pharmaceutical companies are awful beasts, but film companies are heroic! How does that work? Who does more good for society? I'll wait while you make me a drink.

February 23, 2015

Last night were the Oscars, or as I call it, the Super Bowl for short men. It was typical Hollywood, many black presenters, few black nominees. The Oscars were as white as the cocaine snorted in the bathroom. But Patricia Arquette deservedly won for her role in *Boyhood*. And she said this.

PATRICIA ARQUETTE: To every woman who gave birth to every taxpayer and citizen of this nation, we have fought for everybody else's equal rights. It's our time to have wage equality once and for all and equal rights for women in the United States of America.

Now, one could point out that single childless women in their twenties actually earn more than their male counterparts. And that it's not really about equal rights.

Wage discrimination, after all, is illegal. But choices affect pay and life.

Women live nearly five years longer than men. Now if this were reversed, could you imagine the outcry? We'd be talking about "life disparity," not wage disparity. We'd protest against the life ceiling, not the glass ceiling, and demand that men die sooner just for the sake of equality.

But if Hollywood wants to talk about equality, look at their two worlds—one of dramatic concern at the Oscars, and the other of absurd luxury. Their gift bags cost $125,000 each—that's more than they pay their maids, their drivers, their leaf blowers, and their hookers combined.

Amazing point!

So as the Oscars trash America, the world outside is going nuts.

Women are being enslaved by a death cult, or stoned to death for adultery.

True, there may be women in Syria who would have applauded the Oscars speeches if ISIS hadn't chopped off their hands for using cellphones.

> There is no better example of misguided concern than that of a movie star's take on the world when accepting an Oscar. It's a moment that fully exposes a celebrity's imbecility—a sort of dumbass X-ray. Leftism in Hollywood

is gravitas for the lightweight, intellectualism for the stupid. Reading, facts, critical thinking . . . that's for the little people—those normative losers! So rather than actually assess the various injustices around the globe, they pick what they can handle without having to read much, or digest statistics. There are all sorts of inequalities, but in America, everyone is better off than anyone pretty much anywhere else. But that is overlooked, in favor of hammering home the same mundane, inaccurate assumptions about the world's greatest invention—America. Instead of exposing true injustice, they feed into the false ideas that fuel the anger of the people who hate us. They target those who happily tolerate their silly ideas, meaning American moviegoers, while ignoring followers of ideologies who would kill such brave artists, if given the chance.

The argument over inequality is a complex one, and often ignores the more obvious concrete cases of disparity.

For example: height. Taller people are afforded more opportunities than the short. Studies bear this out. If you're taller you're more likely to get a raise or get that job. But also, let's not forget the prime target of inequality: the plain. If you're good-looking, you'll always do better than those who aren't. But sadly, the unattractive do not mobilize, or protest. And what about the good-looking? Hollywood KNOWS that good looks are truly more important than anything. For example, it's amazing how attractiveness is used in movies to undermine one's judgment regarding good and evil. I think it really caught fire the moment Warren Beatty and Faye Dunaway played Bonnie and Clyde—how could you not love two murderous bank robbers when they're so damn hot? Mind you, it's not the obvious, grotesque villain who is portrayed as handsome [typical vicious henchmen always have scars and bad teeth]. It's the "cool" villain who is hot. And that villain is somehow granted a certain leeway, simply because when he's doing the killing, he looks so great doing it. It's why *Rolling Stone* put the Boston Bomber on its cover—he was cute. It's why every young psychopath in movies is portrayed as uniquely "complicated" when they're just psychopaths. We can talk forever about the inequality between sexes and races, but ugly people get the shortest stick of all, and we accept it as a fact of life. I've said this in previous books (it's a cause of mine). We need a Gandhi for the homely. An MLK for the plain. Until then, they will suffer in silence, as we continue to judge such books by their pimply covers.

June 17, 2015

So, on some talk show, comedy powerhouse Judd Apatow said it's crazy to think rich people care about other people.

Well, unless they're rich leftists.

JUDD APATOW: I just think it's ridiculous that anybody thinks that rich people care about other people, all right. Just as simple as that. Like when the Koch brothers like give—like new—a billion dollars for the new election cycle. It isn't out of a great concern for the masses.

When asked if this applies to rich Hollywood liberals like Apatow, he replied:

JUDD APATOW: I think the difference is that Hollywood liberals would be willing to change the entire system if we all would get money out of it. And I don't think the conservatives would do that.

So do you get that? Rich Hollywood liberals care, rich conservatives don't. Now, I could defend the Koch brothers easily. David has given more than a billion dollars to medical and cultural causes. But why bother with such facts? With Judd, you're talking to a wall—an ideological barrier that can only endure as long

> This guy actually thinks that? Wow—it must be nice to be thirteen years old forever, Judd!

as you believe your opponent is driven by ill will. So it's one thing to say you think someone's wrong. But it's another to say that person is just no good. Judd does that—which allows for his hypocrisy.

To him, a rich liberal can flood politics with money because it's for the greater good. Your rich people are evil, my rich people . . . good. This is a conviction driven by the insecurity prevalent in novices playing catchup with newfound politics.

But consider the person who allows the possibility of being wrong. He ends up with sharper ideas. For conflict exercises your muscles of logic and reason—rather than playing patty cake with a salivating fan base.

So Judd's not evil. He's sometimes right, he's sometimes wrong. But he'd probably never say that about us. Which makes you wonder how far his side might go to hurt its opponents. If all disagreement is rooted in malice, then everything's permitted when you're fighting evil. Demonize, ostracize, and pulverize, all in the name of the greater good.

It's one thing to disagree—we do that all the time. It's a different thing to root the disagreement in morality—to claim that you don't agree with me because you are evil. It's the kind of tribalism that leads ultimately to excuses for oppression. Remember, there are those on the left who believe you should be able to imprison those who question their extremely inflexible beliefs on climate change. There are those who believe you can "punch a Nazi"—which most of us would like to do—except that their assessment of who a Nazi might be is anyone who departs from their political assumptions.

I'm writing this little note in January 2018, just after Trump used the phrase "shithole" to describe economically rotten countries. Apparently, Hollywood finds that outrageous, but had no problem with their favorite nominee calling half of America "deplorable." In Trump's case, he was referring to the state of a country, in the other, Hillary was referring to *actual* people. But when you're a liberal, you're exempt from your own high-horse mentality. You can accuse me of being vile, while employing a far more vile vocabulary. A perfect example is Chelsea Handler, who despises Trump for his behavior, yet makes far more insidious attacks on people she hates than he does. For example, she just tweeted a particularly vile comment about Senator Lindsey Graham being blackmailed over homosexual behavior. If a right-wing commentator had said something similar about, say, Oprah Winfrey, he or she would be crucified. People like Handler and Apatow see standards as something that applies only to the little people. Not them. They're special. They're liberal and rich. But not evil. I will never deem them so, even though they would not extend me the same courtesy. I'm fine with that.

September 22, 2015

My feelings about Bernie Sanders have changed a bit since I wrote this. I still detest his progressive beliefs, but I do realize that he was far more likable than Hillary, who treated him like a white-haired speed bump on her way to the White House. I'm glad he's not president; but I can still kind of like the guy, right?

So look at all the cool kids flocking to Bernie Sanders. He got Will Ferrell, Jeremy Piven, Sarah Silverman. It's a gala for the gullible. But really, all this Bernie love is a status marker. In an attempt to appear authentic among their peers, they performed the least authentic act ever, embracing a stupid ideology simply to appear real. In the 1970s, Hollywood types embraced albums with singing whales.

Bernie is just another kind of singing whale. A novelty used by guilt-ridden faux intellects to shame their personal trainers. You can credit historical amnesia when you forget the horrors of previous deadly strains of socialism.

This one is different, you say. But it never changes. The primary engine of socialism is a force of leveling outcomes from above, through the power of punitive revenge, fueled as always by envy. Anyway, it doesn't matter to celebs. It didn't matter when they glorified deadly communism.

Yet here he gets love from the intellectually empty in the land of the plenty.

So after all the prosperity that America's free market system brought them, they flock to an ideology that would have prevented such outcomes. Fact is, without capitalism, there would be no Bernie Sanders. If this country had been under socialist rule, Sanders would have been chased out of town long ago. Capitalism really enables the survival of beliefs that damn capitalism

Let us not forget: The love for Sanders among the rich is meant to excuse the rich for being rich. This is their penance, their indulgence, for living a life of gated luxury, expensive pot, and more expensive therapy. That's the difference between a Hollywood leftist and an underground Hollywood righty like Gary Sinise or Clint Eastwood. The Hollywood leftists got their pile of money, and now it's perfectly fine for them to prevent you from getting the same—they can extol a proven disastrous idea because they're doing so sitting on a million. But the underground Hollywood righties want you to get as rich as they are. That's not greed, that's opportunity. But try to explain that to Sarah Silverman. The only thing she really cares about is her next bong hit—since the other hits are so few and far between. Skeptical? Ask yourself why socialism has only ever been considered on American coasts—with a stopover in Chicago. The truth is that rich celebs don't understand socialism. They don't realize that they'd be the first to go. That level of understanding would actually require reading something beyond the Chateau Marmont late-night menu.

February 18, 2016

On Tuesday, Secretary of State John Kerry met with Hollywood studio heads to hack a plan to counter the ISIS narrative. It's a great idea, if I don't say so myself, years ago. Imagine if Hollywood channeled this energy into something else—like death cults currently killing thousands. Imagine what Hollywood could do to degrade, mock, and marginalize the useless, lurid tools who flock to loser magnets like ISIS. They could use special effects to scare the hell out of these idiots.

For forever, Hollywood has pumped out propaganda for presidents' pet causes, from obesity to climate change, while ignoring the real threat to their total existence. And that threat is a suicide cult with a great story. They are hordes of marauders racing across the sand to their sex-crazy apocalypse.

Meanwhile, our creative minds in Hollywood often side with our critics, portraying our free-market system as a greed-driven, power-mad evil. America is the only target left in which blaming the victim is actually cheered.

So this could help—maybe other companies, like, maybe, Apple, could join the fight. Consider the contrary narrative we could supply. Is ISIS a real fighting force? Or losers? And what of those seventy-two virgins you were promised? Who might they be?

Granted—they keep you warm at night.

Now, this plan could work. But there is one problem. How do we know about this plan? Kerry tweeted it. Yes, he tweeted to the world about our plan to fight ISIS. What in God's name is he thinking? Isn't the whole point of propaganda to make the enemy think that it's real and not manufactured? Well done, John Kerry: Announce our intentions, then wonder why our enemy is always one step ahead.

> This is where I show a clip of bleating goats.

Poor John Kerry. It was also his job to sell us the Iran nuclear deal also. This guy makes Willy Loman look like Warren Buffett. Bottom line: Portraying ISIS as losers is what Trump happily adopted. These are not revolutionaries, but the world's detritus—sad sacks who can't get laid, so they're opting for an afterlife of nonexistent virgins. Trump called them losers, then crushed them, like termites. This is important: By exposing the lie, by showing that the Islamic State was not inevitable, but rather just a mad group of douchebags destined for a loser's death, Trump shrank the appeal of ISIS to a nonexistent fleck. No one wants to join a loser. But keep those lectures going up at the Kennedy School, Mr. Kerry. They've definitely been the difference! [The other advantage Trump had over his competition: his refusal to telegraph his plans beyond "We are coming to get you."]

Another thing that bites my ass: Hollywood has no problem creating villainy out of whole cloth—it's usually an executive at a nuclear power plant or a pharmaceutical executive. But hand them the greatest villain since Hitler, in ISIS, and they drag their feet like they're being forced to sit down and eat a pot of boiled broccoli. But I don't blame them—they have a definite problem identifying evil in their midst. ISIS is just Harvey Weinstein without a car service.

December 19, 2016

Last week, we told you about some has-been celebs who released a video imploring GOP electors not to vote for Donald Trump—after he won the election.

These celebrities are now targeting one elector, Ashley McMillan, the vice chair of the Kansas Republican Party.

Here's actor Martin Sheen:

MARTIN SHEEN: As you know, Mr. McMillan, our founding fathers built the Electoral College to safeguard the American people from the dangers of the demigod and to ensure that the presidency only goes to someone who is to an eminent degree endowed with the requisite qualifications.

See what Martin did there? He called Ashley a man. The only problem, she's not.

But what do you expect from sexist Hollywood that can't see women in positions of power? He just assumed if it's a vice chair, it's got to be male.

> Yes, we get it, Martin, you own a thesaurus.

Hollywood, where once a woman hits thirty-four, she's stuck playing the crazy spinster neighbor while casting agents try to get new talent only born after 1995.

Forgive Martin if he thought Ashley was a dude. At her age, she might as well be. But these stars are anti-influencers—when they tell you something, you got to do the opposite.

Getting political advice from them is like getting dating tips from ISIS.

And don't they remember all those celebrity videos before the election accelerated Hillary's defeat?

They are the ones who finally cleared our political system of Clinton constipation. So you think that maybe after that humiliation, Hollywood would take a moment to self-reflect between indulging their outsized egos and gaping insecurities? Hell no, they are like a guy who has been dumped, but refuses to believe it, so he's lurking outside your apartment, hoping to change your mind. Hollywood, it's time to move on. There are other fish in the sea, probably in Canada.

It's always a pleasure to expose the underlying sexism of those who pretend to be so enlightened. It's also been somewhat of a joy to see the implosion postelection from people who would often portray the right as being "insane" over Obama winning way back when.

When Obama won, we got on with our lives—even if we disagreed with his weak foreign policy, pernicious progressivism, and his teachers' lounge politics. Sorry, no one on the right was "broken" by Obama the way the left was by Trump. None of us needed therapy; none of us needed to march; none of us needed to scream at the sky.

Why is that? Because for normal people, politics plays only a small part in our lives. Sure, we can be pissed that our guy didn't win, but then we shrug and have dinner with our family, read stories to our kids, get up for work in the morning. [Note—I do none of those things, but I'm assuming you do!] For the libs, the Trump election destroyed their entire world—because their entire world is political. What a horrible world to live in. Politics should occupy less space in your brain than thoughts about your favorite *Golden Girls* episodes—which for me is a rather large space, actually.

But Sheen's actions were a precursor of all the impeachment hysteria that followed from his side. When the electoral tricks failed, then it was on to impeachment. Or collusion. Or the Twenty-fifth Amendment. The Dems were willing to try anything—Stormy! Dementia! Diet!—to undo an election—a sign of an overemotional response rooted in a life too drenched in team sports politics. The fact is, of the nearly twenty Republican candidates who ran for president in 2016, Trump is the closest to a Democrat you could have ever gotten.

And the idea that somehow they would be happier with Ted Cruz or Rubio is laughable. They'd be vicious to every single alternative to Trump. They would likely have been worse to Cruz, actually.

Which is why the best thing one can do since 2016 is laugh hysterically at their hysteria. Of course, this doesn't mean everything Trump does must be met with applause simply because it's the joyful opposite of the meltdown madness. But the irrational anti-Trump response is a strong hint that things aren't as bad as we're regularly told on an often overboard CNN or an apocalyptic MSNBC, and in fact, it could end up being damn good—fingers, toes, and vestigial tails crossed.

April 26, 2016

Lena Dunham became the latest lefty lass who threatened to move to Canada if Trump wins the White House.

If you don't know who she is, I envy you. The recipient of entertainment welfare, Dunham got famous mining a self-indulgent mountain of feminist navel-gazing crap. Her favorite topic is herself, and being a cookie-cutter leftist, she's as daring as flatulence.

Dunham is one of many celebrities threatening to move to Canada over this election. Maybe that country should build a wall.

Now, I'm assuming Dunham wants to leave because she feels Trump is a bigot because of the stuff he said about Mexicans. But could it be that she's the real bigot? If she was offended by Trump, why didn't Dunham say she was moving to Mexico? Why did she pick the white north over the darker-skinned south? Talk about microaggression. I guess our Mexican friends are not worthy of her lily-white coddled presence. Well, unless they're delivering food to her doorstep.

But also her threat to move just shows how lazy entertainers become when nothing is expected of them. Dunham has coasted on these same banalities, because they're the same banalities the media shares. The threat reveals how vapid hokum passes for edgy intellectualism, the kind that gets you into the clubhouse of the mediocre hipster.

Poor Canada, sending them Lena Dunham. That's like a missile strike. Then again, they did send us Justin Bieber.

> I feel bad about that. Bieber, for all his faults, is nowhere near as bad as Dunham. A better comparison would have been rickets. People still get rickets, right? [And Canadian rickets—that must be bad, right?]
>
> It's a shame that I actually have to know who Lena Dunham is. But I had no choice. Remember the bizarre, unsubstantiated accusation she made about some flight attendants, who she claimed made disparaging remarks about a transgendered kid? She tweeted an accusation, naming the airline—and the airline conducted an investigation. They realized that none of their flights were in the terminal where Lena claimed the "incident" took place. But since Dunham has appointed herself to the role of the nosy neighbor who narcs on people when she overhears their conversations, who cares about such details? And for her, if she hears that conversation in her head, that's good enough for her. She would have been a hero in the East German Stasi—creating conversations and hauling people in for punishment. Then she moves on, weaving another tale to impress the sycophants around her. One couldn't imagine a less positive, more pernicious influence on American public life than Lena's Twitter feed. It's as if every tenth-grade social justice warrior in the country who is trying to overcome braces and zits suddenly had a

transcontinental megaphone. It's the rhetoric of the student council election, on a national scale. The fact that this awful, unoriginal, hectoring jackass is tolerated puts the lie to every charge of "intolerance" this nation has ever faced. If we'll put up with her, we'll put up with anything.

I have to admit, though, I did like a few episodes of *Girls*—especially the one where she squats and pees in a train station. It's always good to get a glimpse, from afar, of the horrible things you're missing.

July 27, 2016

This monologue foreshadows the next chapter on terror. If you'd like to know what that is, you could skip ahead—but then you'll miss this delightful piece of writing!

If you blinked during this Democratic National Convention, you would have missed any mention of ISIS. If you didn't blink, you would have missed any mention of ISIS, too. Of nearly 120 speakers during the first two days, five brief hits of it were heard, a batting average that should disqualify you from the world of reason. But who's counting? There are many more urgent things than a zombie jihad slitting the throats of priests, running over children, and blowing up families. Just like the left enabling communists, decades ago—the Dems fret over the police, big corporations, big air-conditioning, while terrorists thrive. Sorry, your greedy banker didn't cut the throat of that priest. In a world beset by mass self-activated terror, the Dems come off as wee children, singing la, la, la, la, la, loudly to drown out the weeping victims of France, Orlando, Istanbul. Here are two self-described celebs echoing that old refrain.

AMERICA FERRERA, *UGLY BETTY* **STAR:** Let's forcefully reject division.

> Lena: Love the sentiment, but you don't make it easy.

LENA DUNHAM, *GIRLS* **STAR:** Let's say with one voice that we all have worth; we are all a part of this country.

FERRERA: Let's put Hillary Clinton in the White House.

DUNHAM: And let's declare.

BOTH: Love trumps hate.

Love trumps hate. ISIS is quaking in their blood-soaked boots—oh, I hope they don't come at us with love!

> And reality trumps Hollywood horseshit.

What a battle cry, but for what? Here's a new pro-Hillary star-studded video. It's so fighty. Begin video clip:

JOHN MICHAEL HIGGINS, ACTOR: My power's turned on.

ELIZABETH BANKS, ACTRESS-TURNED-DIRECTOR: Starting right now I'll be strong.

CROWD: I'll play my fight song.

UNIDENTIFIED FEMALE: And I don't really care if nobody else believes.

> Poor Jane—it must be hard to devise a way to turn traitor to an enemy that would slit your throat on sight. Why can't ISIS be more like the Viet Cong!

> Maybe that was the problem.

JANE FONDA, ACTRESS: Because I've still got a lot of fight left in me.

It's called "Fight Song." Why, because it's totally okay to wage war against Americans over politics, but not ISIS—that's too much.

How sad: Artists will be the first to die under a caliphate, and they don't even know it!

Anyway, Obama had eight years, and ISIS is spreading like a malignant tumor. The evidence is written in the blood of innocents every day. Too bad the Democrats can't read anything but their own horoscope.

The Democrats' "fight song." I'm still laughing over that one. So is al-Baghdadi, I'll bet. When I look back at this, I realize how lucky we were that Hillary lost—because these idiots would be the people who own the conversation. Well, okay, they still do own the conversation—telling the world day in and day out in interviews that Trump is causing the end of the world.

Note: These are not stupid people—they're just sheltered, misinformed, misguided elitists. And unfortunately, they will run the conversation either way. But if Hillary had been elected, she would actually be listening to them, so she would have their cool shiny approval, and that's the scary part—and the reason for some relief that Trump beat her.

Such celebrities know only what they prefer to know; they refuse to even tolerate the possibility that they might be wrong. It's a combination of cognitive dissonance and confirmation bias. They're looking at the world for evidence that they're correct [confirmation bias], and when it doesn't happen, they end up acting like idiots [the dissonance].

Again—imagine if Hillary had won. We'd have to hear from these idiots every single day. Wait. Trump won. And we still have to hear from these idiots every single day. That's America!

Which leads me to my old refrain: All of these sore losers claim that Trump has been a threat to free speech and a free press. Yet they've never been more vocal. If anything, they should be grateful to Trump. He's the best thing to happen to the media since the printing press.

November 9, 2016

Pop stars are crying. Comedians clutch their Xanax. Trump has won.

Cher says she's moving to another planet, as if she wasn't already living on one. Sarah Silverman mourns, making her even less funny than before, if that's indeed possible.

It's the end of the world as we know it, so why do I feel fine?

Because this hysteria validates last night.

The stars did everything they could to get Hillary elected. And now they're freaking out because their entitled arrogance flopped.

> i.e., the election results

SNL's Taran Killam tweeted "Rural = stupid" about Trump's victory. To think . . . that's probably his best material.

By the way, how did that guy get a gig on *SNL*? It says a lot about that show that they'd give this guy a job—he's about as funny as head lice, and I know how unfunny head lice can be.

Lady Gaga looked sad in a Rolls-Royce Phantom, which is hard to do, after protesting at Trump Tower. Such a woman of the people!

And though Republicans snared the presidency, kept the House and Senate, at least the Democrats still have Katy Perry. She just threatened revolution. She's Che in a thong.

> . . . meaning conservatives who wanted someone else . . .

So you can criticize Trump for lots of things. I did. (Believe me.) But you've got to love him for the enemies he made, because they're our enemies, too.

It's a fact: You may not like Trump, but you know Hillary's fans hate you. And boy, did they make that clear.

> This is the most important point to be gleaned from the election. So many of the people who hate you lost. You could have despised Trump, or like me, been very critical of his rhetoric. But the other side, the hard-left Democrats, actually think you're morally and intellectually inferior—if you're lucky! They also think you're a Nazi racist who personally deports anchor babies in your free time. Now, I may have had a problem with Trump's behavior, but he doesn't look down on me. I don't think he looks down on anyone. Well, except for "shithole" countries. But so do liberals. Trump's just more honest about it. Last time I checked, Rachel Maddow, Anderson Cooper, or Joe and Mika aren't going to spa retreats in Port-au-Prince. In fact, did you notice that not a single celebrity claimed they were moving to Haiti after the election? They only want to move where white people live! Racists!

But last night the unpopular kids told the cool kids, "Up yours." For once, Republicans won a culture war. And it was against smug celebs who felt that you were inferior. But I guess now the feeling is mutual. To us you're just overpaid preachers.

So thank you, Mr. Trump, for making Lena Dunham move to Canada. She'll be the least popular Canadian export since acid rain. I'm not even sure. I think she might be worse than acid rain.

I have said this before: I had my problems with Trump—and I made them clear. But what cleared the slate for me were these things:

I despised the arrogance and entitlement of the Hillary machine.

I knew that Trump deserved more of a chance than Hillary. We knew Hillary. We didn't know Trump—at least, as a political leader. It was a gamble. But it was a gamble based on the fact that we KNEW what Hillary already was. So we were willing to roll the political dice with this funky-haired orange Godzilla from Queens.

I was able to forgive the small things [his personality, for example] for the big things [he knows ISIS is a priority, not the caribou endangered by pipelines]. Being on top of national and domestic security makes me forgive whatever idiosyncrasies you may possess. Crush ISIS? Then eat all the well-done steak with ketchup that you want! Reduce the influx of gangs from down south? I'll take your crass language and sick jokes and chalk it up to a different, more rough-and-tumble era. I mean, who would you rather have as president: someone who understands old truths, or one who sees the past as an encyclopedia of our sins? Who would you rather have: a skittish substitute teacher like Obama, or the scary gym coach who runs detention (Trump)?

The reaction of Hollywood Hillary cultists made me substantially relieved over the outcome of the election. Do this simple counterfactual: Imagine their sorrow in reverse. Imagine if Hillary had won. Imagine their inevitable throwing it in your face. Trump voters aren't rubbing this in anyone's hair. They're too busy packing their kids' lunches. But you know the liberals would have gone nuclear with their glee. Because when it comes to the team sport of politics, they're petty. You can tell by the way they handled this loss. Every day that I watch Hollywood overdose in sorrow over this election is one more day I am happy he won. I may not have been on board during the primaries when there were other choices, but America made the right decision. They didn't just elect Trump, they gave a beautiful, monumental "SCREW YOU" to all those coastal celebrities who, for so long, had it coming. If only they could stop prattling long enough to hear it. And learn something from it.

Where Are We Now?

Our celebrities are still here, and more unstable than ever. And thank God for that—because as you can tell, without them, I would be out of a job. Seriously, the previous seventy pages would have been blank were it not for them! And I would have to write about something else—like geopolitical issues—which would suck, because I don't know anything about that crap. Celebrity instability is my wheelhouse, and I hope it never goes away, for my sake. And I don't think it will.

President Trump has succeeded in triggering the entire town of Hollywood into full-blown hysteria. It's something I haven't seen in my lifetime, and I grew up in California during the infamously evil Reagan era. I won't go on about Trump Derangement Syndrome, because that cliché is already overplayed. But one cannot ignore the contagious delusion that's taken hold among our nation's fragile entertainers. I worry about them. They need therapy llamas! I think they should pull back and take a deep breath, and realize that it's physically impossible for Trump, or anyone, to be as evil as they claim he is. But then again, if they were to do that, I'd be without good material. So by all means, carry on!

I finished this chapter on March 5, 2018, the day after the ninetieth Oscars—an event at which political pronouncements against Trump were handicapped by their own #MeToo sins. You can't throw stones in a glass house—especially a glass house with so many casting couches.

But watching the Oscars makes me ask: Why do people like me, who love movies so much, hate the Oscars so much?

I grew up with the 1970s Saturday matinee, where you arrive in the morning, in daylight, and leave when it's dark.

I would watch back-to-back sci-fi double and triple features.

The Planet of the Apes trilogy, odd films like the *Neptune Factor*, or *Food of the Gods*, or that great classic with Bruce Davison about rats called *Willard*.

I positively lived for disaster classics—*Earthquake. Poseidon Adventure. Towering Inferno.* These movies were the escape for a kid in suburbia, when there wasn't much else, other than dismal playgrounds and parks littered with pull-tab beer cans.

But times have changed. Everywhere you go, you're now being informed, instead of entertained.

Hollywood, through the Oscars, has relegated cinematic escape to the backseat, as virtue signaling replaced shared human experience.

Traditional story lines are so old—as old as humanity. Which is why they worked.

Movies used to be about entertaining us—all of us. Yet the Oscars recast the industry as an engine for the new religion of identity politics.

But I remember the original reason for watching the Oscars on TV: to see movie stars.

There was nothing better than seeing Charlton Heston, or Jimmy Stewart, or Cary Grant—as themselves, and not the characters they played!

Now, actors simply assume another role at the Oscars: that of the caring automaton who sees the world in exactly the way you would predict. It's crushing to see someone cool be so meek.

The Oscars are no longer a parade of creative individuals.

It's a corporate offsite retreat for an industry adrift, something you accidentally walked into at a Marriott convention center.

So as the Oscars try to explain why movies matter, you end up hating everything about movies. It's not fair to the movies, frankly. In short, if you hate the Oscars, it's because you love the movies so much.

Bottom line—the only real big American "star" right now is Trump. He stole the bullhorn from Hollywood, and now he's speaking to the world—in language *they* understand. And by "they," I include our adversaries. A few pages back I said that Hollywood was how America "speaks to the world." The message: We are sinful oppressors. Not anymore. Since Trump came in and wrestled away the megaphone, the message has dramatically changed. No longer is it "Hello, we're America and we're sorry," it's "Hello, we're America—deal with it."

It's a message so potent and refreshing, no wonder Hollywood seems so irrelevant, and why Hollywood is so pissed off.

CHAPTER FOUR

ISLAMIC TERROR

It's what caught the eye of those of us on *The Five* way before it interested President Obama. This pesky thing called ISIS, which he deemed the JV squad. Remember the quote? It was from a *New Yorker* profile of the president by David Remnick back in January 2014. Remnick had pointed out that the flag of al Qaeda was back up and flying in Fallujah—referring to ISIS, which wasn't yet infamous enough to go by its own name. Obama said in response: "The analogy we use around here sometimes, and I think is accurate, is if a jayvee team puts on Lakers uniforms that doesn't make them Kobe Bryant."

Maybe I could cut him some slack on this . . . if heads weren't cut off afterward. So this remains one of Obama's big screwups—ignoring a new kind of terrorism that was about as far from JV as I am from playing for the Lakers.

There was something way different, more insidious, and chilling about this new kind of terrorism. It was a tech-savvy propaganda machine that delighted in revealing its atrocities to the world. The beheadings, the drownings, the immolations—this was their overwhelming message. Join or die. It was compelling, well thought out, and perfectly executed—no pun intended. How Obama missed this is beyond me. My only thought is that perhaps he didn't miss it, but his allegiance to Islamophobia-phobia (fear of being called Islamophobic) left him paralyzed. He could not diagnose the most obvious ailment the world had seen since the Nazis, because it would just be in bad taste, and upset the global, progressive audience he so deeply preferred over us American rubes. Islamophobia was a term created to describe "what racist redneck white people feel who are scared of different religions and people," a diagnosis used as a way to misidentify a legitimate distaste for death cults that behead and burn people alive. If that's Islamophobia, then we all should be Islamophobic. But it's their rhetorical diagnosis that is incorrect, not your instincts.

The ironic thing: Those who accuse you of Islamophobia for being antiterror are the actual bigots, for they are the ones conflating Islam with the radical Islamists creating piles of mutilated bodies. True Islamophobia is what plagued President Obama—he saw radical Islam as part of Islam, so insulting that part meant you were insulting all.

So, given Obama's weakness, who becomes the leading candidate to be president of the United States? The one who condemns ISIS the loudest and clearest. That would be Trump. Clearly being called Islamophobic, to him, was a point of pride. Because he knew the accusation was bullshit. It was like calling a fear of stabbing "stabophobic." It's true and somewhat understandable.

These monologues tell the story of ISIS from beginning to—we hope—its end.

The campaign year of 2016 was all about distinction. Perhaps the starkest difference was that one man (and one party) refused to call evil by its name, but another party (and especially one man) was happy to shout it from the rooftops.

So we're talking about coming face-to-face with radical Islam, and the false charges of Islamophobia levied against anyone who expressed concern over the terror threat. Every time a terror attack occurred, the left focused its energies on *not* judging evil, and instead worried more about backlash than the initial victims.

That sentiment is what has paralyzed our country's response to ISIS, and what enabled Trump to take the stage.

So, after repeated terror attacks, and the emasculated response that followed by our leaders, the public had had enough. And the Republicans—primarily Trump, Lindsey Graham, and Marco Rubio—had had enough, too. Running toward the evil, instead of running away, gave the right the upper moral hand in the fight against terror—a fight abdicated by identity-obsessed liberals more worried about serving ham in cafeterias where Muslims might eat than bombs detonated at marathons. (Which is where we begin.)

April 26, 2013

So, it's true, the Boston bombers were here on a visa. A visa made available by a government fearful of accusations of profiling, a media fearful of accusations of profiling, and an academia fearful of accusations of profiling.

Let's take that last one first. The terror attack occurred in the ultimate college town. Now that this dorm room utopia has been punctured, by one student who went from filling a pressure cooker with ramen noodles to filling one with ball bearings, academia faces two choices: Do you still keep a worldview that all cultures are equal, and extremism is part of the rainbow that already includes violent professors? Or do you wake up and recognize the poison in your system?

By the way, enough with calling these killers "kids." They're adults. One killed an eight-year-old boy.

So, while we can't rely on the campus, we also can't rely on the FBI. Old-school agents would have crushed these twerps. But now, they are more like social workers, risk averse and scared to identify evil. They have been infected with the same virus, Islamophobia-phobia. It's a terror of the mind that seeks to blind you to the objective reality around you. It's in government, media, the schools.

So, who is left to protect us? Us. You and me. It's our job to remain symptom-free and quarantine our families so none of us succumb to the disease. Because it's going to get worse before it gets better. The only vaccine we have is our spine.

It's kind of crazy, in my mind, that we are told to "say something" when, or if, we "see something." But if we "say something," we run the risk of "being something," which is racist. The Scarlet Letter of Islamophobia-phobia allows attacks like the one targeting the Boston Marathon to occur for this simple reason: If you had called the cops on these "kids" beforehand, there's a sizable contingent of folks who would mock and demean you. The irony of ironies: You're only right to "see something and say something" after the something has already cost lives. It's the same with mass shootings. You're told to "say something" after you "see something," but what's the point if no one "does something"? See the Florida mass murder in February 2018. Multiple tips were offered about that madman before the act, and no one took them seriously. Why? As this goes to press, Sheriff Israel is still employed, which amazes me. He was in charge when the most preventable mass killing in history occurred.

By the way, before the marathon bombing, the Boston Police Department had planned a terror training exercise, paid for by the Department of Homeland Security. The terrorists, however, were fictitious creeps called Free American Citizens. No mistaking that for al Qaeda or the Weather Underground. So, why take a name that sounds like a cross between a Tea Party group and a poorly translated *Rambo* sequel? Well, some might call it risk aversion, others might say cowardice. Let's face it. While the police know they're not on the prowl for middle-aged Americans dressed as Ben Franklin, they also know the hell they'd get if they concocted a Muslim terror group. Screw realism, that would be Islamophobic—something you avoid if you don't want to get fired.

Does it matter if they play pretend with false enemies, if they keep their eyes on the real ones? Well, we missed the Boston bombings. We missed Fort Hood.

Mind you, in both cases, we didn't miss the attackers, they were there in plain sight, but we missed stopping the bloodbath, because of fear of targeting the bad guys, and calling them out by name. In the name of protecting oneself from activist groups and a PC press, the citizen becomes vulnerable to something far worse, Islamists with evil in their hearts and bombs in their hands.

April 24, 2014

So, a new film that will run in the National September 11 Memorial Museum has ticked off its interfaith advisers. Called *The Rise of al Qaeda*, it uses the words "Islamic" and "jihad" when referring to terrorists!

I know, disgusting!

Said the imam in the group, quote: "Unsophisticated visitors who do not understand the difference between al Qaeda and Muslims may come away with a prejudiced view of Islam, leading to antagonism and even confrontation."

In short, facts will cause us rubes to beat Muslims up.

However, FBI stats show anti-Muslim bashing is rare. It is not like the museum smears Muslims at all. It shows that they were also among the victims and the rescuers that day. Look, if you feel that basic words harm your beliefs, that's more about your insecurity than our rage.

> I went back to read up on the FBI stats and found a lot of recent media reports claiming a 20 percent increase in incidents of anti-Muslim backlash. This stat was cited everywhere, but from what I read, the total reported bias incidents, counting all kinds of victims, in 2016 was 6,121, and of those, just 361 were targeting Arabs or Muslims. I know, I know, one incident is one too many, but let's remind ourselves: This is a country of 330 million. I would try to do the math, figuring out what 361 is, in terms of a percentage of 330 million, but I haven't done any math since senior freshman calculus, and I got a D.

And what would the imam prefer us to say? That 9/11 was caused by men unhappy with tall buildings, or that terrorists were really Mormons posing as Muslims to smear Islam?

My guess is they wish 9/11 were cleansed of all things Islamic, which ain't happening. At some point, you have to say it out loud—9/11 was done by Islamic radicals and they're still killing all over the world.

They are fiends and they are your problems as much as it is ours.

So, that's the first step, admitting you have a problem. Other religions have done it, too. So, why not join the club? We won't bite.

Once again, if you're conflating any criticism about Islamic terrorism with criticism against the entirety of Islam, then it's you who's painting that religion with a broad, bigoted brush. I hate radical Islam, but joyfully admire Muslims in our NYPD [roughly three hundred cops] who protect our city . . . from, among other things . . . terrorism.

Having said that, I get it—I don't blame a religion for being embarrassed by its worst practitioners. And 9/11 was the worst thing to happen in my lifetime—if it were done by weird cultists from my club [agnostic wine drinkers in bathrobes], I'd feel shame, too. But you really shouldn't. You should feel power in condemning such actions, for it strengthens the perception of your religion around the world. A strong religion should be confident enough to expose and shame and condemn its worst elements. If imams, however, see such vocal actions as a smear against their beliefs, then it makes you question what kind of beliefs they have.

August 13, 2014

Shark Week is here. You can thank *Jaws* for that. That flick made us think that shark attacks are common, when really they are quite rare. But humans prefer their fears to be tangible, which is why large threats are avoided.

Let's change that. Instead of Shark Week, why not—Radical Islam Week?

After all, sharks may be scary, but they won't end civilization. Sharks might want your foot, radical Islam wants your head on a stick.

I love this mono.

So, here's the schedule. Monday let's begin with al-Shabaab, a nasty bunch who slaughtered sixty-seven in a Kenyan mall. And it wasn't because the Nike store ran out of shoes. It was because they ran from Allah.

Tuesday, we got Jemaah Islamiyah, Indonesian scum behind many bombings, including a 2002 attack that killed 202 people. Their weapon of choice: potassium chloride and religion.

Wednesday, we got Boko Haram, killing hundreds in Nigeria and enslaving girls. Their weapons of choice were bullets, fear, and YouTube.

Thursday, remember al Qaeda? The godfathers of gore, they knocked down the World Trade Center, bombed London and Madrid. Choice of weapons: planes, trains, and automobiles.

And it's "casualty Friday." Lashkar-e-Taiba unleashed the 2008 Mumbai attacks, killed 164 people with both bombings and shootings. They were truly varsity, never jayvee.

Finally, it's ISIS Saturday. No one saw them coming. Well, except for everyone. Intent on a caliphate, they are called the jayvee squad—but tell that to the headless.

> This really is an important, daring idea for a week of horrific programming.

Now, I've left out the Muslim Brotherhood, Hamas, Hezbollah. I figured six days is enough.

Oddly, there seems to be a really persistent thread that runs through all these terrors.

Maybe they saw *Jaws*!

Say anything else, and that would be Islamophobic.

The idea for this mono came to me after becoming bored with all the crap on TV about sharks. Sure, sharks are scary, and they'll attack surfers [mistaking them for seals], but it's not like they want to end the planet, or at the very least end your life. Sharks are just being sharks. Radical Islam, on the other hand, is just systematically working its way to heavenly utopia, and your death is the stepping-stone.

Just reading this now, I'm rekindling a thought I often have about radical Islam. If you stripped their activity of its religious underpinnings, and just saw them as an isolated biological phenomenon—men who without rhyme or reason butcher or maim dozens or hundreds or thousands of people—then how would we actually perceive that? What you're left with is the plot of every zombie film. Divorced from ideology, the terrorist actions of jihadists come off as products of some sort of brain virus that drives men into a murderous frenzy. If these were truly zombies, we'd actually have a better, more concrete way of responding. Sadly, because their actions are tethered to religion, we stutter in our response. Worse, we look the other way. And looking the other way gave us 9/11, and most recently, ISIS.

August 14, 2014

The British police are investigating pro-ISIS leaflets said to be found in London, asking Muslims to join their merry band of death cultists, which makes me miss the good old days when it was the Hare Krishnas handing out the leaflets. The worst thing they did was chant. There was never a beheading.

> And they co-opted one of my favorite musical instruments—the bongos.

So these flyers aren't about finding peace or even pizza. They're offering a way out for bitter weirdos, a promise of revenge in an evil world.

> **This was the new wrinkle of Islamism—the impressive propaganda machine, operated by savvy Western-trained fiends who knew exactly what insecurities to prey on, something that Obama completely overlooked.**
>
> **By reacting lamely to this initial appearance of evil, Obama gave them the early sense that they were winning—and could win—in the war for the existential apocalypse.**

Not that I care. If you want to join a death cult, go ahead. I hope you die in a cloud of dust. Which is why, when one asks if these leaflets should be stopped, I say never. We need this activity out in the open, because recruitment does us a big favor. It gets the evil out of our country. If radical Islamists leave to fight in Iraq or Syria or Afghanistan, that's far better than the reverse. I'd rather America fight them over there, converting these terrorists into a sticky paste, than have them decapitating citizens here in the street.

ISIS could be their magnet, a glorious roach motel that attracts the very worst of this planet, where they die in large groups. Of course, this all depends on whether the West is willing to do the dirty work to keep them from returning.

Because for every time we say no boots on the ground, you can hear the footsteps of their boots right behind us.

This point was largely ignored until Trump started running for president. Telling the enemy what you AREN'T prepared to do is the perfect prescription for your loss, and their victory. It doesn't matter how many losers join ISIS if we keep killing them. We must realize *it could go on forever*. But telling them we aren't prepared to do that incites more to join their murderous frenzy. No one likes to join a losing team, and we kept telling them that they were winning.

And, my God—I don't understand why we would stop anyone from joining ISIS. Let them join! And kill them! The key is to NOT let them join and THEN RETURN TO THE U.S.!

If you want ants to get away from your food, put some food where the ants could flock to, then spray 'em with Raid.

Trump also understood that the followers of radical Islam are going to figure out the porous parts of our southern border and take advantage of it. For long-term preservation, we gotta plug the holes. If you noticed, all of Trump's concerns are for long-term survival that create unpopularity for him now. He sacrifices short-term stability for long-term survival.

August 25, 2014

Today I ask, what happens when you dismiss the devil, yet the devil continues to grow? I speak of ISIS, a fight we don't want—but a fight that wants us.

Is wanting war on them actual warmongering? Not these days. If you think concern for the survival of our world is warmongering, then you gravely misunderstand the purpose of our nation's defenses.

Even more: The belief that war must be waged does not require the believer to be a soldier. Let's simplify: Would you not call the police because you never served as a cop? Do you need to be a fireman before you pull a fire alarm? It's that logic that helps encourage this evil.

The "chicken hawk" argument is the kind of leftist claim that ends civilizations. If only people who fight wars can have opinions about war, we would not be aware of future threats. Soldiers are too busy fighting to analyze the nature of global threats. They're the guys you call when you decide to act. And get this: They have no problem with it.

The point of our military is to act with ruthless efficiency against current and future dangers, that's it. And before you scream "chicken hawk!" remember that our military didn't just stumble into this lifestyle. They actually chose it. I suppose for a media obsessed with a grievance, it's hard to understand that kind of service.

That really is a key point, for it pollutes every part of life. People are now confused by the nature of service, because they're too busy feeling aggrieved to think anyone else deserves their time or sacrifice. I wonder how many young men look at other young men in uniform and wonder, "Why on earth would you do that! You can't play *Call of Duty* when you're actually on duty!"

I ask those who repeat "no boots on the ground" like it's some kind of mantra, why are we telling evil what we *won't* do? When you say it's not our fight to those whose only goal is to fight, who exactly are you pleasing? The very animals who find solace in our suffering.

The time for binge watching *Homeland* while surfing the web for Kardashian's butt is over. The wolf is knocking at the door and he's hoping that we don't answer. It's time that we do.

If Obama had listened to this monologue, I imagine that thousands of people would be on this planet, thriving, right now, who instead are dead, after experiencing horrible, brutal ends. It takes a special kind of naïveté not to recognize a sword at your throat. I think they teach it at Harvard Law.

The countless terror attacks, the raids on towns, the mass killings that happened as we just sat on our hands, wondering how best to agree on rules of engagement— it was the paralysis of analysis, and ISIS gleefully took advantage of it.

Fact is, also thwarting Obama's will to act was his own misunderstanding over serving one's country. He didn't understand that our troops actually WANT to fight. They want to do good. They don't see fighting ISIS as some sort of intrusion in their lives. Obama finds America's power so distasteful that he just didn't feel comfortable wielding it. I never met a single serviceman who didn't want to destroy ISIS quickly and completely. And they certainly didn't mind that I expected them to. Three of my best sources on this are also three of my favorite friends: Terry Schappert [a former Green Beret], Joey Jones [who lost both legs detonating bombs in Afghanistan], and Rob O'Neill [the SEAL who offed bin Laden]. Trust me, they'd tell me to shut up if they felt I was over the line on any of this. The phony concept of "chicken hawk" is just a ruse to keep you from wanting a strong military.

By the way, around this time, the *Washington Post* claimed global warming was the defining issue of our time. Not terror but warming. It's like being on fire and worrying about your halitosis.

The idea that global warming is somehow a greater concern than terror might be one of the most dangerous ideas of our time, for it funnels money, time, and attention toward a problem that may or may not occur, and away from something that is happening now, and could kill hundreds of thousands now. Fact is, it might be true that temperatures are increasing [albeit insignificantly]. But we KNOW there are individuals on the planet who are seeking the means to end this planet NOW. So you can think that CO_2 is evil, but we can tackle that—we have time. CO_2 isn't actively trying to find a dirty bomb to unleash over a stadium in an American city. How anyone can not see the difference in priorities is both tragic and hysterical.

Trump saw that difference and made terror a key issue, one that got a lot of people to support him who otherwise might not have.

Fact is, for the Obama administration to take ISIS seriously would have been to dress them up as the *Duck Dynasty* guys and label them "cis-gendered."

October 6, 2014

So Friday, Ben Affleck became a caliphate crusader, attacking Bill Maher and the great author Sam Harris on Maher's talk show over Islam. Maher and Harris argue that liberals are cowards when it comes to facing radical Islam's horrible acts, out of fear of being labeled a bigot by others. Affleck proved their point by calling them bigots.

SAM HARRIS, AUTHOR: I'm not denying that certain people are bigoted against Muslims as people. And that's a problem.

AFFLECK: Bigoted.

HARRIS: But the . . .

AFFLECK: It's gross. It's racist.

MAHER: You're not listening to what we are saying.

HARRIS: We have to be able to criticize bad ideas.

AFFLECK: Of course we do.

HARRIS: But Islam is the mother lode of bad ideas.

MAHER: It's the only religion that acts like the mafia that will (EXPLETIVE DELETED) kill you if you say the wrong thing, draw the wrong picture, or write the wrong book.

AFFLECK: What is your solution? Condemn Islam? We killed more Muslims than they have killed us by an awful lot. And yet somehow we're exempt. Because it's not really a reflection of what we believe in.

So burdened by lack of facts, Ben relied on that emotional crowd-pleaser, cries of racism. What you see is the crisis that takes hold when liberal orthodoxy faces off with real attacks on liberal orthodoxy.

Affleck's tantrum proves Sam's point. The inability to separate identification of evil from platitudes on tolerance is what enables evil to thrive. Affleck doesn't help. Worse, he didn't see that where his point ends . . . is where the rest of us begin.

> I also think Ben had a few in the green room, but who hasn't?

Yes, we get that it's wrong to stereotype. But then we study the facts. We could all pretend the world is a Benetton ad, but that does nothing to stop genital mutilation, beheadings, slavery, or genocide.

Behind those crimes is a sick ideology that preys upon the passivity of the West. Like the tussle over communism that fractured traditional liberals from anti-West leftists, radical Islam is repeating this dance among the modern progressives. Where Affleck is reduced to a sputtering, bitter scold, soaked in self-righteousness, in need of a script because his words ring hollow.

And in a shock to even himself, Maher becomes the sanest man in the room. How's that?

> When I look back at this monologue, I realize that the transcript of Maher's show does not do it justice. I ask that you look up the Affleck/Harris back-and-forth on YouTube, just to see how angry the actor was. You could see him shaking with righteous rage [or bourbon]. I also notice that Affleck made this point: "We killed more Muslims than they have killed us by an awful lot." I'm assuming he's referring to the wars that followed 9/11. But he's conveniently over-

looked that the primary killers of Muslims are other, more extreme Muslims. We're just on the outside, as Westerners, hoping that this sectarian shit doesn't get worse. My gut tells me that Affleck will never make it better. The more we deny that extremism and violence are a problem, the more their practitioners seem to demand it. It's also refreshing to see liberals like Harris and Maher remain resolute in their often unpopular stances regarding radical Islam. Both pay a price for it. . . . I've heard that Harris's life has been threatened [he's talked about it]. And with radical Islam, having your life threatened isn't something you take lightly. I'd tell you to ask Theo van Gogh, but he's dead— murdered by an Islamist, on a street, for voicing an opinion.

October 24, 2014

They made it fake for publicity's sake. Two video bloggers got press, after posting a video they said showed the Islamophobia of the New York City Police Department. The video starts with the guys wearing Western clothes, arguing and pushing each other, as the cop stands by and does nothing. And then the pair did the same thing, but dressed in Muslim garb, and they got a different reaction.

In this video, an alleged police officer who ignores the men in Western clothes begins harassing the men now that they're in Muslim garb—to show that cops are more willing to harass practitioners of Islam than Western-dressed, quarreling men. The officer demands that they "get against the wall," put up their hands, and "open your legs." He repeatedly shouts at the men. It's as poorly acted and as contrived as your basic *Saturday Night Live* skit.

So the video was tweeted out by the Council on American-Islamic Relations and picked up by the *Huffington Post*, which called it a small glimpse into the ugly world of racial profiling. Maybe so, *if it was real*.

But surprise, it's not, and yes, these cop-smearing dopes eventually came clean, admitting it was a hoax. They released a video in which they said, "We sincerely apologize to anyone that might have been misled that it is not a national event. Over the dramatization, our reenactment on what happens to us, when we film the traditional clothing on. . . . Our intention was not to make the NYPD look bad. If you feel like it was such, then we do apologize to you."

> Wait, so your intention was to make the police look *good*?

So they're really sorry, but for what? For being caught? After all, if the stunt was indeed a dramatization, why didn't they label it as such? They didn't, because they assumed that they could get away with it.

Even more, to justify their fakery, they claimed that profiling happens a lot to them when they film. Which is weird. I mean, why aren't *those* incidents on film? And if it happens a lot, why did they have to *fake* one? They seem to be implying: It doesn't matter if it didn't happen. It's the thought that counted.

> I'm thinking the NYPD should have sued these assholes.

Again—if it happens constantly, why create a fake one? Just show the real thing. They couldn't because they couldn't.

So, of course, they did this to raise awareness of racial profiling.

Yes, the all-purpose excuse to defend deception and wrongdoing: raising awareness. It worked: They raised awareness that they're morons.

This is a case where I should have sworn on *The Five* and called them "assholes" instead of "morons." But then I would have been sent home for a day, which isn't so bad. Day drinking in your pajamas is pretty awesome!

These losers thought they could get away with it based on one perception: that NO one would nail them on this ruse, even if it was an obvious one. They knew the media and the public are too worried about being labeled bigots to call them out. Luckily, their work was so amateurish—their acting was terrible—they accidentally called out themselves. They only managed to trick those who wanted it to be true—like the untrained mediocrities at the *Huffington Post*. Pranks like these work as idiot detectors. If you fall for this, then you are an idiot. And you should never be trusted again. As for the hoaxers, may they never work again. I would look them up to see what happened to them, but I can't be bothered. My guess is that they are probably interning at the *Huffington Post*.

February 6, 2015

Yesterday at the prayer breakfast, President Obama brought up the Crusades, in light of modern evil, and it was something about our high horse . . .

BARACK OBAMA: Unless we get on our high horse and think this is unique . . . to some other place. Remember that during the Crusades and the Inquisition, people committed terrible deeds in the name of Christ.

What's with this relativism reflex? Even if you agree with the point—yes, we were bad once, too—how does that solve a problem exactly? How does it solve Islamic extremism? It doesn't. It just allows you the excuse to not acknowledge present-day problems that upset your like-minded peers.

Wow, talk about a slight!—comparing modern-day Islam to medieval atrocities. Shall we accuse Mr. Obama of Islamophobia?

He's right, though: the Crusades were an awful thing responding to another awful thing, an Islamic holy war. But he left out three key points.

- They happened like seven or eight hundred years ago.
- It stopped.
- This is 2015 . . . so you should stop, too, or else.

The fact is President Obama spoke the truth. When it comes to religion, Islamism is the slowest runner in a millennium marathon.

We're here, they're still back there—and some of them want to stay there and take us back with them. Now, maybe during the Holocaust, some academics said these horrors happened throughout history. But how is that any comfort? When you compare something happening now to a time before indoor plumbing, it reminds you where the president's head is—in the sand—and why he sees Islamophobia in his sleep.

The Crusades were brought up to remove our victim's status and make us the aggressor, which works for an academic . . . that we are the bad guy. The president indeed condemns terror, but relativism leads to ruminations that waste precious time needed to fight terror. Instead of leading, he's educating us on our own transgressions, as though his presidency is a college course.

I just hope we don't get graded for it. I dozed off after the second year.

It's either an amazing example of naïveté or stupidity—I can't tell!—to downgrade radical Islam by saying that Christianity was nuts five hundred years ago. This "what-aboutism" argument actually does more damage to your own position, for unconsciously, you are comparing what you're trying to defend [Islam] to something barbaric that occurred centuries ago. I mean, yeah, I'll give you that, Obama: The Inquisition and the Crusades sucked! They were absolutely horrible. I learned that from Monty Python. But how does that help us now, when dealing with radical Islam? How does it help their current victims to remind them that other religions were awful, too! Right then and there, Obama became a clumsy apologist.

Meanwhile, somewhere on the globe, a few hundred or thousand people are butchered because they aren't as lucky as you to sit in a free Christian country, engaging in such pretentious babble, protected by the law enforcement you hold so much disdain for.

February 16, 2015

A trend that refused to die, as innocent people did: Even when terror announces exactly what it is, and what it intends to do, we choose other ways to explain it.

A gunman shouts "Allahu Akbar" on a rampage through Copenhagen, killing two. The root cause?

Obviously, a criminal gang.

Check out this clip from the news:

UNIDENTIFIED MALE: New details emerge about the twenty-two-year-old gang member who killed two civilians and injured several police officers in a frightening attack over the weekend.

> I love acronyms even if they waste even more time trying to explain what they mean.

Yes, you see, he's a gang member! And here we have the latest installment of NIDNI. "Nope, it's definitely not Islam."

It's the reoccurring game show where a paralyzing case of Islamophobia dictates no linking Islam to terror. Yes, whether it's beheading Christians, or murders at a synagogue, there's never a thread—not unless you count climate change, which creates a brutal heat that drives men to murder. If we hadn't been driving all those SUVs, those folks might have lived. So never mind the shouts of "Allahu Akbar," or a killer targeting the Muhammad-drawing cartoonist, the synagogue is totally random. He thought it was the Best Western!

Because for the media and our president, Islam is that scary neighbor who plays music too loud and we're all too petrified to tell him to turn it down.

So, we're a country more worried about our reaction to evil than about evil itself, which leads to one question. Who guards you from the maniacs we cannot name? The answer won't be found on CNN—but maybe at the golf course, where you'll find Obama's head still buried in the sand trap.

Yeah, he golfed a lot. So does Trump. But I'll forgive Trump's golfing habit, as long as he keeps killing terrorists by the buttload. It's the philosophy that helped Trump win: You forgive the little stuff if he delivers on the big. But let me be clear: I HATE GOLF. Here's why: How much land should a sport require? It's why I favor Rock, Paper, Scissors. You can play that anywhere.

But maybe if the Syrians and Iraqis had put a few putting greens up amidst all that desert, they might have gotten Obama's attention.

Said before: 2016 wasn't about politics, but priorities. The Dems offered an inverse pyramid, with the least important issues up top, and the real scary stuff at the bottom, in a tiny space marked "other." All Trump really did during his campaign was invert that pyramid—putting it commonsense right side up. Then he dropped it on the Democrats' politically correct head.

February 26, 2015

Jihadi John, the ghoul from the ISIS videos, was from a well-to-do family and graduated with a computer degree. Mohammed Emwazi, clearly an Irish Scientologist, had a breezy upbringing before cutting off the heads of captives.

It's funny. Every time I make a joke like that—"clearly an Irish scientologist," viewers—either Irish or Scientologist—will write in to complain that I demeaned them. I realize when you're part of a group it's hard to take a joke even when it's meant to be complimentary to said group. Obviously he is not Irish, or a Scientologist. The compliment being that he is NOT Irish or a Scientologist.

Now, remember when a White House spokesperson said that if there were more jobs, we'd have less terror?

It's so true! I mean, a degree in computers? It's not like that expertise is in demand these days!

So, when the normal turned evil, what's the "why?"

You could think religion, which provides one with purpose, but come on, there is no Catholic ISIS.

Let's be honest, ISIS offers thrills. You, charging across a desert, gun in hand, full of zeal and certainty, facing infidels, plundering homes. When death is a step to nirvana, what's the downside?

> I probably should have said heaven, no nirvana. Nirvana is a different religion. Oops.

So, the issue is our counteroffer. It's hard to champion a free society when our own leaders in media find it gross.

Heartfelt patriotism, the belief that this place is worth dying for, is now seen as something silly, an option for the ignorant. Our military now fights propaganda from the cynical country that it defends! So when a leader explains the roots of terror, remember, it's what we no longer root for, the root cause is our absent will— when fighting is viewed with ridicule.

Be all that you can be, that used to be a rallying cry for the army; now it's the rallying cry for *American Idol*.

This monologue touches on a key theme: We could say we're great, but that would be rude and ignore our ugly past. Which fuels the decline in patriotism, at least among the media, celebrities, and academia. It used to be that they expressed their distaste for love of country amongst themselves, but now they are telling the rest of America to feel the same way. In the fight against ISIS, offering a compelling alternative to the excitement of mass murder would be propaganda. The rejection of assimilation in favor of multiculturalism, coupled with the cynical mockery of patriotism, got us here—which likely explains why a simple phrase like "make America great again" resonated for so many across the country—except in the teachers' lounges. Consider: Why do so many on the left find that simple phrase offensive? Why did the media laugh at something so clearly positive?

The inability of our leaders to happily offer a persuasive defense of this country gave us 2016. Within our own borders, we have the left telling us that America is the real oppressor; beyond our borders, we are told that we are the infidels. It's no wonder ISIS thought it had the U.S. on the run.

March 9, 2015

How do you portray evil? When it's so evil?

Alex Gansa, producer of *Homeland*, said ISIS will appear on the show soon.

After all, *Homeland* for the past four seasons has tried so hard to portray our adversaries and try to humanize them, right?

ALEX GANSA, PRODUCER OF *HOMELAND*: *Homeland*, for the past four seasons, has tried so hard to portray our adversaries and to humanize them. That is very hard to do with ISIL. What they are doing on the ground feels so medieval and feels so horrible that to give them a platform on television, I'm a little wary of. To try to make what they are talking about understandable or relatable is very difficult. So yeah, we are struggling with that. . . . It may be that we don't understand them well enough. It may be that they are just too evil to dramatize on television.

So if you can't humanize the bad guy, then you can't show the bad guy? No wonder Hitler is in no movies! This is an industry that has no problem with evil if it matches its politics. There's no ambiguity when it comes to evil cops or a greedy oilman. Hell— the TV show *Scandal* just did its version of Ferguson—and had the cop arrested because that is their happy ending. Yet here, actual reality offers you the worst villain ever and you say, sorry, he is too villainy.

I guess to Hollywood, the objective evil is like a relic. Like your granddad's chompers floating in a glass of water. But ambiguity, that's cool. It makes you look deep.

Still, you'd think *Homeland* would reflect the ugly truth. It is about terror, after all. The problem is entertainment has changed, but evil hasn't. Since the movie *Bonnie and Clyde*, Hollywood has romanticized evil. And *Reservoir Dogs* broke new ground, turning cop mutilation into a dance number. So as we embrace these sexier evils, real evil persists. If we can't depict that evil, then how can we beat it? I do have a solution for *Homeland*, however.

Make ISIS the villain, but one that is funded by a secret group of evil white climate change skeptics. You will knock that script out in an hour.

This story drove me nuts—that the guy had a problem depicting evil because it was so obviously evil. He needed a gray area, perhaps to help assign blame not just to a pernicious twisted cult, but to us as well. But give it time. I'm certain when the books are written on ISIS, the origins will be firmly rooted in our own imperialism. And these ghouls will be seen as troubled revolutionaries trying to right the wrongs of the West. Because that's what our entertainment does best: take our deadliest threat and make it our fault. And hire the best-looking people to play those threats in the revisionist blockbuster.

But understand one thing: Mr. Gansa is not unique in Hollywood, he's the norm. What's Arabic for "useful idiots"?

May 4, 2015

I love this story. That is all.

Last night's "draw Muhammad" contest in Texas did not just draw Muhammad, it drew two Islamists, who drew return fire. Let's roll this clip:

JOE HARN, GARLAND POLICE OFFICER: Both of them had assault rifles, came around at the back of the car, and started shooting at the police car. The police officer in that car began returning fire and struck both men, taking them down.

So, the dudes ended up as a chalk outline—or what Texans call "etchings." You know you're down South when even the art shows come holstered. It's a contrast with *Charlie Hebdo*, whose editors died helplessly. Terrorists in Texas, however, found a far deadlier lead than what's inside your basic pencil. They were dispatched—but the idiocy of the press still stands.

New York Times reporter Rukmini Callimachi tweets, "Free speech aside, why would anyone do something as provocative as hosting a Muhammad drawing contest?"

Well, the answer is in the question, and you expect a reporter whose beat is Islamic extremism would get it. The First Amendment means zilch if it only protects "hello" and "have a nice day." Protecting free speech is like protecting an empty safe. And also, when you begin your take on free speech with "free speech aside," you kind of lose the point. But hey, maybe they were asking for it. *(Begin video clip.)*

JOHN VAUSE, CNN CORRESPONDENT: No one would ever dispute the right for people to have freedom of speech, especially in their country. . . . You know it is a constitutional right. But, are questions being asked in some ways, were they asking for some kind of an attack—that is obviously not that anyone deserved it, but it was some kind of an invitation for an attack, if you like.

There's always that "but." This is where we are. Remember, the attacks on our Libyan outpost were blamed on a film by our own government, including Hillary.

But if you're a journalist and don't get the contest, then it's you who is the real cartoon.

> I get it—I have better things to do than host a Muhammad drawing contest. But that's not the point. The point is that such an endeavor could cost you your life in other parts of the world—but in our country, it shouldn't. It's a keen lesson that in Texas, an attack against such speech is not that easy. If that guard wasn't there, armed, this would

have ended far differently. What kind of message does that transmit? It's one that the press refuses to hear—that the Second Amendment exists, in part, to protect the First.

This story explains, succinctly, the solution to preventing every school shooting. But the media will just mock you for making that key point: Hardening soft targets is a moral imperative and also should be a trillion-dollar industry. The entertainment industry, the media, and tech companies all employ high-level rings of security to protect themselves. Why shouldn't the business of "soft target hardening" be larger than all those industries combined? How is a media corporation more important than a school? Nope. We need to harden soft targets. Couple that with a civil tag database in which names of troubled individuals are placed to prevent gun ownership—and you'd never have another example of carnage like the Broward County horror.

Now, around this time, the media was pushing a new study saying that American extremists have killed more people than Islamic extremists. There's just one problem. The study omits 9/11. Yes, they started counting the bodies after that date. That's like saying, since Japan attacked Pearl Harbor, attacks on Pearl Harbor by Japan have decreased. It's like my saying, you know, since breakfast, I haven't had another breakfast. So why do they start counting deaths after 9/11? Two reasons: It magically removes three thousand victims from the Islamic terrorist side, but it also ignores the facts that it's our response to 9/11 that may have reduced further attacks by radical Muslims.

The point is simple: The media wants to downplay the Islamic threat by playing up others. It's all born from the same "oppressor vs. oppressed" polarity taught on campuses for the last forty years: Damn the evidence, it has to

> be America that is truly at fault, for it's much more powerful, and therefore more evil. You can't be evil if you're the David to our Goliath.
>
> The reflex to blame the West for everything bad is a luxury one can enjoy only in the West. Well protected by our defenses, apologists can indulge our own liberal guilt when we're attacked by those who view us as infidels.

August 20, 2015

> I have to say, the Pope ticks me off. And get this: It has NOTHING to do with religion. The guy's more leftist than Catholic, and in his heart sees America as somehow the Goliath to the subversive radical Davids all over the world.

In a CNN interview, Donald Trump was asked what he would say to the Pope if he were to meet him next month. Roll it, Sven.

CHRIS CUOMO, CNN'S *NEW DAY* COHOST: The Pope believes that capitalism can be a real avenue to greed, it can be really toxic and corrupt, and he's shaking his finger at you when he said it. What do you say in response to the Pope?

> Here's my response: If capitalism is the offense, I'm sure Kim Jong-un or the Castro family has room for you on state-sponsored television. I bet you'd look great in grainy black and white!

TRUMP: I'd say ISIS wants to get you. You know that ISIS wants to go in and take over the Vatican. You have heard that. You know that's a dream of theirs to go into Italy. And you look at what's going on, they better hope that capitalism works because it's the only thing we have right now. And it's a great thing when it works properly.

> By the way, as I edit this, what Trump said then is still true today. On the news last night [November 17, 2017], we were warned that ISIS was planning to strike the Vatican. Note to the Pope: It's ISIS, not climate change, that wants to kill you.

Well done. Now, I think it's great for Donald to meet the Pope. Here you have together an outspoken leader of a major religion—and the Pope.

But Donald is right, especially since the Pope has bashed capitalism, which has lifted millions out of misery—and he's also said that *Charlie Hebdo* victims should have known better. That's not good.

> Ugh. That was obvious.

As for ISIS, they do want to kill the Pope, but they want to kill everyone, including themselves.

But Trump should take his own advice, too, and put all focus on those who wish to destroy us.

Just for fun, let's ponder these headlines from the past.

> Which he ends up doing, and wins an election.

"Clinton sees crisis from global warming."

"It's time to fix America's broken immigration system."

Now, both of those headlines were from September 10, 2001, *the day before 9/11.*

> DAMN, WHAT A POINT.

There were no headlines on Islamic terror, but lots on immigration and global warming. So while those concerns matter, it's the stuff we never see coming that gets us. We're facing a new age of terror.

Today's technology, married to today's hate.

When ghouls master new methods of mayhem, today's barbarism will seem like the good old days. So if you're ever going to be a single-issue voter, that's your issue. Our next president must put aside platitudes and come to grips with a new threat that's almost too horrid to contemplate. A store-bought drone with aerosol spores offers ten 9/11s at a fraction of the cost. If that doesn't get the Pope's or Donald's and America's attention, then nothing will.

This last point might be the most important—and perhaps repetitive!—point of the book: that it doesn't matter how flawed a leader might be. If he understands the nature of terror, and how to fight it, then he's going to be the right choice. I think Trump figured that out, early on. The Pope, sadly, still hasn't. Which is why he's really not worth listening to about anything that might contribute to our safety. He hates guns, air-conditioning, and the war on terror. Remove all three, and there is no civilization. At least in my neighborhood.

Ultimately, nations form to provide citizens with one thing: safety. It's the first principle of countries. Trump understood that Americans cared more about the safety of their children than about the smog in Beijing. The Dems still can't get around their own sanctimony long enough to see that.

November 23, 2015

After the Paris attacks, President Obama pleads with the media to offer some perspective.

BARACK OBAMA: The media needs to help in this. I mean, I just want to say, you know, during the course of this week, a very difficult week. It is understandable that this has been a primary focus. But one of the things that have to happen is how we report on this, has to maintain perspective and not, you know, empower in any way these terrorist organizations or elevate them in ways that make it easier for them to recruit or make them stronger. They're a bunch of killers with good social media.

> When you hear someone offering a "perspective," what follows is usually a word salad.

That's our O. His first reaction is always about over-reaction. I think he overreacts about overreaction, and it is underreaction about action that's the infraction.

> That was good!

I await a retraction.

He's right, though, it's been a tough week. But it's strange how he never asks the media for perspective when emotional responses help him out, with climate change, guns, or even his own popularity.

When the press fell head over heels for him, he never said, "A little perspective, guys. I'm not all that." No, when it's his crusade, you better lick that boot. But maybe he's worried that terrorists steal his spotlight from climate change, which, as you know, causes all terror.

True, high temperatures create jihadists. Just look at the ISIS franchises popping up all over drought-ridden California!

Oh, wait.

But we're used to our concern being smeared as fear-mongering. O's disdain for our priorities feels lifted from

> Good point.

West Wing scripts, where such mockery passes for thoughtfulness, and it blocks any path to unity.

The White House mascot should be the ostrich, head in the sand, and all we see is ass.

Whatever: time to prepare for evil. You aren't living in fear, but learning to be feared. The Islamists are mindless droids, programmed by ideology and evil. It's not about them anymore, it's just an "it." And there is no Islamophobia when you're extinguishing a wildfire. So when the president says, this is not who we are, remind him that it goes both ways. We may not be who you are, either. Good for us.

It's a hypocrisy few people notice: The left loves to harness emotion, outrage, anger, and fear to drum up support for their concerns. Right now [December 3, 2017], assorted liberals on Twitter are announcing the world is ending. Why? Because of some modest tax cuts that are part of a just-approved Trump tax plan. I'm no fan of the plan [to Trump's credit, the plan is transparent and I see everything, unlike Obamacare], but the world is far from ending over this. Yet, when we express legitimate horror and anger over Islamic terror, we are told to keep our emotions in check . . . don't succumb to backlash and bigotry! When something horrible happens to America, we are told to "maintain perspective." But if something terrible happens [tax cuts!] in which America, or Republicans, are at fault, then damn the torpedoes and bring out the pitchforks.

However, I might agree with Obama if he had offered a scintilla of evidence that our outrage fuels terrorism. I seem to remember absolutely no outrage over terrorism before 9/11. How did that work out? Oh yeah, we had 9/11.

December 3, 2015

Researchers now claim ISIS is using Twitter to recruit Americans. Roughly 250 have taken the bait so far. The catch includes teenage girls, college kids, and a dog named Jasper.

PERINO: Hey.

But it's no longer the world, you see. It's actually us.

Through a combination of ideology and technology, terror has grown a new face. Evil needs no air force to cause mass death. All it needs is a drone, a man, and anthrax. It's not a palindrome, but the plan.

Which is why Rubio has it over Cruz on surveillance, and Donald Trump agrees, saying that when the world would like to destroy us as quickly as possible, I err on the side of security. It's true.

> That's a reference to the "a man, a plan, panama" palindrome. Which no one got, nor should they. Sometimes I embarrass myself.

But again, it's not just the world. Today killers are often homegrown. They are the new needles. And to spot a needle, you need tools to sift through the haystack. Sadly, that's miscast as infringing on privacy.

It's a mistake born from a zero-sum fallacy regarding freedom and security. We have freedom because of security, the Second Amendment, our military, rule of law—even the luck of our oceans around us to provide us with security that has its own benefits and limits to our freedoms.

> Super awesome great point!!!

The oceans make it tough for ISIS to get here. But I also can't drive to England.

The new reality is we aren't dealing with China, North Korea, or the old-school USSR. Mutually assured destruction mattered to them. But to a suicide cult, they're *dying* for it. Until we embrace the tools to engage the new enemy, we will die with them.

This raises the point that I end up repeating over the next few years: that security and freedom are not adversaries, as libertarians would have you think, they are actually siblings who help each other out. Without security, you cannot have freedom. If you want any practical examples, look at hellholes like Somalia, where there is very little security, and accompanying it, almost no freedom. [For a smarter analysis than my own, check out the fantastic, chilling, horrifying book *The Future of Violence*, by Gabrielle Blum and Ben Wittes.]

Lack of safety creates its own prison. We just don't know that, because we're living in the safest, freest place ever. And there is the second point: You can hate Russia and North Korea all you want, but their endgame is not predicated on martyrdom. They actually want to achieve their goals, here, on planet earth. They actually operate on something that approximates rationality. Even when they're blowing the propaganda horn, they're not ACTU-ALLY going to rush into war [as much as the media freaks out any time North Korea farts in our direction—as if they aren't aware of what war would mean for a country that has mostly starving people in it to "fight" their war for them]. The modern terrorist, however, with his beyond-earth assumptions, just wants to get to the afterlife as soon as possible—which is why they're far more danger-ous than any previous adversary.

Say what you will, but Trump looked at a suicide cult and cut right to the chase. "You guys wanna die? Here, let me help you." That's the sort of approach that wins wars. And presidential campaigns.

December 9, 2015

So the director of national intelligence, James Clapper, told Congressman Michael McCaul that ISIS is now using the refugee stream to come here. Which is odd, since the White House dismissed such claims, but what else is new?

The White House is now no different than the neighbor who suspected terror, but didn't report it out of fear of looking racist.

> Here's a case where the possibility of terrorists slipping into migratory masses—which led to the terror ban that's often called xenophobic—had been warned about earlier than Trump. Turns out Clapper said it was a problem, too!

Since the DOJ thinks namecalling is worse than terror, can you blame them? Pair that with our "secretary of stone," John Kerry, a man whose stiff face makes the Burger King mascot seem relaxed, tweeting pictures of him and James Taylor in Paris just days after a terror attack. I would call him a tool, but that's wrong because tools are useful. Add a media and celebrity cesspool cheering gun confiscation, and you've got a raging case of terror denial. The war on terror becomes an immigration or gun debate, because within those realms we are the ones at fault. It's the escape hatch from casting moral judgment on our enemies, because if it's about them and not us, then all that academic brainwash was a waste.

> Note: I was comparing Kerry to that creepy Burger King mascot with a mask for a face. I still don't understand the commercial value of that grinning monstrosity—I look at it and I don't think, "Let's eat hamburgers!" I think, "Let's get out of here before he eats the skin off my face."

But we don't have to talk about terrorists anymore. We can just kill them. Good PR fuels recruitment, inflating prowess without proof of battle. So it's time to shut up and shoot. One humiliating defeat for ISIS, and the bandwagon loses bandwidth.

> This is the point Navy SEAL and bin Laden killer Rob O'Neill had been telling me for years, which I repeated on *The Five*. Maybe someone listened! Because that's what went down, with blazing success.

After all, the road to Armageddon is paved with political correctness and the only thing we have to fear is fear itself. I think Trump said that.

But ISIS "fighters" are, all along, exactly what you suspected—a pack of chickenshit bullies who just needed a smack to pierce their air of invincibility. What irony—they actually were the JV! Problem was, Obama had resigned us to the freshman intramural squad. Trump now has a varsity letter in kicking ISIS ass. Who knew it would be Donald who'd end up the Big Man on Campus? Could anything irk Obama more?

> Key point: If we start killing ISIS in large numbers, then it's over, recruitment-wise. Because from a propaganda standpoint, they've had a free ride at this point in time, because we didn't take to battle, we haven't seen any evidence of ISIS being fierce in battle. We only see their brutality against the unarmed. If we were able to show a humiliating defeat, that would help ruin their recruitment efforts. And now, after Trump stepped up our attacks dramatically, you see that it has. Once we started piling up the ISIS corpses, it's absolutely amazing how their recruitment drive waned. Funny, that. Who could have predicted it? Oh yeah—ME!!!!

February 15, 2016

Last night on *60 Minutes*, a show that lasts an hour, CIA Director John Brennan admitted ISIS has chemical weapons, and he expects them to use them on us.

JOHN BRENNAN, CIA DIRECTOR: We have a number of instances where ISIL has used chemical munitions on the battlefield. . . . There are reports that ISIS has access to chemical precursors and munitions that they can use.

QUESTION: You're expecting an attack in the United States?

BRENNAN: I'm expecting them to try to put in place the operatives, the material, or whatever else that they need to do, or to incite people to carry out these attacks, clearly. So I believe that their attempts are inevitable. I don't think their successes necessarily are.

Great. So . . . Brennan implies that we cannot stop ISIS until they attack us. Not because we lack the ability, but because we lack the reason. Meaning we need a mountain of American corpses first. Then *we're going to show you!*

Check out this exchange from the same program:

QUESTION: If there was a major attack here and we had ISIS fingerprints on it, certainly, this would encourage us to be even more forceful in terms of what it is that we need to do if our policy after an attack in the United States would be to be more forceful. Why isn't that our policy now, if there were an attack?

BRENNAN: I think we're being as forceful as we can be in making sure that we're being surgical, though, as well. What we don't want to do is to alienate others within that region and have any type of indiscriminate actions that are going to lead to deaths of additional civilians.

So there you have it. Rules of engagement, which is code for, put them before us. It's not only preventing us from stopping ISIS. It's paving the way for its inevitable attack against our own country.

> "Alienate others"? Omigod—this was the guy in charge??

Imagine a cop saying to you, "We can't help you out until that crazy guy murders your family. Then by all means, call us." That's the logic, and it's brought to you by the hypertolerant folks behind Islamophobia.

This is not wait and see. It's wait and die.

And it's not a moral stance, nor one that protects America. It's a stance that leads to the death of your loved ones. And it's not going to be small. It won't be San Bernardino, and it won't be a machete attack.

> And this is basically the highest cop in the land saying this!

Thanks to the modern threesome of technology, bioagents, and suicidal ideology, the next attack could make 9/11 look like *9½ Weeks*.

> I'm running out of these comparisons.

The sad part about this is, we need to wait for it, because it's the polite thing to do. What a White House. They want to criminalize war, even when ISIS won't play along.

When the head of the CIA sounds like a sensitivity counselor, you know you've got trouble. We needed Patton, but we got Deepak Chopra. Can't believe that didn't work out!

No wonder ISIS was able to thrive—because those in charge were more worried about the backlash that might hypothetically occur if we respond . . . after Americans die! Who thinks like this? Long answer: an idiot. Short answer: See the long answer.

March 30, 2016

After every terror attack comes that naïve response to evil. This time, it is from Facebook's Mark Zuckerberg, who says to fight Islamic terrorists we must have a world where everyone feels cared for and loved. And who would be against that?

Oh yeah, Islamic terrorists, you butthead.

Look, naïve pacifism is the barnacle on the boat of vigilance—meaning it depends on the commitment of others to kill. If we all thought like Zuck, we would be screwed. My solution: The math of terror is simple. They work 24/7 and must only succeed once. Free from the duties of building and preserving civilization, their world is more agile than ours.

For a peaceful America, fighting terrorism is like a whale trying to swat a hummingbird. They are free to act, and we just react.

But the only thing as agile as terror is our creativity, unleashed in the marketplace. What solves history's great horrors, from tyrants to disease to poverty, is American ingenuity.

Terror, like everything else, evolves, picking soft targets as others harden. So the solution is an innovative private industry that hardens everything. In this changing world, as old jobs disappear, "terror control" provides the West with new, meaningful work based on turning sitting ducks into well-armed lions. A chain of vocational schools that saves civilization from heathens. Maybe Zuckerberg should start it.

After all, you can't update your status when you're dead.

> This is a message I return to often: Why isn't there an industry based on security that is as large and vast as media, entertainment, or academia? After all, without security—rather, the hardening of soft targets—none of those three

could operate. There should be a department at every college that offers a major in such hardening vocations, and those vocations should be financially well rewarded once you graduate and enter the real world you protect. The fact is, on a planet where automation may replace most jobs, and existential terror wants to carry all of us from this world to the next, it might actually pay well to create a defense against such violent threats. The solution to the latter, also solves the former problem. And it's not gender studies. It's security studies. And we better start this "terror control," sooner rather than later.

When I go through these monologues, I feel like I'm rummaging through the diary of a person living in a recursive loop—call it Jihadist Groundhog Day. Every day, we catalog another Islamic outrage. And then the next day, we rinse and repeat. I read these monologues, and it's as if I'm just repeating myself. Yet, I'm not—for every day there is a new outrage, and I have to say the same thing again, somehow finding a new twist to make it memorable to those already jaded by the bloodshed. It's a job, but someone has to do it. But I honestly wish I didn't have to.

June 13, 2016

This mono was written after the horrible terror attack in Orlando. It's amazing to me that it seems so long ago—but it isn't. It seems so far away only because these attacks have become so commonplace around the world that we simply move on. I mean, this was truly horrible, and we rarely, if ever, talk about it much. Perhaps because, since

> then, so many other things have happened. And I write this just two months after the Vegas mass shooting—the most well-planned crime, in my opinion, since 9/11. Yet we've all moved on. Are we growing a numbness to ghoulish behavior? So that now it just takes more death and destruction to shock us? Anyway, back to the mono . . . and you know, if it's a terror attack, it will end up being about guns.

Now, the left labels Orlando as gun violence. Where did they learn this?

BARACK OBAMA, PRESIDENT OF THE UNITED STATES: We are also going to have to make sure that we think about the risks we are willing to take by being so lax in how we make very powerful firearms available to people in this country.

HILLARY CLINTON (D), PRESUMPTIVE PRESIDENTIAL NOMINEE: I believe weapons of war have no place on our streets. We have to make it harder for people who should not have those weapons of war. And that may not stop every shooting or every terrorist attack, but it will stop some and it will save lives, and it will protect our first responders.

But if Orlando is gun violence, then what was 9/11, box cutter violence? Shall we blame hardware stores for that act? Pressure cookers caused the Boston bombing? Shall we blame Crate and Barrel?

> I hate to bring in Crate and Barrel into such a grim topic. I love that store. Everything is reasonably priced and the sales staff is beyond helpful!

Blaming an inanimate object absolves you of actual guts. It wasn't the availability of weapons that caused these acts. It was a hateful, murderous, homophobic, misogynistic ideology, one that sees murdering gays as an act of compassion. And it's a belief ignored by multiculturalists.

Islamism has killed gays for a while. So lefties, if you never spoke out about that, shut up about guns.

> So, if we condemn radical Islam—a belief that deems homosexuality a sin punishable by death—it's the left that then labels us as bigoted! Then, when a terror attack kills dozens at a gay club, they shift the argument to gun control to skirt past the homophobic hatred of jihadists. They can't name the culprit, because that would violate their politics: It's always our fault—never anyone else's.

Now the Pope is lashing out at guns.

But if the Vatican were as unarmed as Pulse, the club, the Pope would not be alive. But ISIS knows that the Pope is surrounded by a military force consisting of one-hundred-plus ex–Swiss soldiers, who carry muskets but also submachine guns, with heavily armed agents nearby.

If that club, Pulse, had 3 percent of the Pope's arms, he wouldn't be lecturing on guns.

The Pope complained that aid and food to poor countries are often blocked, but guns are not. Doesn't he see that, if it weren't for armed men from our country, most aid would get nowhere?

He says he's prolife. Not here, I'm afraid.

> I think this is the weakest pope we've ever had in the history of popes, and I include Olivia Pope from *Scandal* [though she is extremely tough]. How can a man be so

> high up, and so absolutely naïve? I mean, this guy has absolutely no idea how poor countries get their aid. If soldiers aren't there to keep the peace—no one gets a piece of cheese. And if there were no guards in the Vatican, if there were no armed security along the pathways to the Pope, the Pope would be toast.

Anyone with common sense understands the trade-off: Owning a gun protects the people you love, but guns can also end up in the wrong hands. That's the deal we made. Pointing it out as a risk rarely advances your gun criticism, because we've assumed the risk already.

June 15, 2016

> This monologue was also written after the Orlando attack.

When Islamic terror strikes, blossoms of blame erupt. *Rolling Stone* blames guns, of course, the tool a terrorist uses, rather than the terrorist himself. So better to disarm than defend. No thanks.

Guns don't cause terror, but they can surely stop it.

Trump blames terrorists, but *The View* blames Trump.

Huffington Post and others somehow blame Christians; yeah, Christians. Their point is, it's not just Muslims who are bad, it's this guy who won't bake cakes. This is what identity politics has done. An attack on Americans used to be an attack on Americans. Now we just can't hold it together, even our president seems more worked up over reactions than over realities.

Here's President Obama: "The main contribution some of

my friends on the other side of the aisle have made in the fight against ISIL is to criticize this administration, and me, for not using the phrase 'radical Islam.' What exactly would using this label accomplish? Calling a threat by a different name does not make it go away. This is a political distraction."

> **Question: Would specifying a serious illness as cancer be distracting? Um, no . . . it kinda helps to clarify things, don't it?**

Hmm. Yeah, he's ticked. But it's us who should be mad. Here's more blame from the *New York Times*. You're going to love this. "While the precise motivation for the rampage remains unclear, it is evident that Mr. Mateen was driven by hatred towards gays and lesbians. This is the state of American politics, driven too often by Republican politicians who see prejudice as something to exploit."

> **You gotta throw up at this point. This may be the precise point future historians will identity as the *New York Times'* final break with reality. Who could have predicted they would morph into a campus humor mag? The only difference—the latter is actual satire. Also note: Mateen may not have even known the place was a gay club when he chose it. He had targeted other nongay options prior to his attack.**

This is amazing. See, it's Republicans, it's not terrorists. The orgy of blame generated by competing identities obscures a gleeful enemy that now nails soft targets at will. Deflection is denial, as we can't admit the problem, which is—Islamism. The consequence: The fight is not engaged, it goes on longer, more people die. The sooner we admit the problem, the sooner we can get help. Send everyone to "Islamophobia-phobia Anonymous" to get over their fear of being called Islamophobic because it's not just fear, it's going to be our doom.

One of the great victories accompanying Trump's election was the ability to call evil by its name—followed by the swift and brutal decimation of ISIS. Sometimes you gotta name something before you can kill it. See "polio" and "Salk, Jonas." And Trump, in this case, followed through. By humiliating ISIS, we removed their only selling point to new converts: that ISIS members were fierce fighters, refusing to surrender until death—bent on the inevitable establishment of an Islamic state. When they were crushed, it was amazing how many of these fearless martyrs surrendered. It was the public relations blow necessary to stem the conversion of losers into terrorists. No one wants to join a losing team. Well, except for the line outside Jeff Zucker's office.

So how was ISIS so quickly decimated after Trump took office? Well, we had the men and the machinery, but what was missing was the "go-ahead," which is the will to tell everyone that it's okay to kill the bad guys!

It was missing no more—I refer to this Facebook comment by senior enlisted adviser to the chairman of the Joint Chiefs of Staff, Army Command Sergeant Major John Wayne Troxell, who said, "If they surrender, we will safeguard them to their detainee facility cell, provide them chow, a cot and due process. . . . HOWEVER, if they choose not to surrender, then we will kill them with extreme prejudice, whether that be through security force assistance, by dropping bombs on them, shooting them in the face, or beating them to death with our entrenching tools."

In a nice reminder that war is not a game of nude Twister, a leader told troops that if ISIS didn't surrender, they should feel free to beat 'em to death with a shovel. A man after my own heart, while stopping the beating of theirs.

June 20, 2016

Again, below you'll find an example of our government trying to cloud over the link between Islamic radicalism and terror. Islamism has no problems boasting of this connection, but our leaders would rather talk about other "assertions" rather than face the politically incorrect fact that their cowardly tolerance has led us to this grim juncture.

Yesterday, Attorney General Loretta Lynch said they would only release a partial transcript of the Orlando 911 calls. My word, I wonder, what could they possibly leave out?

LORETTA LYNCH, ATTORNEY GENERAL: What we're not going to do is further proclaim this individual's pledges of allegiance to terrorist groups, and further his propaganda. We will hear him talk about some of those things, but we are not going to hear him make assertions of allegiance on that. This will be audio, this will a printed transcript, but it will begin to capture the back-and-forth between him and the negotiators.

But after much outcry, they caved, releasing the whole transcript, claiming the controversy was becoming a "distraction," distraction being another word for "embarrassment."

So what's the lesson? While the terrorist should be forgotten, its link to Islamism should not.

I'm against releasing 911 calls, because that violates the privacy of victims and their families. But if you are going to release this one, don't leave out the key parts. Those people were killed because of radical Islam.

Removing that from the call is like removing the shark from *Jaws* or the Nazis from *Schindler's List*.

And what if the killer hadn't mentioned ISIS, but the KKK, would this even be an issue? Today, identity trumps security, which brings us to, again, "Islamophobia-phobia," that accusatory hall pass to horror.

What if the terrorist's name was Joe Smith?

It's not.

So they focus on guns, not a death cult that infects the planet like a growing malignancy.

It's like blaming arson not on the arsonist, but on fire.

We're told many times how the left loves science. So here's some science: Islamism preaches the murder of infidels. Then if an Islamist murders—by his doctrine—infidels; I think that's cause and effect.

How could you deny that science, Mr. President?

No wonder Obama could declare ISIS the "JV." In his world, they barely existed. I guess that's one way to counter a threat: Put your fingers in your ears and hum "We Are the World."

I hate releasing 911 calls in general, because I believe it dissuades people from helping others in need. Example: Let's say you're out with friends, and one of them overdoses. You might be too scared to call because it's an illegal activity. And 911 calls also reveal people at their most vulnerable, when they're crying and helpless. (The one mentioned above *does not* apply.)

But really, if any declaration were in support of a media-accepted villain, releasing the information in its entirety would not even be a question. The fact that they considered holding it back because it involved Islam should piss the hell out of all of us. They are lying through omission and pretending it's for our own good. Screw 'em. Imagine, for example, if it were an NRA official on that call. You wouldn't hear the end of it. It would be on a twenty-four-hour loop on CNN.

August 16, 2016

Take it from me, when the left deems something "McCarthyesque," it's probably a good thing. Like Donald Trump's proposal on extreme vetting, which sounds like something Tom Cruise did to potential wives. But Trump's plan for questioning potential immigrants is, for the *New York Times*, quote, "an uncomfortable echo of McCarthyism," meaning it's mean and intolerant. The fact is, McCarthyism is the default button that liberals push whenever we demand fighting an external threat, be it yesterday's communism or today's ISIS. It is this clichéd smear that leaves us vulnerable.

Plus, you know, if there are actually communists in government, it's not quite a witch hunt, is it? And let's not forget: Communism did affect our lives. More on that below.

The fact is, you wouldn't need a new antiterror campaign if previous attempts hadn't been handcuffed by PC screams of intolerance. Express concerns about attacks or terrorists sneaking in as migrants, link mass violence to those who actually promise mass violence, and somehow that makes you Islamophobic. But how is wishing to halt mass murder bigoted? It has nothing to do with race, and everything to do with deadly ideas.

I get it, Trump often tarnishes legitimate concerns with impulsive, crass rhetoric. But that's not McCarthyism. It's carelessness. However, it is the media that is guilty of a different kind of McCarthyism—Charlie, not Joe—parroting mindless claims one expects from a dummy on a string. As they focus on Trump, they ignore Hillary Clinton saying she won't send troops to fight ISIS, a presurrendering to evil. How bizarre. But the *Times*—the *Times* is okay with that, and always on the wrong side of history. The media cannot read the handwriting on the wall, even when it's written in blood.

Islamophobia is the current "anti-anti-communism"— meaning it is designed to demonize people who are passionate about stopping something bad. If you believe radical Islam is bad, the Islamophobic label is meant to portray you as a bigot, the same way that if you had, decades ago, pointed out that communism killed tens of millions of innocent people, then you were the extremist. The only difference: Today, it's worse. Communists just wanted to destroy our system. Radical Islamism wants to end the world. And don't take my word for it—for Christ's sake— take theirs.

August 23, 2016

After every recent ISIS-related attack, we're warned not to go overboard in the war on terror. We're told that you're more likely to get struck by lightning than offed by a jihadist. That's the thing with statistics. They can be right until they go very wrong. Let's take lightning. While it's true it's a common threat, there are things you can do to escape it.

Don't stand in a field during a storm, holding a five-wood. Not so much with a suicide bomber. Unlike lightning, a terrorist goes out of his way to seek victims.

A terrorist has a brain. Lightning doesn't. When you close one door, the terrorist finds a window. Also, lightning hasn't changed in billions of years. Terror changes more often than climate. As it adopts new technology, the body count rises.

> This concept of "terror change" is something that must be taken more seriously than climate change, which is slow and incremental. But "terror change" happens fast, and daily. Terrorists learn not simply from their successes, but also from their failures. They even learn from actions they didn't take. For example: The Vegas terror attack instructed a whole new league of terrorists on the methods of death from above. It may be that, in the near future, open-air events will be obsolete because of that. Terror change should be on all our minds, not the dangers of unleaded gas.

No longer involving a plane and a box cutter, it will be done with drones and anthrax. You can expect a major attack (using such weaponry) hitting a big city in the next decade.

Sorry.

Meanwhile, lone wolf attacks continue, caused by a zombie virus called radical Islam. So, don't buy in to the binary choice between panic and relax. We need vigilance and a willingness to fight. The same goes with terror; we have to be right all the time. Terrorists, only once.

It's a logic lost on so many leaders armed with statistics, but little else.

I get it—more people die from lightning than terror. But it's a noncomparison. Fact is, no single strike of lightning is going to kill thousands [unless it sparks a fire] or millions. But one sole terror agent, armed with a dirty bomb, or a clever way to paralyze our power grid, can incapacitate an entire city population. So spare me the pseudo-intellectual stats. Cars kill more people. Opioids kill more people. But only one entity wants to end the planet. And they can be woefully inept—failing in 999 attempts out of a thousand. But when that thousandth attempt, which occurs after, say, a decade of trying, hits the target, we will long for the days of thunderbolt and lightning.

September 28, 2016

> Around this time, a Skittles metaphor erupted on Twitter as a way to describe extreme vetting: To paraphrase, would you eat a bag of Skittles if you knew one Skittle was toxic? This was analogous to terrorists sneaking in through migration—one person among many is all you need to kill you, which explains the entire science behind security . . . yet everyone in media thought the comparison was evil. How silly and awful it is to compare people to candy! But they conveniently forgot how a metaphor works—especially since that metaphor makes a point that they cannot refute.

FBI Director James Comey said the U.S. should expect a wave of terrorists once we get ISIS out of Iraq and Syria—roll it.

COMEY: They will not all die on the battlefield in Syria and Iraq. There will be a terrorist diaspora, sometime in the next two to five years, like we've never seen before. We must prepare ourselves and our allies, especially in Western Europe, to confront that threat.

Diaspora. I think I caught that at Chipotle. I was on the toilet for three days.

So what's he talking about? He's talking about Skittles. Remember the meme, would you eat a bag of Skittles if you knew some were deadly? It describes how one might look at refugees in the age of ISIS.

Today it's easier for bad people to infiltrate good places and kill good people by blending in with good people fleeing bad places. So we've got to sift through the Skittles to make sure the good get in, not the bad.

Wait. Did I just say humans are Skittles? No. I used a metaphor to describe the risk, which upsets the media. The media whose members likely majored in humanities in college, where they ODed on metaphors and similes, writing bad poetry in coffee shops.

To the left, similes are like guns. They're evil unless they have them. Note: That's a simile. They're not really guns.

But Comey's other warning: The killers aren't abroad, but they're now within. With homegrown evil, the Skittles thing doesn't work anymore.

What metaphor does?

Our immune system.

We spend time and money strengthening our body's own defenses against threats within and without. Left or right, we all harden this soft target with exercise, nutrition, preventative checkups. Why do we embrace this with our health but not with our nation? It's a good question, one we must answer before our country catches something terminal.

> Comey got this one right. Too bad it wouldn't last! But the human immune system is exactly how we should view our borders. We need to harden our bodies against illness—so, why not harden our country against foreign invaders [which, in a way, are like toxic bacteria and viruses]? Ideally, in my perfect world, America would be domed. And by domed, I mean protected by lifesaving killer drones that protect us from incoming attack. Maybe it's what Ronald Reagan had in mind with the Strategic Defense Initiative. But he was too ahead of everyone else. But if you look at our country as a human body, SDI is no different than wearing SPF. Just very, very, very, expensive SPF.

I loved that monologue because it illustrates the hypocrisy of the media/academic/entertainment complex, which allows them to indulge in metaphors and analogies—but no one else has that luxury. Hell, I took classes at Berkeley devoted to nothing but metaphors! And now they're mad when I want to use one! It's the only thing I'm able to remember from my education!

October 25, 2016

In case you missed it, we're at war.

Now, if there's any group deserving our destructive wrath, it's ISIS. They are basically Nazis without the fine tailoring. But the challenge isn't their fearlessness. It's the collateral damage. What we are seeing are heathens taking advantage of our own goodness—using human shields, knowing our humanity prevents us from wanting to harm them.

It's their lack of morality taking advantage of our wealth of the same. So what do we do? Sadly, the math. Human shields provide ISIS opportunities to continue fighting another day.

So, will backing away now pave the way for a worse existential evil to come later? Their goal is martyrdom: The more dead, the merrier the afterlife.

It's a sick belief that sooner or later takes all of us with them. For when primitives replace pointed sticks with dirty bombs, their road to heaven is soaking the earth with blood.

A plane flown into a building becomes quaint compared to the effect of a nuke on a major city.

So, imagine that hellish decision made before dropping the bomb on Hiroshima.

To prevent more deaths, involving hundreds and thousands or even millions, do you inflict a smaller but substantial horror?

Now, no one wants to make these decisions. But do we have a choice?

There's no room for pacifism in the era of jihad.

For while it's true that no one wants a holy war, what if the holy war wants you?

Hint to the left: It does. This monologue covers familiar ground, but it's ground one must never get tired of covering. The fact is, we've never dealt with an enemy that not only wishes to win, but also to die. Built within this ideology is "victory as death, and death as victory"—and the more bodies you take with you to the afterlife, the better and faster your magnificent transport to heaven. Right now, radical Islamists just massacred three-hundred-plus fellow Muslims in Egypt [I write this on November 23, 2017]. Do you think those killers felt bad for their victims? Absolutely not. They assumed they were doing those men, women, and children A FAVOR by blowing their young lives to shreds. So when you realize the ugly reality, then you see that this isn't so much an ideology as it is a disease whose main goal is to poison and kill the host, that is earth. Earth is just a way station for the miserable, waiting to die.

The math is, sadly, against us. An average human lives on this planet for twenty-seven thousand days. Give a terrorist ten thousand days to plan his heavenly exit and multiply that by—on a conservative estimate—one hundred thousand terrorists, and you see that it's not out of the realm of possibility that we could die at the hands of an existential maniac. Unless we come to grips with this mad reality. (Sorry if I ruined your day.)

December 22, 2016

It was big news. A Muslim man kicked off a Delta flight for speaking Arabic on the phone to his mother, freaking out Islamophobic passengers and the evil, evil airline. This outraged celebrities. Even actress Olivia Wilde vowed to boycott Delta. Yes! The great Olivia Wilde! And CNN's Brian Stelter, who rails against fake news all the time, retweeted the victim's video, which fanned the flames.

> He's our nation's hall monitor, his concern as sweaty as his forehead.

But hold on, you heroic warriors of social justice! Stop indulging your assumptions for just one moment and you'll find that this so-called victim is a renowned hoaxer who fakes events on planes. On his YouTube channel are videos of him, with titles like "Arabs on a plane," "Speaking Arabic on a plane," and "Counting down in Arabic on a plane."

I sense a trend here.

Recently he staged a fake video with a New York City cop harassing men in Muslim dress. It was fake. He even faked the story about board-

> And one that was so damn obvious—how did a CNN anchor fall for this?

ing a plane in a suitcase. Fake. And there's the time he claimed the Boston bombers were framed. He's also a 9/11 truther. And still celebs in the media buy his shtick. This ghoul says that even though he's cried wolf many times before, this time it's real and he's consulting a lawyer.

So should Delta. Sue this divisive alienating a-hole.

We must finally declare war on hoaxers, because once again, without evidence, so many swallow an attention-seeking drama, happily smearing a company and the innocent people that it employs. So who is worse? The hoaxer or his prodding enablers in the media? Hard to say. But in the meantime, until further notice, let's make all of them walk.

Can you imagine some jackass pulling this on your flight? I'm not a vengeful guy, but in a perfect world, after such incidents, every passenger gets to kick the guy in the shins as they exit the plane. It's also amazing how none of the well-known sympathizers ever really have to answer for their slack-jawed gullibility. They can sympathize with this clown, publicly, but when he's found out, they simply slink back into darkness. I'm sorry, if you supported this jackass, then you owe everyone an apology for being such a fundamental jerkwad. Final note to Olivia Wilde: Just because people know you're a famous actress doesn't make you smart, it only makes you a famous actress who is easily tricked.

And you notice how Twitter warriors rarely delete the original tweets that got all the original "likes" and retweets? And of course, the follow-up tweet saying it was a hoax never gets as many eyeballs. But the attention-seekers wouldn't have it any other way. [I include myself in that bunch!] Bottom line: We're so addicted to the rush of adrenaline we get from mounting an attack on a perceived oppressor—we don't bother to second-guess an obvious lie. We want to believe it so badly that we turn off all our tools of skepticism.

Where Are We Now?

I would love to end this chapter on an upbeat note. But that would be dishonest and dangerous. ISIS, for now, is crushed. But I say "for now," for good reason. We know that ideology is deathless. When one form is crushed, another far more gruesome kind takes its place. ISIS, after all, was just a bastard offspring of the creeps who came before them.

So, what scares me? That we assume this stuff is over. It's never over. Ever. We will live with this kind of apocalyptic existential threat as long as radical Islam exists.

What really scares me? That the marriage of technology and terror makes it simpler for one creep to do the work of millions. You don't need a ton of terrorists anymore. You just need one. Our world has truly become a James Bond thriller. Whether it's attacking a stadium with a drone packed with anthrax, or polluting a water system, or paralyzing a power grid—it's not the number of crazed jihadists that matters but how inventive and surprising the latest enemy is. And the difference between this enemy and those of old is that these aren't playing to win on battlefield earth. This is all about heaven. So they're perfectly fine with dying, and taking thousands, or millions, with them. This is why our diligence must be never-ending.

See, I told you I wasn't ending on an upbeat note.

CHAPTER FIVE

THE ENVIRONMENT

For the eight years before the election of Donald Trump, we were reminded of two eternal truths, drummed into our heads by both the media and the Obama White House:

- Earth was going to hell in a fiery handbasket made of smaller fiery handbaskets.
- And it was our fault.

These coupled beliefs drove almost every moral decision: Somehow our callous treatment of the earth was leading us to a man-made Armageddon ("managgedon"), and unless we disavow our addiction to oil and embrace windmills, solar panels, and edible compost, we are deservedly doomed to die.

After a while, most Americans just grew tired of the tirades. Although, I never got tired of writing about them.

These monologues focus on the absurdity of our modern times: that we had a president, a media, and an academic culture that found carbon more dangerous than Islamic terrorism. Living in a luxury country buffeted by oceans, we could debate about the consequences of plastic bottles, air-conditioning, and cattle flatulence, while families are butchered in other countries over some insane belief. If there's anything I learned from the last decade, it's that the more removed you are from real threats, the dumber you are about real threats.

Back in the summer of 2011, a new report suggested that climate change could lead to mental illness. The *Sydney Morning Herald* noted that one in five people report emotional injury, stress, and despair after extreme weather, which they link to climate change. A lot of global warming science looks like this—hypothetical bias designed to foster guilt, fear, and grant money. Let's be clear. Emotional injury and stress are not mental illness. They're normal responses to bad stuff like natural disasters. The real mental illness comes from other factors. But their key message is this: If you were a little more green, people wouldn't be so ill. Which makes me think climate change doesn't cause mental illness. Mental illness causes climate change hysteria. Or rather, the harmful Chicken Little mentality causes panic-obsessed PhDs to conjure up any harmful problem and link it to climate change, which then leads to junk science. Think about everything we're told that is caused by global warming—which includes acne, bee stings, bird loss, even cannibalism. That's a few, but the list keeps going. Ultimately, hysteria creates a hellish fantasy that addles the brain of its believers. No wonder Al Gore has lost it. He's about four years away from wandering a local parkway in a opened shorty robe with a beard down to his belly button.

That's a segue to . . .

August 9, 2011

So former vice president Al Gore finally blew a gasket at, of all places, a communications seminar. What pushed the gloomy gasbag over the edge? Well, he feels it's getting harder for Chicken Littles like himself to talk about climate change now that we've all wised up.

Here's a rough transcript of his words, and I mean "rough."

AL GORE: "This climate thing, it's nonsense. Man-made CO_2 doesn't trap heat. It may be volcanoes." Bull—! "It may be sun spots." Bull—! "It's not getting warmer." Bull—!

They have polluted this s—t. There is no longer shared reality on an issue like climate, even though the very existence of our civilization is threatened. People have no idea.

It's no longer acceptable in mixed company, meaning bipartisan company, to use the goddamn word "climate."

Wow, that was elegant. Let me tell you: Gore becomes a child who, after defeat, wants to take the ball, that is, the earth, and run home. But what he doesn't see is that it wasn't the skeptics who blocked the debate, but the purveyors of panic—like Gore—who exaggerated the threat and demonized anyone brave enough to question it. No wonder he is hotter than those numbers on his silly graphs.

Anyway, compare him to the deep green resistance and he appears almost sane. In a recent article, these greenies say that to save the earth, civilization must be destroyed violently and replaced by a Stone Age lifestyle. Now, I wouldn't be against this if these earthworms led by example. But somehow I don't think they will be embracing Fred Flintstone's way of living. Sadly for Al Gore, you can't start your million-dollar houseboat with your feet.

I firmly believe that the media felt so guilty over Gore losing that they allowed him to become President of the Planet—an office that holds no real power [except on talk shows], but offers him the opportunity to pontificate more than twenty popes put together. Fact is, if Gore had been right in his first movie, *An Inconvenient Truth*, then there would be no need for his sequel [which came out in 2017], because the planet would already have been destroyed by evil human behavior. That's the irony lost on Gore: For him to have a sequel, he had to be wrong in the first place!

I don't believe you're crazy to deny climate change, or crazy to run around in a constant apocalyptic panic. Instead, I think both positions are defiant responses to each other. The more people tell you that you might be wrong, the more likely you will dig your heels in and shout even louder. Here's what I've realized over the years: There are a ton of smart people on both sides of the debate. It just so happens the really smart skeptics are also the type of people who rightly sense the strong-arming by their intellectual rivals on the other side. My advice to the warmers has always been: If you stop insulting us, and try to convince us, you'll find that we're only really reacting to how the debate is framed.

I read of an analysis spanning forty-plus years claiming that today's young Americans are less green than their elders. How could this be? Weren't they the ones who embraced global warming as scripture and preached that solar and wind power could cure all our ills—including toenail fungus, which is also green? Well, maybe when you get pushed too hard by MTV or self-righteous celebrities or agenda-driven teachers, you realize that you're being manipulated. All this indoctrination, forcing kids to bow to the god that is environmentalism, backfired, as they realized their little green legs were being pulled.

July 30, 2013

Saudi Prince Al-Waleed bin Talal just penned an open letter that the fracking boom is cutting demand for Saudi oil, threatening their livelihood, to which I add, hooray! The less we rely on them, the better. Let's invest all that money here for once.

If I see another sheik with thirty Mercedes-Benzes, I am going to choke a kitten. It's amazing. It's not often in life you encounter something that solves three major problems at once.

> Not true, I love kittens.

But fracking does that.

It ends four-bucks-a-gallon gas, check.

It ends high unemployment, check.

It ends reliance on countries in unstable parts of the world, where people want to kill us, check.

So, where is the president on this? He's busy building a windmill powered by unicorn flatulence.

And what about green celebrities, goofballs like Yoko Ono and Rosario Dawson who demonized fracking, ignoring the positive impact it's had on millions of Americans. That's because people that fracking benefits most, Yoko and Rosie really don't care about.

Obama should hail shale like the second coming of kale, but instead shuns the oil deposits like they're racist, gay-hating Christians. The fact is, Obama didn't really want independence. And he never really cared for easing suffering at the gas pump. More pain and less consumption was always his goal. Now, it's all screwed up, thanks to fracking.

> Remember, one of his fave advisers wanted really high gas prices, which would punish all Americans, as a way to lower carbon emissions. America suffers! Hooray!

So, why isn't it called bigotry? It strikes me as essentially hating the poor and the uncool. After all, working for an oil company just isn't as authentic as community organizing. One makes something people use, another just makes noise.

> "Obama should hail shale like the second coming of kale" is my favorite line of the page. Only because I'm a sucker for rhymes. I'm not even sure what it means, but I'm not letting that get in the way of my enjoyment.
>
> Obama's antipathy toward fracking and pipelines also served up an easy win for Trump. All Trump had to do was be FOR fracking and pipelines, and he wins. Do the math: Obama was merely trying to please a handful of cool celebs; Trump was appealing to millions of people. And, by reversing Obama's misguided mission, we further ease our dependence on Middle Eastern madmen. When you consider that, you realize how consequential Trump might become in the Middle East.
>
> By the way, the idea of banning coal deprives those who burn deadlier substances of it. People who don't get that are "coal-privileged,"—they've had the black stuff all their lives, but now deprive others of it. Trump promising to revitalize that industry helped him beat Hillary, who had no idea what he was talking about. She was too busy laughing hysterically at Trump to notice him walk all over her.

Almost 2 million die each year inhaling smoke from makeshift fuels like animal dung and wood, all because they lack coal. I guess that doesn't play too well in the patios of D.C. or Bel Air, where the only climate change that matters is which way the wind blows.

October 22, 2013

Remember that stupid song that said children were our future?

It was right. Children are our future, which is why they now have none.

According to Stanley Druckenmiller, while today's seniors will get three hundred grand in lifetime benefits from Social Security, children born today, they're going to lose four hundred grand. That's a lot of money.

I try to calm myself about these facts by telling myself that I'll already be dead. But then I realize that I won't be dead. I will have hired a team of scientists to separate my brain from my body and sink it into a vat of delicious nutrients, which will allow me to live, I hope, to the ripe old age of 19,432.

So, Junior still supports Gramps, but since reproduction has been replaced by recreation, the juniors are disappearing. But at least he's on Mom and Dad's health care. But wait, who is paying for that? The kids.

That's justice.

The sheep that voted for change are left with little, except for bragging rights that they voted for the cool guy—and not the Mormon, or the war hero. Sadly, the cool guy screwed you. They always do. It's true—just watch *The Bachelor.*

Finally, 6 million people aged sixteen to twenty-four are neither in school nor working. I'd say they fell through the cracks, but it's more like an economic black hole, leaving them without skills or experience. So, how do you climb out of the hole?

You frack.

Thanks to fracking, America will be self-sufficient by 2020, which means good-bye to the maniacs of the Middle East. Al Gore must be sobbing in his bowl of fried kittens.

No idea what that means, or my recent obsession with kittens. But fracking isn't just creating freedom. It's creating jobs. You want to find young people making serious money? Follow the fracking, which is enriching generations of men and women. And true, this work may be beneath the beta male bloggers who majored in gender studies. But those bloggers can tell the frackers that as they wait on them at Applebee's.

I am a total hypocrite, by the way. I'm telling kids to go frack; meanwhile the last time I got my hands dirty was April 3, 2005. I can't get into the actual circumstance, because it involved a bucket of voles and a chinchilla. I probably could not survive an hour fracking. I would break a nail, go on workmen's comp, and gain enough weight to appear on *My Six-Hundred-Pound Life.*

November 14, 2013

After every major natural disaster you bet some nutcake will blame it on anything but nature.

Now, a professor of theology blames the tragedy in the Philippines on our use of fossil fuels. The dead aren't even buried yet.

> I'm referring to Typhoon Haiyan, which was one of the most intense tropical cyclones ever, killing at least sixty-three hundred people.

Here's what Susan Brooks Thistlethwaite blames the tragedy on: Quote, "The moral evil of climate change denial that is. Those that continue to deny in the face of mounting evidence that violent climate change is upon us and accelerating."

Now, it's foolish to expect science from crazy. She's so nutty she qualifies as a Snickers bar. Her assumptions are no different than those of others who gloat over people suffering: "Ha, ha, you denied climate change. How do you feel now looking at all those corpses!"

I hated it when evangelists blamed AIDS or earthquakes on sin—and I hate it now. It's done simply for the pleasure of the accuser, to feel superior and right. No misery is too big to fuel your smug satisfaction.

> It's a key point—every outrage on the left has a mirror image on the right. For every climate nut blaming you for the end of the planet, there's some crazy right-winger blaming gun shootings on an angry God. I hate all these people, with equal passion.

The shameful sickness still exists but under a new religion, one of blind faith and flat earth hysteria, and denial of actual facts.

So, congratulations on cementing your incorrect assumptions about man's role in causing typhoons. Grieving families are so happy to oblige.

I maintain that this has been the biggest obstacle to a reasoned argument over climate change. When you indulge those who quickly demonize a side as mass murderers, there isn't much room for actual logical debate. Worse, it does nothing to alleviate the suffering of those afflicted. Instead, it gives one bitter, shallow scold a dopamine rush derived from the misery of others, and gives people like me more reason to remain skeptical about the side that supports them.

You see the same routine after every mass shooting. Once one side demonizes another (like, say, implicating law-abiding gun owners, by the association of gun ownership, in the acts of one madman), all it does is cement the divide, rather than thaw the chill. We all need to step back and take a deep breath before we start condemning the other side to some hellish destiny. (I include myself in this advice.)

December 11, 2013

The North Pole is melting, and it's your fault, which is why for Christmas, Greenpeace has barfed out a fundraising video featuring Santa looking like Saddam trapped in a spider hole. In it, he says, "I bring bad tidings. For some time now, melting ice here, in the North Pole, has made our operations and our day-to-day life intolerable and impossible. I have written personally to President Obama, President Putin, all world leaders. Sadly, my letters have been met with indifference. My home in the Arctic is fast disappearing. And unless we can all act urgently, then I have to warn you of the possibility of an empty stocking, forevermore."

And here lies the lesson: Once someone's trying to scare the kids, it's because they lose on facts.

This is true in most issues in our time, the drug war, satanic heavy metal music, DDT hysteria, day-care abuse, rising gun crime. Once you focus on actual stats, the story dies. Far better to stoke fear than state the facts.

We used to call this propaganda. Now, it's called "raising awareness." It's where Al Gore and global warming hysterics live. It's not about a tiny blip in temperature over a century. It's that the debate has been stained with lies, panic, and fear.

The hysterics cried wolf so loudly that the wolf croaked. But the facts are finally winning. Global temperatures are flatlining. That's not to say we shouldn't care. A gradual rise in temperatures will save lives.

> This is a point many neglect to mention: People thrive in warmer, rather than colder climates. There's a reason few people live in frozen climates, and it's not because of the lousy internet. Just a gradual uptick in temperature, however, leads to a better, healthier climate for growing vegetation. And volleyball, as well as margaritas and coconut-scented tanning spray.

And the use of coal, which hysterics hate, would save millions of lives in third-world countries where people burn far deadlier stuff.

So, it's not this Santa we need to worry about. It's the Santa in the White House. Fresh from trashing one-sixth of the economy, he's now eyeing climate change.

Do you think he's actually read the science? I doubt it. Like Greenpeace's Santa, he's being kept in the dark.

The apocalyptic response is rampant among the left. It's their only weapon in their desperate tool kit, when it comes to every issue they engage.

Tax reform? It kills the poor. Deregulate? It kills the planet. Drill in barren places? It kills reindeer. Repeal Obama's net neutrality BS? Ends the internet as we know it! It leads me to a favorite rule of thumb: If the left claims that something will lead to widespread devastation, it's likely the opposite will happen. If liberals were alive at the time of the birth of the universe, they would have argued against the Big Bang.

But I have to admit that at times, I might be overplaying my hand as a response to the aggressive, coercive elements of the pro–global warming side. I often wonder, if they had not been so shrill, would I think differently about the issue? I have to be honest with myself about this: Maybe my response is driven by my hate for their arrogance. So, in fact, I could admit that I may be wrong, and adjust my views accordingly. But that's almost impossible to do when the other side declares that such a response STILL ISN'T ENOUGH. [Again, you see this in the gun debate. If you say you want a database, a ban on bump stocks, and an age restriction on certain guns, still, you'll be told, IT'S NOT ENOUGH. And the media mocks the fear of staunch gun owners that "sensible gun laws" are a Trojan horse meant to usher in total gun confiscation.]

January 17, 2014

The UN could be the worst thing ever to contain the letters U and N since untreated rabies.

Case in point, their climate chief says communism is tops at fighting global warming.

> That's a decent line, but then again, it's 2:30 a.m. and I'm three tablespoons into an expired bottle of Nyquil.

Christiana Figueres claims that America's political differences prevent passing laws to fight rising temperatures. While in commie China, "They actually want to breathe air that they don't have to look at. They're not doing this because they want to save the planet. They're doing it because it's in their national interest."

Translation: To get what we want, we need a dictator, because then we can murder the dissenters.

It's the same logic behind left-wing fantasies here and abroad. A dictator Obama could take our guns and make us watch PBS. Why not?

> Sounds like the old argument about the positive attributes of a tyrant—at least he's "making the trains run on time."

So, never mind that in China, the smog is thicker than Michael Moore's thighs, for with the UN, evidence is a drag and so is history. Communism slayed in the twentieth century—over 100 million dead, 65 million in China alone. They're the McDonald's of massacres.

But I get it. Think of how much less carbon is emitted when the emitters are reduced to crushed bone. Using this logic, all killers are environmental heroes. Genghis Khan becomes a tree hugger, and Hitler wrote the first *Inconvenient Truth*, called *Mein Kampf*. Perhaps Ted Bundy was killing locally but thinking globally.

But look, the desire for someone or something to take over and fix things, even if millions die, is not new. It's the nature of the left. If you wish to remake, you first must undo, which spells doom for me and for you.

> Nice unintentional rhyme—I'm the Doctor Seuss of politics!

> There is an underlying assumption to the far left's obsession with the environment: Humans are bad, and the fewer there are, the better. Of course, this rule doesn't apply to them.

May 7, 2014

The science is settled: If we don't do something now, we're all going to die.

> And so begins a video clip montage of the media response to the National Climate Assessment report.

ANCHOR 1: Torrential rain, flooding, heat waves, drought, and wildfires. It's all getting worse.

ANCHOR 2: On the heels of America's warmest decade, more heat waves and periods of severe drought.

ANCHOR 3: All these are set to be more severe, according to the latest National Climate Assessment put out by the White House Tuesday.

That's the media's loving take on the White House's new climate change report. I'm telling you, the incestuous bond between the media and Obama makes Norman Bates's crush seem wholesome.

So why does this report call for a course of panic? To beat you into cowering submission, so your wallet is more easily lifted? Perhaps.

Or it could be that the data just isn't enough. The computer models have failed, as most predictions flunked. The prior hysteria didn't help. They put politics before science, so trust is essentially dead.

The scientists used to embrace skepticism. But global warmers marshal only those who agree to ostracize the rest. It's intellectual bullying by government and media together that's meant to silence others.

The panic, the doomsday rhetoric, is so in sync, with such suffocating superiority, that you're a leper just by questioning it. I'm one now.

See, the media used to ask questions. Now they're a megaphone for their masters on everything from climate change to gun control, Benghazi, Obamacare, and the IRS. Which leaves only one real question: What can the average person do when he's this outdone? Where do you go when no one speaks for you?

The beach? We've got the weather for it.

I'm trying to think of an example where the American public was ever persuaded by a panic to do the right thing. In just about every instance where we were told that something wicked would come if we didn't change our ways, nothing happened. Or things simply got worse because of the panic. The Alar Scare? Artificial sweeteners? DDT? SARs? Any issue linked to the end of the world never is. But if you're able to argue coherently armed with facts about something that concerns you, you make more headway, and come to some reasonable conclusion about what to do next. It's how I look at terrorism. Rather than scream "We're all going to die," I focus on ideologies and technologies that make it easier to achieve goals. That's how you deal with a real fear.

Panic never solves a problem. It only makes it worse—like truffle oil [which has ruined French fries for me in most neighborhood restaurants].

February 12, 2015

So last night, I had this nightmare. It was about a president who believes the media overstates the alarm people have about the threat of terrorism, over the threat of climate change.

I realized it wasn't a dream when I saw this clip:

MATTHEW YGLESIAS, EXECUTIVE EDITOR OF *VOX:* Do you think the media sometimes overstates the sort of level of alarm people should have about terrorism and this kind of chaos as opposed to a longer-term problem of climate change, epidemic disease?

BARACK OBAMA: Absolutely.

Well, it's almost as if the president's saying, as he seems to be imply-ing here, that the threat of climate change is greater than the threat of terrorism.

> And they say Trump shouldn't be in charge? This was a president whose view of national security apparently came from reading Hallmark cards.

JONATHAN KARL, ABC NEWS: As the president is saying, as he seems to be implying here, the threat of climate change is greater than the threat of terrorism.

JOSH EARNEST, WHITE HOUSE PRESS SECRETARY: I think, Jon, the point that the president is making is that there are many more people on an annual basis who have to confront the impact, the direct impact on their lives, of climate change or on the spread of a disease, than on terrorism.

> Christ, I need to throw up.

So the media's ignoring global warming—the same media that blames climate change for shrinking sheep, increased shark and cougar attacks, cow infertility, and even global cooling. You think maybe this absurd obsession is why our president missed ISIS?

> Uh, yes, Greg—you're absolutely right on that . . . the more we focused on Celsius, the more we overlooked the mass murders propagated by an ideology that doesn't fit neatly in the "blame America" box. Climate change was the acceptable threat because it was OUR fault. But ISIS? If only we could make that our fault, too. And in time, they do, by linking the rise of terror to . . . climate change!

Sorry, that's not a cold front that kills innocents with machetes. Those aid workers didn't lose their heads to drizzle.

Fact is, if climate change is a huge threat, what do you do about it? We know the temperature models were wrong. Scientists dispute both cause and harm.

Sorry, that 97 percent consensus was bunk. Exaggeration occurs when facts escape you.

I'm referring to what might be the most overused statistic on the planet about the planet. From what I gather, and I could be sloppily right, it was taken from a general questionnaire regarding *opinions* of academics on whether man might have an impact on climate change. To rephrase it better, the number from the survey is not "bunk," but that it reflects overall agreement that we are heading to environmental armageddon *is*. And that the academic arena demands obedience to a set orthodoxy, I'm surprised it wasn't 99 percent.

But with terror, you know what to do, the threat is palpable. We see the forecasts every day and it's 90 percent bloody with a 50 percent chance of beheading.

So, why climate change? Well, it's an ideology built for American blame. If the villain isn't the West, then why bother with unrest? The result: snow blindness, where our president calls Yemen a success, right before our embassy evacuates—and says ISIS morale is low, as their forces grow. Seriously, how does Obama miss all these storms? He is not just a weak president, he is a crummier weatherman.

We haven't had a worse prognosticator in the U.S. since Custer. How wrong Obama was on ISIS will never enter history—because it's the liberals who write the history books. And also, Trump cleaned up Obama's mess. But Team Obama couldn't have gotten this one more wrong if they emptied Gitmo and expected the prisoners to go straight. Wait a minute . . . oh.

I do believe that Obama's obsession with climate change has one origin, and one consequence. The origin: It's an issue where one can blame the U.S.—and if you can blame us, you're on safe ground with everyone else [who hates us]. The consequence: By keeping his eye on climate change, he took his eye off terror and allowed the rise of ISIS. And the fact that the media still clings to the idea that an incremental increase in Celsius is deadlier than a raging mass of murderous ideological zombies speaks to their blindness. This trend, for now, was reversed by Trump. He took the foot off the gas of climate change hysteria [pulling out of the Paris climate accords], while throttling up the wholesale elimination of ISIS by easing rules of engagement. We could now win a war by actually TRYING to win it. Which meant killing. The result—we eliminated, for the time being, an apocalyptic death cult, and saved countless lives in the immediate future.

Even during horrible events—like a Jordanian pilot being burned alive by ISIS—our government still prattled on about its climate change obsession. It's not like you can't hold two different thoughts in your head [one about terror and another about the planet], it's just that one thought commands so much space over the other. It makes you wonder that if ISIS had actually grown and spread to a force that could take over the West, annihilating hundreds of millions of Americans, our government would be saying, "Well, as long as they're recycling!"

April 22, 2015

So at an Earth Day thing at the National Mall, activists made an unearthly mess. I guess if your heart's in the right place, the trash can go anywhere. But it's never about the earth, but about ego and retribution. Take Bill Nye, the denial guy, bragging on Twitter about flying with President Obama today. See, for him, it's all about status. The attention bestowed for parroting the right platitudes.

> My "side" can also be guilty of this—when the dude in power decides to anoint you with his admiration or friendship, your ego expands and you suddenly pull back on your usual sober critical analysis. I've seen it: The president says something nice about you, and it changes you. We're all susceptible to flattery from above (and below).

The scarier belief, however, is that climate change poses a greater threat than terror. It's fine coming from loons, but the president . . . yikes.

BARACK OBAMA: Today, there's no greater threat to our planet than climate change. The Pentagon says that climate change poses immediate risk to our national security. Climate change can no longer be denied or ignored. (How is this not a cult?)

I call this the strawpocalypse, a mix of straw man and Armageddon. Sure, it's the earth and it trumps everything, but with that absurd comparison, then we should devote nothing to fight present danger and fight only figments of imagination. It's nuts.

But Republicans must be better. If you say the science isn't settled, then you cannot dismiss warming out of hand.

You need to be persuasive, even when they mock you—and they will mock you. Earth Day is Christmas for earth's avengers. For most climate change activists, it's less about carbon and more about consumers and consumerism and trashing the systems that save countless lives.

For the green movement believes that the root of every evil is a beating human heart.

Their bile toward human enterprise is the howl of the nonproductive—nurtured on bitter slogans. "I'm here to help," they tell the earth. If the earth could talk, she would say, "Please, get lost."

> Slipped inside this monologue is some sound advice to Republicans: Going "whole denial" is not a strategy. It gives the opponents too much turf. And if you believe the science isn't settled [and it isn't], then you must allow for the possibility that there is truth to the climate change claims, even if the claims are often exaggerated. And, yes, it forces you to take the high road: Though even if you're willing to meet the other side halfway, they'll still want to run you over in their Teslas. The good news: Your F-150s will crush them.

December 1, 2015

Did you know that the Paris climate talks emit three hundred thousand tons of CO_2? Here's some of that gas.

BARACK OBAMA: This is an economic and security imperative that we have to tackle now. Everybody else has taken climate change really seriously. They think it's a really big problem.

> Thanks, Einstein.

CHARLES, PRINCE OF WALES: Your deliberations over the next two weeks will decide the fate, not only of those alive today, but also of generations yet unborn.

> Oh, stop it, Dumbo.

DAVID CAMERON, BRITISH PRIME MINISTER: Let's just imagine for a moment what we would have to say to our grandchildren if we failed. What was it that was so difficult when the earth was in peril? When the sea levels were rising in 2015, when crops were failing, when deserts were expanding. What was it that was so difficult?

And then the media added their own stink.

> I'd say your flowery panic made it unbelievable, chap.

SCOTT PELLEY, *CBS EVENING NEWS* ANCHOR: The president warns it will soon be too late to stop climate change. We find evidence in China's pollution emergency and in the melting Arctic.

DAVID MUIR, *ABC WORLD NEWS TONIGHT* ANCHOR: Overseas United to Paris into that unprecedented Climate Change Summit tonight, a major gathering of world leaders, nearly 150 in all, including of course President Obama, who said today the United States deserves some of the blame for climate change.

> Seriously, it's like they all got the same phone call.

What self-perpetuating poop. You've got to wonder why such drama hasn't been directed at terror. Maybe it's the difference between those who fight for such causes. The climate crazies are elitists—lavishly educated, expensively caffeinated, and predominantly white. The older and richer they are, the more this elite status becomes obvious. See Prince Charles, Leo DiCaprio, Al Gore.

But I beg you, try finding a poor Indian, a working-class Asian, or a struggling Latino on this activist front. No, they are almost entirely white European elitists who wish to deny cheap fuel to the billion in the third world not on the electricity grid. Maybe they're racist!

As Prince Charles falsely links drought to terror, this war on cheap resources is more likely linked to terror—for when you ensure the poverty of a billion people, a death cult becomes viable. So climate panic helps terror in two ways, by diverting resources from the fight and punishing the poor.

Now let's look at those who see terror as a bigger threat than climate change, they aren't in Hollywood, they aren't in the media, they're not tenured. They don't have private jets, they don't drip with royalty or party with Leo on a yacht stacked with topless supermodels. They aren't chic. They look like you and, sadly, me. Could that be why the climate crusade gets the summit and the attention and the accolades that terror warriors never get? Imagine if we flipped this and made the war on terror the glamorous one. ISIS wouldn't stand a chance.

This script finally got flipped, and as I edit this in early October 2017, ISIS forces are surrendering by the hundreds to the Kurds. It proves the point: What if a new leader shifted emphasis from climate apocalypse to the more urgent existential threat of ISIS? It shows you how climate blindness was preventing us from fighting terror, and in turn ushered in a leader who wanted to change that.

And all of this climate hysteria blather really was about securing $100 trillion bucks for the climate accords, which would have again diverted precious funds from solving more urgent problems to capping the temperatures by a fraction of a degree over a century. When Trump pulled out of the accords, the outrage told you everything you needed to know. It lasted a few days, then everyone went on their merry way. Everyone—perhaps even the environmentalists—knew it was a scam. There may be a better deal to be made, but only Trump had the guts to say so, out loud. And we all pretty much knew he was right. Including his critics. God bless the orange Godzilla!

December 14, 2015

This is a monologue on the great triumph of the Paris accords. The good news: It didn't last long.

Good news. The Paris climate thing was a smash.

Hmm, I wonder if Captain Planet said this agreement represents the best chance we have to save the one planet that we've got, and believes that this moment could be a turning point for the world.

> I love doing this. Although it works better on TV than on the page.

BARACK OBAMA: This agreement represents the best chance we've had to save the one planet that we've got. So I believe this moment can be a turning point for the world.

And the media loved it, greeting this deal with wild applause. It's like they won a car on Oprah. And you wonder why terrorists enter America unnoticed. It's because these adults are too obsessed with Celsius to see the real threats. But it's no shock, they all fester in the same campus swamp where prosperity is deemed evil, but violence is a means of the powerless. So while these fools whoop it up, our government—out of fear—won't review social media posts for people who are applying for visas here. Political correctness stops vetting of potential terrorists, so we die. I can't cheer for that. And what about that drywall with Botox known as Secretary of State John Kerry? What are his thoughts on the accord?

JOHN KERRY, UNITED STATES SECRETARY OF STATE: I think it actually sends a very powerful message to the marketplace, but one of the reasons why there is no enforcement mechanism is because the United States Congress would never accept one. So it has to be voluntary. And a lot of nations resent that, but we have accepted that because we believe it's going to move the marketplace, and already you see countless new technologies, a lot of jobs being created, and I think it's going to produce its own form of oversight.

What is he talking about? What an oaf. They didn't solve anything. It was a consensus of the senseless.

The liberal reply always is "We can chew gum and walk at the same time." Meaning, we can tackle climate change and terror—but where is the proof? Forget walking and chewing gum, Obama's climatism is like texting while driving. He's not doing two things well, but doing the wrong thing instead of the right thing at the wrong time and endangering all of us.

He's driving a packed Greyhound around a tight corner, while texting Leo about the weather. Forgive us, dear media, but we aren't cheering, we're screaming.

Now, I do think we can handle two things at the same time, but in an era of terror, let's get those things in the right order. Which is when something like ISIS happened to cross. But instead of hitting it, they hit us.

Right now [late February 2018] someone floated a rumor that Kerry is considering another run for the presidency. I'd love to see that! The debate with Trump would be the equivalent of a race between an Olympic sprinter and an Adirondack chair.

March 28, 2016

Like a rusted garage door needing a gallon of WD-40, John Kerry opened his mouth this weekend, defending Obama's recent terror response. I bet he says the president's schedule isn't set by terrorists.

JOHN KERRY, SECRETARY OF STATE: The president of the United States' schedule was not set by terrorists. The president of the United States has major diplomatic responsibilities. He has to engage with other countries. That was an important part of trying to build a relationship and achieve some of our goals with respect to human rights, with respect to transformation in Syria, in Cuba, and elsewhere. Life doesn't stop because one terrible incident takes place in one place.

Says the man so wooden, Orkin sprays him weekly. But he's right, life doesn't stop unless you're in Brussels or Pakistan, and it's shredded to pieces. But for Kerry, there are bigger fish than ISIS. Climate change, wage gaps, Argentinean dance instructors. Here's the talking tree on how the world views Trump.

KERRY: Every leader I meet, they ask about what is happening in America, they cannot believe it. I think it is fair to say that they are shocked. They don't know where it's taking the United States of America. It upsets people's sense of equilibrium about our steadiness, about our reliability. And to some degree, I must say to you, some of the questions, the way they're posed to me, it's clear to me that what's happening is an embarrassment to our country.

> What a sputtering jackass. So let me get this straight: We should act in a manner that makes the world feel better? A world that can barely keep up with us? Please stop, you walking plank of repurposed wood.

Yes. After so much terror, this is the world's concern: Trump. I think I can speak for all of us. I don't care what the world thinks. They don't have the best track record. Just eight years ago, a new leader received the Nobel Prize for just being him. His vague "hope and change" was lauded for ending the America of old. Tired of being the world's policeman, Obama buried its badge and gun. Now, in 2016, the world quakes—where's that gun, that badge? Sure, Trump's an impulsive hydrant. But can the fear he causes worldwide be worse than Obama's aloof uselessness? This is the pendulum swing coming after eight years of odd priorities, favoritism toward enemies, dismissal of our own safety—all in the service of world acclaim for Obama. After swimming among a globe of ghouls, maybe it's time for us to be the scary guy on the block, that heavily tattooed lug with a pit bull and bloodshot eyes. Because if we learned anything this weekend, it's that all love gets you in this world is killed.

A more-than-decent prediction. Trump's unpredictable ambiguity is inspiring new thinking among our adversaries and our allies. And terrorists are dropping like flies. I used to say this a lot on my old show, *Redeye*: It would be nice if the world saw us as the crazy guy on the block for once. Now we are, and it's working out nicely.

Also, as I write [March 2018], North Korea is signaling it wants to talk about denuclearization. I think that's only happening because Trump could speak Rocket Man's language. The language is "Our country first, yours second . . . if that." But Trump's salesman strategy worked: Create chaos to start a new process in which your position cannot be predicted. Then, negotiate. So far, it's worked. You always do better when the other side is off-balance.

June 30, 2016

Yesterday on *CBS This Morning*, a correspondent noted how the recent terror attacks were diverting attention from more urgent matters, like our special friend, Mr. Climate Change.

MARGARET BRENNAN, CBS CORRESPONDENT: President Obama, though, this is the third time in the past year that a major summit is being overshadowed by terrorism. Here in Ottawa, Mexico, Canada, and, with President Obama representing the U.S., were all supposed to sit down and tackle tough climate change issues, including a pledge to switch to renewable, clean energy and tackle immigration issues.

Poor thing. Instead of discussing how to devote billions of dollars and countless hours of time to slightly adjust global temperatures with little or no evidence that it's realistic, possible, or even beneficial, we must tackle an evil that's causing mass death now. Oh, the pain. Having to deal with such an inconvenience, especially when you've already printed up that elegant climate agenda on fake organic stock and hired a mime troop to act out the horrors of carbon emissions.

Terror always rains on their parade. That murderous guest, always uninvited, refuses to leave until you're dead. What a pain. Because it's not like we ever discuss climate change or have global summits where self-obsessed celebrities and blowhards show up to outpanic each other! Imagine if we had the opposite: that we had a leader who saw terror as the chief threat, galvanizing the globe to fight these ghouls. Imagine if celebrities understood that they would be the first to die under a caliphate. Imagine if they understood terror change, how the threat expands based on advancing technology. Imagine if they could understand true evil. Of course, they just blame it on SUVs, guns, and Christians.

> **Yes, I keep making this point—but I would happily STOP making this point if they stopped avoiding real threats and just agreed with me! That really is the answer for everything: Agree with me!**

Where Are We Now?

We're still here. I mean, the planet, that is, unless we were blown to bits in between my writing this sentence and publication of this book. And if that's the case, this book was a phenomenal waste of my time; I could have been in Aruba drinking Dark & Stormys on a clothing-optional beach with my good friend Lorenzo Lamas. The highlight for me, brought to us by the Trump administration, was the Paris Accord Pullout, or PAP, for short—what can I say, I like acronyms! PAP didn't make me happy because I think climate change is a hoax (I don't), it's because it was a lousy deal predicated on peer pressure, emotional arguments, and bad stats. It was also going to cost us $100 trillion over a century. By my calculations, that's "a lot."

And that's money that could help a lot of other people.

This is where I turn to the great Bjorn Lomborg, a Luke-warmer who crunches the numbers as part of his sane Copenhagen consensus group.

What could you do with a fraction of that Paris accord money? According to Bjorn, whom I asked about all this via email—the UN organization UNCTAD has "estimated that the full extra cost of solving all humanity's problems in the world (living up to the UN's sustainable development goals, eradicating poverty, hunger, diseases—while fixing air pollution and climate, and almost any other issue) would cost about $2.5 trillion a year until 2030, which comes to $37.5 trillion." To deny that money, and instead pour all of it into chasing a goal of preventing an incremental change in Celsius, seems criminal.

Fact is, there are 2.8 billion people who need to get onto the electricity grid. They suffer from indoor air pollution, which according to Lomborg, is ten times worse than the outdoor pollution in Beijing or Bangkok. According to the World Health Organization, it's the equivalent of smoking two packs of cigarettes every day (without the pleasure of smoking). Put those people on the grid—which would be powered not by windmills or hairless unicorns but fossil fuels—and that would prevent 2.8 million deaths every year. So the next time a hardcore climate changer says it was evil for Trump to pull out of Paris, simply use their stereotypical argument against them: Their stance kills people.

CHAPTER SIX

THE CAMPUS

For this batch of monologues I've included a few more recent ones, in order to cover the recent trend of barring conservative speakers from campus.

It's an obvious point, but it bears repeating until my beautiful head explodes: The campus, once designed for free exchange of ideas and expression, is now intensely intolerant of both. I fear that it's spreading beyond the leafy quads to the real world.

It boils down to this: If your ideas do not fit perfectly with the hard left's assumptions, you must be silenced. And they are justified in doing so, for—as the old saying goes—they believe that you aren't simply wrong, but evil. That means they can use any or all means necessary to stop you. The end result is that the intermediate step between disagreement and chaos, which is dialogue, is removed. And that leaves only violence to "solve" the problem. It's why the phrase "safe space" is so absurd. If you're a freethinker hungry for challenging ideas, the campus can be the most unsafe place around.

Note: One of the most obnoxious campus trends is attacking anyone for cultural appropriation. How dare you wear a sombrero on May fifth? And so on. I get why some isolated incidents can seem silly—but cultural appropriation is actually cultural *appreciation*, meaning it's what people do to survive. Everything comes from somewhere. If someone steals something good from one culture, it's a compliment—and I say this wearing pajamas (culturally appropriated from Indian Muslims). So sue me.

December 9, 2011

> This is an oldie, but a goodie.

So, at Iowa State U, the college Republicans started their holiday care package drive to send goodies to troops overseas. We're talking candies, socks, toothpaste, and puzzle books, basically the stuff Bob shoplifts on a Saturday night.

And normal people would embrace this, but academics are not normal people. Take instructor Thomas Walker, who penned a note to the school paper mocking the drive.

> A reference to our dear old pal, Bob Beckel—hope you're doing well, Bob.

In it he said, quote, "Aren't GIs paid enough to buy what they need and even what they want? . . . What are the troops doing for us? Nothing. But against us, they are doing a lot, creating anti-American terrorists in the countries they occupy."

Oh, yes, there is that "occupy" verb again. Why does the word come from tenured self-absorbed twits who consider a nose ring an achievement? And why is it so many academics are full-on clowns? Is it because carnivals no longer hire?

> I realize at times I fall back on clichés that now make me wince. For example, every time I mention a progressive on campus, I always have to bring up "nose rings" or "patchouli." It's hacky. I hate it now. From now on, every time you hear me do it, punch me in the butt.

Now, I could say that the jerk wrote this letter just to impress naïve coeds, but maybe he needs a real education. How about everyone watching this show now who has a loved one in the military, send him a Christmas card, care of XXXXXXX. And include a photo of that loved one inside. Be sure to add a note explaining what they are doing for us.

> I'm blocking out the address here.

It's not so much a care package, but a "why you should care" package. It may not matter to him, but it's really for you.

> This is an example of a jackass picking a terrible battle to fight. You can have a stupid opinion, like "Why send these jerks care packages," but if you're smart, you just mutter the notion to yourself and move on. This dope actually felt compelled to make his idiotic thought immortal in a letter. Next time, Tommy, count to one hundred before you put finger to keyboard, jerkwad. (By the way, I give the same advice to myself, which I still often ignore.)

April 2, 2012

A new study by the California Association of Scholars reports that the UC system is rife with left-wing bias. The "system head" rejects these findings, of course. After all, they come from conservative scholars.

So, that's got to be biased!

Of course, the college head will think it's biased in the same way a suspect might accuse a witness of bias, because the witness caught him in the act.

But how do you know the bias is real? Talk to your average professor. If he doesn't utter the word "patriarchy" in five minutes, he's been dead for six minutes.

Ask a student about patriotism—feel free to yank out his nose ring when he mentions Halliburton.

Look how conservative speakers are handled on campus. Ahmadinejad gets way better treatment.

> There I go again. Nose ring. I am punching myself in the butt!

Look at the jobless grads. They majored in crud that guarantees teaching the same crud to another clueless kid.

As Thomas Sowell points out, students can exit top colleges learning nothing about science, math, or economics—all the stuff that protects you from demagoguery.

So you have grads with a dummy education that makes them vulnerable to bad ideas. See Occupy Wall Street.

But this isn't news. We know college is commie central. So, conservatives have to stop whining and start crashing the party. It's time to stop pointing fingers and step on a few toes.

Let's see what happens when a professor finally meets someone who thinks America is a positive force in the world. He'll probably choke on his tongue stud.

> Well, I apparently moved off nose rings to a "tongue stud." I have now punched myself twice in the butt, and once in the throat for good measure. I apologize for these stale cliches.

November 21, 2012

So, according to a new poll, 63 percent of college grads think the American dream is dead. I'm surprised they knew what it was. For this dream, once defined by equality of opportunity, has been replaced by the morally superior equality of outcome.

So why is that? Well, for the dream to work, you had to get American exceptionalism. After all, there is no Belgian, Mexican, or Hawaiian dream.

> I make that Hawaiian joke to invite viewers to write in to tell me that Hawaii is indeed part of the Union. And some people do write in to correct me! (Note: I love Hawaii. Ever since the three-part *Brady Bunch* episode, I've wanted to live there in a cave with Vincent Price.)

But even our president thought that was academic. Exceptionalism, it's so *Leave It to Beaver*.

See, the dream requires thinking that our system is better. And that's *mean*. The American dream of selfish individualism makes the world mad.

So now, "exceptionalism as exploitive" is coming back. It's never a new idea. It's sprouting from the same leafy campuses that gave us an administration that sees government as the dream's replacement.

As young folks are saddled with debt and unemployment, Obama wishes to expand the government's reach, raising taxes on those who spent decades laboring under that old dream.

> It is weird that after four years of "hope and change," a poll suggests there is no hope for the "dream." Was that the intended effect?

So, how can anyone believe in a dream when our leaders don't? They look at stagnant Europe and say that's better. America may be entering a nationally recurring nightmare. And I don't mean the one where Dana and Jasper show up as house guests.

> If you watch *The Five*, then you've seen Dana's dog, Jasper. But it's a lot bigger in person than it is on the flat screen. And it has no sense of "space," meaning if you're sitting in a single chair, it will lumber over like a drunk construction worker and climb up on the same perch, assuming both of you will fit. Invariably, you don't, and you end up giving up the seat to the dog, who may have had that goal in his head from the very beginning.

March 5, 2013

Stanley Kurtz in *National Review* is reporting on the left-wing campaign to have college endowments divest their holdings in fossil fuel companies. The movement so far has affected 250 campuses, featuring the crown jewels of hipster protest, sit-ins, building seizures, and hunger strikes. Which leaves me to one point about student hunger strikes: Let them starve—for a while. Seriously, they could stand to lose a few pounds.

> **Easy, lame joke. But the fact is, young people are getting fatter and paler. The good news—it's temporary. Once they leave college and realize that playing video games and watching the Housewives of Whatever does not pay them a living wage, suddenly they're making themselves presentable. I went in the opposite direction. I was in amazing shape in college. Now I'm a ball of carbs with a belly button.**

But divestment is part of a larger goal, found in teachers' lounges: killing America. It's a movement to upend progress, which, to them, is code for American domination.

Look at its leader, Bill McKibben, who is blocking the Keystone pipeline. It's a coercive ideology, forcing you to return to a communal lifestyle—no cars, no stores, and no clean underwear. For climate changers, it was all kind of a ruse, forcing you to bend to their primitive utopia. So far, Obama doesn't seem to mind.

Anyway, remember how the goal of the radical Islamists is to force existence back to a time when Muhammad walked the earth? The only difference between them and the divesters is the radical Islamists cut to the chase.

But I endorse this divestment movement, and would like to see Harvard, where the students favor divestment overwhelmingly, give up oil entirely. Let the kids and their idiot professors freeze their Marxist asses off next winter. May they keep warm perhaps by burning copies of my book, *The Joy of Hate*.

> **This point could have been made clearer: The radical Islamic dream to return to a seventh-century belief system is somewhat similar to the dream of those greenies who**

wish us to return to the life of Luddite simplicity. To be clear, this point isn't about terrorism, but about a distaste for progress that disrupts your own ideology. Yet the other hilarious thing they have in common: They both use technology to preach their return to primitiveness. Every green celebrity who flies a private jet to expound on climate change deserves a nuclear wedgie.

May 6, 2013

Weather Underground terrorist Bill Ayers was at Kent State giving a keynote talk when he was asked what made him different from the Boston bombers. It is a fair question. Ayers had tried to kill innocent Americans with bombs forty years ago, just like the jihadists of today.

But he claims that the Muslim supremacists were nihilistic, while back then he believed in something. But also, Ayers points out, all of his terrorist pals did back then was property damage.

About that property damage . . .

During the Kent State talk Ayers left out how he lost three of his pals. Bombs they were making actually blew their heads off. Yes, property damage. The bombs were intended for a dance at the Fort Dix Army Base in New Jersey. So, the right people died that day. Thank God.

A harsh line, but factually true, agree? Just nod for yes— I've embedded microscopic cameras in these pages capturing your every move.

Ayers wanted to kill innocent people. So the only difference was that the Boston guys were good at what Ayers was bad at.

Ayers said it would be, quote, "inappropriate to include that in his talk," meaning it would expose him for the scumbag that he is. When faced with the immorality of his action, he championed relativism by saying, and I quote, "The United States is the most violent country that has ever been created." I guess he'd know.

So as the authorities struggled to find a place to put the corpse of the Boston bomber, I have one suggestion—why not in Ayers's living room, as a constant reminder of what could have been, or maybe what should have been.

Just think about it: It's entirely possible that if that Boston bomber had lived, he'd get a teaching position at a top college in America. (Maybe there's still a chance for his younger brother.) Because over time, we start to "empathize" and "identify" with those who want us dead. It must be us who are at fault! How else could Ayers have a job, when in reality, he should be in prison until he's dead. Remember, he's only free because he failed. He's only around because the people who died were on his team. He teaches because they're dead. Some hero. And another thing: Not too long before Andrew Breitbart's death, Andrew bought a dinner ticket to dine with Ayers at his home as some part of a charity gimmick. Andrew told me that Ayers and his wife maintained an aloof, bemused politeness. Poor Ayers: It must have been weird to be in the presence of a true revolutionary, a real bomb thrower who changed the world for the better.

April 29, 2014

So, two Dartmouth Greek groups have nixed a fundraiser for heart patients, because one student didn't like the Mexican theme—the "Phiesta" was to have burritos and guac. But Alpha Phi and Phi Delta Alpha scrapped it after a self-described Mexican-born, United States–raised first-generation woman of color called it "cultural appropriation" and won, because that's all you need these days to kill the fun.

Said the Phi Delt president, quote, "The possibility of offending even one member of the Dartmouth community was not worth the potential benefits of having the fundraiser."

> There's nothing less fun than championing your identity, unless it's hanging out with someone who champions their identity

You wimp.

Now my buddy Joe traces this idiocy to two words that start every self-absorbed student's complaint, "as a." You know, "As a Native American lesbian, I'm outraged," "As a feminist ambisexual pole vaulter, I am speechless," "As a sequential hermaphroditic Icelander, I am devastated." It's too much.

> Plus, I get this weird rash. Go to my website— the photos are all high-def.

And, as a height-challenged loudmouth of German descent, I've had it. No more Oktoberfest, then. I find the tight-fitting hosiery a mockery of my people.

As a rule, we should all be outraged by bigotry. I get it. But this ain't it. Students seem more consumed by identity than by industry. And the campus feeds the attention-seeking, which is why a place once safe for speech is now the flagship for the feeling fascists.

> I get paid extra for alliteration— it's in my contract

College is the IKEA of intolerance, where one comes to build a fragile identity, incapable of withstanding the slightest words. I'd call them a bunch of "P" words, but that's been banned on campus, too.

Identity politics is the enemy of fun. It's cancer of the funny bone. What kind of entity would kill a charity luncheon meant to help sick folks? An engine of antifun, of course. And it wouldn't end there.

Think about killing a fundraiser because only one person is offended. Isn't this insane? Does that mean that anyone can complain about anything the university does and it gets canceled? What if someone complained about football? Does that just go away? Highly unlikely. Especially if the complaint came from a non–justice warrior. No activity would ever be canceled because a conservative was offended. Which is cool. Because why would we give a damn?

IKEA of intolerance . . . it's true. You go to school and build a flimsy bookcase of stacked identity defenses. All identity and no work ethic—the modern-day social justice crybabies, swaddled in sweatpants and clutching iPhones, have only one talent: shout at strangers just trying to get to their real jobs.

July 16, 2014

A Pew poll, my favorite kind, finds that 43 percent of eighteen-to twenty-nine-year-olds think socialism is okay. Meanwhile, 86 percent of their grandparents don't. So, why the gap?

Well, *Reason* magazine reports that millennials think socialism is better than a government-managed economy, even though socialism is a government-managed economy, and that's the point. As long as you don't know what socialism is, you're fine with it.

Once you explain it, however, people run. Again, like President Obama. Which explains why older folks detest this crud. They remember history and its bad guys all too well. These days, socialism is the sugar-coated answer to coldhearted capitalism. Socialism is "let's share" to capitalism's "don't care."

No surprise. This silliness peaks in college. That incubator filled with academics who disguise coercion as compassion. They probably celebrated July Fourth because it's Tokyo Rose's birthday.

> I always find it a good thing to rhyme at least once or twice a week. I learned that from Nipsey Russell when he used to be on *Match Game*.

> Score!

On campus, it's the leftists' job to keep kids in the dark, because when they're in the real world, the drugs wear off. Except in the media, where bad ideas are kept alive by the incubator's star pupils, which leaves the real work up to you and me, all of us here. To deprogram the brainwash, you must persuasively show them why capitalism means freedom, how a paycheck is yours and not Obama's, and that real compassion is defined by opportunity and not entitlement.

We've got our work cut out for us.

> I admit, for a while there, Obama was my personal piñata. And I actually like the guy. I just hated his policies. And I hated the way he expressed them—as if you were not to question them at all, as if they were just naturally right, and his opinion was not to be questioned. The complete opposite of Trump, who treats his opinions as simply that. Opinions. If you don't like 'em, you might be right. So what. He changes his mind as often as I change my socks (three times a week).

September 1, 2014

A website created a list of rookie mistakes that freshmen make in their first week in college. Most of it was stupid stuff like locking yourself out of your dorm room. The real mistakes, in my opinion?

Not forcing students to learn these four things:

Number one, where stuff comes from, or rather how things are made.

Number two, how stuff gets paid for—like your tuition, iPad, and prescription medication.

Number three: Why most of the world is still a mess, as America prospers—for now.

If you teach these three things, then every anti-West professor on campus looks like a moron, which is why they avoid such truths. And you must learn them on your own.

Shit—did I forget the fourth thing?

The fourth thing one must learn, and it's important: Do not mistake sheep for rebels.

You'll be swamped by people who claim that they're outspoken and edgy. They will try to impress their differences

Whew, there it is— that gave me a scare!

on you as a method of expressing their fake uniqueness. They will wish to raise awareness and debate gender politics loudly. They will wear victimhood as a badge of honor, when it's just a substitute for identity. It's an alluring shtick, and weaker minds and spines fall for it.

Identity politics is the 7-Eleven of self-esteem, a quick stop where you choose to become whoever you are. But if it's so easy, how could it be unique? How could it mean anything? Like all ideologies, it creates a dead mind. It stops thought, the kind that challenges their narrow view.

So while they go to college, their minds atrophy.

So here's my tip, when the lockstep comes lurking, masquerading as rebellion, tell them you got over that in kindergarten.

A pretty weak ending; but a strong message for college students: Proclaiming one's identity, if it's done by everyone, is merely sheep in wolves' clothing. If everyone's doing it, how is it in any way dangerous? You're following the herd.

Anyway, I find both sheep and wolves deeply disturbing. It's why I moved to the city. Where the rats are the size of sheep and wolves. Bottom line: When we make the "group" more important than the "individual," it never ends well. For more on this, see "Stalinism."

October 1, 2014

Hooray, cold-blooded cop killer Mumia Abu-Jamal has been picked as commencement speaker at Vermont's Goddard College. Now, if you never heard of this college, here's why. They suck balls.

Again—I can't believe I said that. I wonder if the transcription is inaccurate. If I actually said "They suck balls," I think I would have been sent home for the week, and as punishment forced to watch nothing but *The View*.

Sacrificing morality before the altar of cool, using dialogue to mock the dead, they claim that their graduating students had decided that they wanted Mumia to be their commencement speaker, and it's the policy as a college "that advocates for complicated dialogue around complex issues."

> So based on that: Would they invite, say, Newt Gingrich to speak? Or even President Trump? No? Not "complicated" or "complex" enough? What academic BS.

Here's a quote from some dude on Megyn Kelly's show:

The graduating students believe that Mumia has a message coming from prison, from a unique perspective, and speaks to issues that are important to them, that are important in a world where we have Ferguson . . . where we have police brutality, where these issues are real and in their lives.

> The old show from her FNC days.

I think the technical term for that is "hooey." So you call a cop killer's words "a unique perspective"? You just became a heinous cheerleader for a criminal whose victims still walk the earth. Like Maureen Faulkner, the widow of the officer Mumia had killed in 1981.

> Yeah, he does have a lesson. Don't shoot cops if you don't want to die in jail.

Here she is, on Megyn's show.

FAULKNER: My husband was in a community college. He was getting ready to graduate with his bachelor's degree when Mumia put a bullet into his back and then between his eyes. But does anybody talk about that? No.

Now I get why it's cool to invite this loser, this murderer, to speak. Radicalism is what many of today's college students have instead of actual achievement. But would they have cast their vote in front of Maureen? Of course not; they're cowards who likely don't know real suffering, because if they did, they wouldn't do this.

Meanwhile, Yale is welcoming an Islamist cleric, who's preached death against us—weeks after students there protested the invitation to Ayaan Hirsi Ali, a victim of that ideology's gruesome mutilations.

So campuses embrace bombers like Bill Ayers, cop killers like Mumia, and misogynist creatures of death, and they charge parents thousands for this privilege. Only in America: where you can earn a degree in hate and still call it tolerance.

> That earns a "nice line" award from the Nice Line Award Association.

Forget quarantining Ebola: Quarantine Yale and Goddard. That kind of thinking is deadlier than any disease.

> **Why parents continue to shell out big bucks to send their kids to these hate factories is beyond even an evil genius like me. I think, maybe in ten years, we won't even be talking much about colleges anymore. Colleges will become like magazines. Cute to have around, and pass the time until something more interesting comes along.**

February 17, 2015

A student at Brown University wants the ROTC banned, calling it state-sanctioned violence and its cadets, criminals.

Last week Brown partnered with the navy and air force ROTC, prompting junior Peter Makhlouf—or Maklauf, who cares—to vomit this in his school paper, quote, "By outlawing our ROTC, we have the opportunity to maintain a tradition of refusing to capitulate to the increasing demands of military engagement in today's global agenda."

What a joke. And what language. That lockstep cultspeak that marks an all-brain-free rhetoric that's often passed on like a pox from its petulant professors. He could be a White House spokesperson.

Now, this is just one brat, but it would be fun to see such kids experience life without an American military. No cozy dorms, no iPods, just them and ISIS. The only selfie stick would be their own head on a stake.

> I can't remember who I was knocking with that joke.

But this little hack represents the vapid ideology that lets evil grow. It's an anti-West movement that gives tenure to terrorists, while condemning those who protect them.

Dismiss it if you must, but given that campus-approved progressivism offers a zip-line from school to statecraft, it's just a leap from the paper to the presidency. Seriously, how else did we end up with so many lightweights in the White House? Lightweights who stand between us and the heathens. This kid, after all, is just a chip off the old Barack.

> There I go again, hitting Obama. Although, it's not entirely unjustified. Obama is a progressive, and part of being a progressive is the belief that America is an oppressive monolith, and the military helps maintain its oppressiveness. Still, that last line was only there for pun purposes. Although it's true—he was surrounded by lightweights, who, when compared to Obama, seemed a little heavier. I mean—how was Ben Rhodes dictating policy? He should be running a Foot Locker. [Actually, that's an insult to Foot Locker.]

March 6, 2015

Questions were raised whether a Jewish student should be allowed to join a student council at UCLA. She was temporarily blocked by students who felt her Jewishness would cloud her judgment. Take a close listen, close listen takers.

UNIDENTIFIED FEMALE SPEAKER: Given that you are a Jewish student and very active in the Jewish community, how do you see yourself being able to maintain an unbiased view as your position?

Yes. That actually happened. In 2015 on a campus in America, a Jewish student being told her Jewishness is a conflict of interest as if she was in the Klan or something.

So here's a game. Let's replace "Jewish" with "gay" and repeat the bigotry. Quote, "Given that you are a gay student and very active in the gay community, how do you see yourself being able to maintain an unbiased view?" You can only imagine saying that, because you'd never say that. If you did, you'd be expelled. Not from school, but from the galaxy. You'd have to relocate to Andromeda under an assumed name and face.

> This "imagine if you said this about X" argument is repetitive, but only because it's a fair point. Imagine saying what Chelsea Handler says about Republican women, but about liberal women. Imagine saying what celebs can say about Trump, but say it about Obama. Imagine saying what you can say about rats but say it about hamsters! Yes, it's getting tiresome, but that's what you get when your beloved author overdelivers!

Suddenly, the diversity that lockstep leftists once loved is now loathed, an example of how they reject dogma when it conflicts with their own bigotry. Different backgrounds before meant new perspectives. But Jewish, your background, that equals bias.

You can blame the rise of anti-Israel fervor on activist groups, professors, and outside agitators. The same people who show up at anticop rallies, as well. And they use that issue to excuse plain-as-day prejudice, which is really an expression of these bigots' own failures. To put it bluntly, they blame the Jews for not falling for the same PC crap they did.

> An update to this story: The four members who voted against her actually apologized. But—this is the best part—they did so after a faculty adviser had to point out that it's okay to be in a Jewish organization! I think they apologized because they were caught. But what do I know? Spoiler alert: a lot!!
>
> Meanwhile [or rather, right now], some prominent Democrats are finally having to answer for their lovefest with notorious anti-Semite Louis Farrakhan. I kid, they're actually not having to answer for a damn thing. Unlike David Duke [his white racist counterpart], the media doesn't mind Lou's bigotry. Kudos to Jake Tapper for dogging everyone on this story. Here's my observation: Ask any liberal about Farrakhan, and he'll say, "He's a marginal figure; no one takes him seriously." Ask the same liberal about David Duke or Richard Spencer, and he'll say, "Oh, he's representative of the sizable racist wing of the Republican Party!" Why do they do that? Because they're trying to cover their asses, and protect their own.

March 25, 2015

Last week the *New York Times* examined safe spaces at colleges, which are secluded spots made for students to keep their feelings from being hurt by different viewpoints. In these comfort bubbles, people refrain from making jokes for fear of bruising someone's delicate sensibilities. This is not shocking. As the modern era shows, if a fact hurts your feelings, the feelings win.

In fact, safe spaces are designed to turn emotions into medical conditions.

> That's the clearest diagnosis: We've turned emotions into medical conditions! And that, in turn, is now a medical condition. I call it "Gutfeld syndrome," since I invented it. I want something named after me, so it might as well be an illness.

If you can claim that an idea scars your well-being, fearful administrators will suppress the point of view. Ultimately, that leads to speakers' being disinvited and apologies made about everything.

It's crazy this is happening on campus, where the free flow of ideas is the whole idea. But that's changed. As the lunatics run the asylum, all the walls must now be padded. Free speech begone, words are weapons that hurt like hurled rocks. It's the new strategy to suppress competing ideas. And it's working.

But as we criticize, we must police this stuff among ourselves. A demand for lockstep exists in all places where discomfort from dissent is recast as offense. After all, the only way to strengthen an argument is to make it vulnerable to criticism. It's called learning.

Demanding consensus is coward's work. And if you can't take the heat or a joke, get out of the kitchen and go back to college.

This was my reason for criticizing Candidate Trump regularly throughout the presidential campaign, rather than excusing his actions like others did [which I called "Trump-splainin'"]. I kept referring to the "guardrails of criticism," as my method of steering someone in the right direction. The candidate never listened to me—and he won, so maybe that was a good thing.

I hope decades from now we will look back at safe spaces and be deeply embarrassed. But chances are that decades from now we will all be enslaved by robots, so the point is moot. The upside: Since I've been very supportive of robots, they will let me live comfortably while the rest of you beg for food.

May 19, 2015

Commencement addresses are usually garbage.

They're for colleges seeking publicity. So you end up with star-hawking platitudes to an audience suckled on baby formula called *The Daily Show*. I was once asked to do one for a high school in Jersey, but I turned it down because they wouldn't pay my cab fare.

> Wow—great line, Greg. Talk about mailing it in.

So here is my advice for free.

> Crappy joke.

- Take any job, any job you can find. Work your butt off for one solid decade. That will put you ten years up on any pothead backpacking to Europe and video-game-playing drones who think success drops from the sky like a magical Kardashian.
- Modern culture has created a warped view of achievement. Not everyone gets a reality show—so instead, be a workhorse

and by 2025, you'll surpass the famous people you see now. Hard work beats those who prefer identity over industry.

- Also, ask dumb questions and listen quietly for the answers. That's a wisdom stair climber.
- Steer clear of pot. It's an ambition zapper. Wait till you've made it. When you're forty-five, buy a bong. But for now, buy a suit.
- Move somewhere with decent public transit so you don't drive drunk and hit somebody.
- Scalpel your online footprint to a fly's toe. Twitter is the contrail of life. When I'm hiring I don't need to see your naked butt. And I'm pretty open to new things. Real experience beats web activity. Everything is being filmed. So any public rant you do to a clerk at a shoe store, that scars you eternally.

> **I also think at some point we need to invent a forgiveness clause, or "online amnesty," where for one day we can go back and erase everything we've ever done on social media that's potentially embarrassing. Anyway, it's a dream.**

Which leads me to my last point: If you're the person doing the hiring, forgive a scar or two. Remember that when we were young, we were also idiots. There were just no cameras there to catch it.

> **The advice about public transit might be most important of all. You simply do not want to drive regularly when you're young. Because you're young—and you'll be drinking or drugging a fair amount. One arrest will screw you, and if you end up hurting someone, it's far worse for you [and for your victim, obviously]. But this point may be irrelevant,**

once self-driving cars take over, and we can all be drunk 100 percent of the time.

I followed the first point right out of college, taking a job in Virginia, moving from California. And I did it again a year later when I moved to Allentown, Pennsylvania, the same year that *USA Today* voted it the worst city in the country [1990]. It was freezing cold the day I showed up in this gray, hardscrabble town, taking what few belongings I had from my mom's home in sunny San Mateo and moving into a small apartment around the corner from a cemetery on Eleventh and Chew. It's a decision I don't regret, but I can't fathom that I lived there for a decade. The point: I took a job in one of the least appealing cities at the time and made it work for me, until the city practically had to kick me out. I mean, I spent ten years in Allentown, by choice. It's more charming than you think, Billy Joel notwithstanding [or sitting].

September 8, 2015

As students return to school this week, it pays to know what they'll be returning to learn.

According to the *New York Post*, a freshman English class called "The Literature of 9/11" includes the perspective of the Islamic terrorists, portraying them as freedom fighters driven by U.S. imperialism.

> I'm glad I'm too old for school.

One of the colleges, UNC, says it isn't advocating one viewpoint over another. But most students know that to get an A in any class these days, you just recite these four words: "It's all our fault."

Fact is, most curriculum thrives under a phony guise of open-mindedness, a farce, for we often see people with competing points of view denied the chance to speak on campus. College is the only place where intellectual opposition means a duel with a grading pen, wielded by a guy with tenure and a ponytail.

> Ugh—another "ponytail" line. But maybe all these jerks really do have ponytails! Nevertheless, I'm punching myself in the butt.

How do you counter this take on terror? You could ask these questions: By giving victim status to terrorists who are either poor or uneducated, aren't you saying that their victims had it coming? If ISIS were to blow up this class right now, would you say we deserved it? And if it happens, is the final canceled?

> I am intrigued by stories about students who call in bomb threats to cancel midterms and so on. Because, be honest— haven't you once been tempted to do the same? Ever? Come on!! I'm not saying it's right—no, it's wrong . . . but it's one of those thoughts you've entertained, no?

Professors blame violence on previous violence, but terror as a consequence of our actions inevitably turns into a game of what causes what first, a game you can play all the way back to the Big Bang.

So if you're a parent paying a small fortune for Junior's schooling, take a peek at the syllabus, if only to prepare you for the horrible opinions come Thanksgiving dinner.

You can say that this type of class will welcome diverse points of view, but I remember in college, in order to get a decent grade, I had to mimic left-wing deconstructive analysis regurgitated by my professors. Every thesis was supposed to reveal some postmodern take on whatever novel we were discussing that semester. Example: I remember that my freshman year we were studying Stephen King's *Firestarter*. Yes, that was in my college curriculum at Berkeley in 1983! And the theme conveyed by the teacher was that pyromania represented a legitimate response to patriarchal society. I remember the instructor writing on the chalkboard these two words: "phallic death." Which I then stole as the name for my short-lived death metal band. We only recorded a handful of songs in a garage in Richmond, California. We drank canned mixed drinks purchased at a 7-Eleven and my role was strictly as the lead screamer. If we had kept at it, instead of becoming lawyers, engineers, and talk show hosts, we would have been bigger than Metallica. Or at least Poison. Or perhaps Right Said Fred.

October 8, 2015

A Minnesota school is spending thirty grand on recess consultants to improve the politics of the playground, making that break more inclusive by replacing terms like "you're out" with "good job."

Okay—I know—this isn't about "college," it's about grade school. But at this point, what is the difference? And besides, I really like this monologue, so put that in your bong and spill it all over your rug.

Now I'd applaud this, but I fear my clapping might kill harmless bacteria.

But recess is indeed a war zone cloaked in cruelty. We know tag is wrong. Calling a child "it" can only lead to future mental trauma. And freeze tag, well, that mocks paralysis. Tetherball, a brutal sport where one beats a shackled ball, implies you can pummel the defenseless, the trapped ball being the symbol of every victim of American oppression.

- Dodgeball is simply training for life as a callous sniper. And Hide-and-Seek teaches kids the thrill of life on the lam, perhaps as serial killers.
- Blind Man's Bluff? What's next, "deaf guy's charades"? "Let's kick the iron lung"? Please.
- Hopscotch, that mocks those with a limp.
- London Bridge glorifies destruction of monuments.
- Leapfrog makes light of reptile abuse.
- Kick the Can encourages violence against recyclables.
- Keep Away mocks the repellent.
- Patty-Cake encourages obesity.
- Rock, Paper, Scissors inserts competition into hand gestures.
- Mother May I glorifies subservience and is heteronormative.
- And Simon Says reinforces our patriarchal culture.

In short, recess is offensive, because everything is offensive. And as I am a self-appointed recess consultant, you owe me thirty grand.

> **About this particular line: "Now I'd applaud this, but I fear my clapping might kill harmless bacteria."** One of my first articles ever published was in the *Sunday Punch* section of the *San Francisco Chronicle* [back in 1989], and it was about a fictitious concert for bacteria rights. In that satire I de-

scribe how the audience is told not to applaud the entertainment, because it would kill innocent microbes. I wrote that when I was twenty-four. I was living at my mom's house. It was a year between jobs. It was a really weird, tough time. I was broke, and scared. My poor mother. I miss her so much. Fortunately, Peter Sussman, the editor of that section of the paper, took a chance on me and published my writing. Those pieces ended up helping me get a job at Rodale Press, where I ended up working for a decade, culminating as editor in chief of their most successful product, *Men's Health*. Sussman discovered me, and for that I owe him a lot. Side note: One time I sent a batch of my *Chronicle* pieces to two different places: *Forbes FYI* and the *Wall Street Journal*. The editor of *Forbes*, Christopher Buckley [son of the great, late WFB], promptly sent me a handwritten note telling me how much he loved them. It gave me a contact high that lasted weeks. But when I called the *WSJ* to see if the receiver of my work had read them, the person abruptly said yes, and then hung up the phone. I will not say who that person is. So in sum: Christopher Buckley is a generous, sweet person, and the person I shall not name is a miserable creep. You'd know him by name, so ask me when you see me in person during the book tour! That shall be your incentive.

March 29, 2016

Imagine a place that poisons your teens' emotional well-being, targeting their vulnerabilities, laying waste to their spine, inculcating weakness, replacing reason with hysteria. Once designed for enrichment, it's now an ego asylum, where character is reduced to a bubbling stew of anguish.

Guess you didn't see that coming, did you?

That is college.

At Emory University, pro-Trump messages written on sidewalks in chalk have scarred coeds badly. Student organizations are offering counseling—poor things. The school president sent his sympathies.

Now the scribbles could have been solved easily by erasing them. It is chalk, after all. But that's something an adult would do. These are emotional toddlers. Forget about a wall on the southern border—build it around Emory.

This is the new life on campus. One must balance free speech with feeling safe. College must be a haven, safe from words.

But college is supposed to challenge, not cuddle. Doing the reverse just leads to fake incidents of hate that provide spotlights to these attention gobblers.

> **Attention gobblers—I feel like we've all become that kind of creature—more enamored of what others give us than of what we might give back. And maybe that's the name of my next book!**

Now, while this was happening, the U.S. military was evacuating families of defense personnel from southern Turkey due to security fears.

Maybe the Emory students can trade places and find out what a real unsafe space is all about.

> **By the way, colleges have always had safe spaces—they were clubs, teams, and fraternities. Safe spaces were simply where your friends were. It's sad that we've lost the sense of community and replaced it with identity. No wonder so many young people feel lost. I'd try to counsel them, but the authorities still say I'm not allowed within five hundred yards of any campus.**

August 30, 2016

There's so much evil in this world: war, famine, the Red Hot Chili Peppers, and now team mascots.

> Yes, I hate the RHCP. If you're a dedicated fan of Faith No More—which I am—then you have to hate the Chili Peppers. For FNM is what the RHCP tried to be, but lacked the brains, wit, and chops for it. You can't be a fan of both bands. If you are, that's like being a fan of both getting hit in the face and not getting hit in the face. I prefer FNM, which is "not getting hit in the face."

Apparently one such beast doesn't express enough emotional diversity and must be changed. I speak of Herky the Hawk, from the University of Iowa, whose static grimace has upset one professor enough for her to write to school officials claiming Herky's smirky traumatizes students.

Professor Resmiye Oral believes new students need happy faces, not angry, violence-inciting ones. She writes, "I plead with you to allow Herky to be like one of us, sometimes sad, sometimes happy, sometimes angry."

She's right. Look at that face. It's not inviting, I wouldn't want to eat that at Chick-fil-A. It seems like an Angry Bird. We should ban those, too. Imagine what that's doing to your children.

Fact is, these days everything is offensive, from common words to costume birds. It's why we need trigger warnings and safe spaces to protect us from these microaggressions. The world is so scary, it seems the best thing you can do these days is not be born! So is it possible that a student might actually think Herky is a real actual monstrous hawk with a grudge and not just a class-mate in a costume?

It's possible. All this psychological coddling is turning kids into fearful worms. Worms.

Maybe they should be scared of birds!

> The fight over team mascots reveals a large truth about this country: We have so few problems that we need to make up some, just to pass the time. If our country had real calamities—existential terror threats, bloody gang violence, another movie by Woody Allen—we wouldn't be spending so much of our time talking about team mascots. Wait, we do have all those looming problems. We're doomed!

September 7, 2016

So if you think time travel is impossible, then you haven't made it to Cal State L.A., where they're now segregating students based on skin color. Amazing.

According to CSLA, the school's under fire for offering sepa-rate housing for black students in response to claims of racism. Apparently, this new housing was triggered by insensitive re-marks and microaggressions made by professors and students. So get this: The solution to racism is segregation. You know who would agree with that? Racists.

Somehow, I don't think this is the unity that we all had in mind.

So as inclusion is now seen as some kind of appeasement, the left views separatism as the answer to their grievance. The natu-ral result of identity politics, where conflict resolution is replaced by polarization.

After America's grand experiment of inclusion, we now return to tribal splintering, retreating to the instinct of surrounding like with like. It indulges the worst urges. It's based on the toxic assumption that empathy cannot exist between different pigments, genders, and orientations.

> The word on everyone's lips is "tribalism." Mainly because the web allows us to separate faster and cleaner. If I want to, I can easily find someone or a group of someones who will validate me, without ever running into an opposing voice. I mean, for so long I thought I was the only fifty-three-year-old man into totally shaved unicorns. Thanks to the internet, I realized there are eleven of us!!

So where do we go from here? As the country splits into factions, be it through separatist movements or infamy, through divisive symbolism or reparations that reward anger over achievement, it only leads in one direction. Down and then apart.

> This begs for some kind of update.
>
> From what I gather ("gather" is the word I use for "googling in my boxers") this trend of separate living quarters is not only not new, but pretty common. I found a handful of examples in five minutes. Some even have a name for it, calling them "ethnic-themed dorms." (I didn't know dorms had themes!)
>
> But here's the point: Separatism is going to end up being the ultimate ugly endpoint for identity politics, driven by the belief that different people simply cannot empathize with each other, and therefore must be kept apart. Identity politics is evil, for it diminishes the individual in favor of the group, turning communities into warring factions.

Another thought comes to mind: Identity politics always demands virtue signaling on the part of everyone involved. [A reminder of what virtue signaling is: It's the cloying, obvious expression of moral obedience intended only to improve your standing within a specific group, as well as protecting you from becoming a target of that group, by becoming an "ally."] But what you realize is that the more signaling you do, the more signaling you HAVE to do. Because if everyone is expressing the same moral value, then the baseline is always going to be zero. And you have to race quickly up the signaling ladder to appear superior, in that regard, by signaling even more. The end result could be something far worse than separatism.

February 16, 2017

While campus activists and so-called protesters shut down free speech with threats of violence, at least we know there is some justice in the world. Caleb O'Neill, a student at Orange Coast College, has just been suspended. Was it for torching a dorm, or the beating of a motorist? No, he filmed a video of a professor comparing Donald Trump's election to terrorism.

> Here is the audio from the video.

UNIDENTIFIED FEMALE: We have been assaulted. It's an act of terrorism. One of the most frightening things for me and most people in my life is that the people committing the assault are among us. It is not some stranger from some other country coming in and attacking our sense of what it means to be an American and the things that we stand for. And that makes it more painful. Our nation is divided as clearly as it was in Civil War times, and my hope is that we will get some good leadership to help us to overcome that.

For recording that, the student has been removed for one semester. He's forced to write an apology, as well as an essay that explains his actions. Now, that's what I call re-education. He's being punished for precisely what college used to teach you: independent thought.

> So it's as divided as it was in Civil War times! Clearly, this wasn't a history professor.

No word yet on whether the teacher will also write an essay on why she's still allowed to teach.

Anyway, Caleb held the teacher accountable, and for that, he's being held accountable! It's another one of those examples in liberal culture where you're only a whistle-blower if you're blowing the whistle on things liberals hate.

I'm sure if the professor was making fun of fifty-odd gender pronouns or raised skeptical questions about climate change, the student would be exalted. Instead, for shining a light on an infantile example of academic intolerance, he's given the boot, temporarily.

So remember Caleb's name, and when he graduates, hire him.

One of the great by-products of the cellphone is that we can now document idiocy, which for the longest time proceeded without documentation. If more students did what Caleb did, there might be some hope for academia. Although, I wonder if anyone in this bizarre world actually sees such documentation as an embarrassment.

I also realize that this kind of technology could go both ways. God knows I was a jackass when I was younger, and I consider myself lucky no portable technology was around to record it. Right? There is nothing out there? Hello?

March 6, 2017

Last Thursday at Middlebury College in Vermont, Charles Murray and Professor Alisyn Stanger were attacked by a violent mob of left-wing creeps out to stop Murray from a planned lecture.

Stanger was hospitalized with injuries. We contacted the college over their disciplinary response. They just got back to us two pages of nothing.

But without real action against those who use violence to silence speech, the next step has to be anarchy. And you think I'm kidding? Consider this one question. What is the intervening step between silence and violence? It's words. Without words, it's a simple leap from calm to calamity.

Before language, cavemen simply grunted and then they used their clubs. Communication changes that. It's the mechanism that created civilization and prevents its destruction.

> Yes, I've made this point before. But it's true: Remove debate, what do you have left? Violence. It makes me wonder how horrible it must have been for those first cavemen who tried to reason with their slower counterparts. That really is the missing link, in my opinion.

But now it's the left that wishes to go back. Do you ever see a right-wing kid violently jumping lefty speakers? On campus, you either have silent appeasement or a bruise.

It used to be that discourse was a college staple. You could hold a lively debate, and even when it got hot, it was respectful. But now how many speakers have been forced to cancel? Did you lose count? Was it due to bad weather? No, it was the threat of harm. It's either silence or it's violence. This has to be stopped before it becomes the norm.

Imposing a cost like expulsion on violence isn't suppressing speech. It's the very opposite. Someone higher up better find their spine soon, or they will be next—and suddenly their allies will be the very people that they mocked for years.

> Murray's big sin was writing about differences in IQ, among other things. You can argue with him about it, which seems a totally cool thing to do. But to suppress his views simply makes such views more intriguing. It's just like smoking. Tell a kid that he shouldn't smoke—the first instinct is to wonder "Why?" Then you go buy a pack of smokes. If you want to make something sexy, try to ban it. It's why I started eating Tide Pods once everyone was saying they were bad for you.

Right now some colleges cancel speakers based on the "we can't afford the security to protect the speaker" excuse. But once you agree to that, you've established the "heckler's veto" to stop all speech. Create the possibility of a threat, and all speech goes away.

> Now, look what recently happened to Sam Harris, who interviewed Murray for his podcast about his research into IQ. Just for *doing* the interview, Harris was smeared as a bigot by social justice mouthpieces. It's the new weapon—smear by association. It beats thinking for yourself.

April 11, 2017

Another day, another campus speaker shut down by jackasses.

> This is footage from an event at Claremont McKenna College, where conservative Heather Mac Donald was speaking.

UNIDENTIFIED MALE/FEMALE: Shut it down! Shut it down! Shut it down!

UNIDENTIFIED MALE/FEMALE: Black lives matter! Black lives matter! (BLEEP) the police from Oakland to Greece. (BLEEP) the police from Oakland to Greece.

Well, at least it rhymes. So parents, this is what fifty thousand dollars a year gets you—mindless intimidation by anti–free speech cowards. That was Thursday, when an ugly mob of seething snowflakes surrounded a building at Claremont McKenna College screaming and banging on windows, all to block a woman from speaking. She had to flee in a van under protection of security.

> Yep, I'm already tired of the "snowflake" thing. It was a useful word until, of course, everyone abused it. Now it's just a cliché echoed by right-wing blowhards [not including me, of course!].

> I met her once in a TV green room. Smart lady!

Heather Mac Donald's sin was writing a book called *The War On Cops*, which pushes for better community policing and familiarity of the police with the neighborhoods—a book I'm sure none of these petulant protesters actually read.

The tome is saturated with facts, which terrifies these campus cretins. I mean, why shout her down if her words are baseless? The fear of her facts speaks volumes, but the goal here isn't to challenge the speaker but to prevent any speaking at all. Debate is secondary to silence.

Activists called her antiblack, capitalist, imperialist, and fascist, all to camouflage their lack of depth and to shut her up. They also harassed students, and segregated the white protesters. I'd say the lunatics have taken over the asylum, but why insult lunatics? A piece of advice to these activists—and parents and teachers who support them—every action has an opposite one.

Imagine what kind of movement you would create by silencing speech, because without speech, the only solution obviously is violence. Maybe that's what you want. Maybe that's what you'll get.

I realize that my saying the reduction of dialogue leads to violence is now getting on your nerves, but it's only because the practice of speech oppression is spreading! I'd happily stop bringing it up, if campus activists would simply stop trying to silence ideas they find scary. But they won't, so, I shall continue to repeat myself until I'm as blue as a Smurf. I'm already the size of one, so it seems like the next natural step in my transformation.

Fact is, if the left silences speech, you're back at square one, where we settled everything with fists and clubs. Why would they want that? That's the real question. Just this week (end of April 2018), a rapper put out a public hit calling all Crips to punish Kanye West for speaking his mind. Who knew gangs and campus activists had so much in common?

November 29, 2017

It's not often I get to do a monologue where I don't get to say anything. Just quote. Here it is.

A Texas State University newspaper piece tells white students, "Your DNA is an abomination." Rudy Martinez, the writer, begins, "When I think of all the white people I've ever encountered, there is perhaps only a dozen I would consider decent."

Now, if you think that's mean, try the ending of the piece. Rudy writes, "Whiteness will be over, because we want it to be, and when it dies, there will be millions of cultural zombies aimlessly wandering across a vastly changed landscape. Ontologically speaking, white death will mean liberation for all. Until then, remember this: I hate you, because you shouldn't exist. You are both the dominant apparatus and the void in which all other cultures upon meeting you die."

> **Note: I had to look up "ontologically." I still don't understand what he means by it. But this is the essence of academia: Use words that sound impressive to hide the thin ideas that are behind them.**

I've got to say that is some amazing writing, as evil as it is.

According to the *Washington Examiner*, the writer of this piece, Martinez, was arrested in D.C. during Trump's inauguration and tried to crowdfund for legal fees. That's not surprising. That figures.

What's surprising is that in an era of safe spaces, where students get out of classes or ban speeches because of diverse opinions in words, a college paper in Texas can run this savage call to violence. And as Hollywood creates movies and TV shows that push the myth that America is a sexist, racist tyranny, a college paper would happily run a piece that essentially calls for genocide. But I guess if the color's white, mass murder is okay.

> **Weird thing:** The original ending to this was "But I guess if the color's white, then mass murder is right." But at the last minute I said "okay" instead of "right." Maybe I felt that the rhyme was so obvious I had to change it. This happens when I tend to overthink things, and ruin them. Sometimes the decisions I make confound even myself!

December 14, 2017

To help fight the stress of upcoming finals, colleges are using therapy llamas. The University of South Florida and Radford University are trucking in llamas and other beasts to help students cope.

So this is great for the students, poor things. But what about the llamas that have to absorb the noxious, annoying angst of fragile idlers as they moan about their insulated existence and perhaps the easiest phase of their comfy lives?

Yes, some studies show that pets lower stress, but what about the stress of the pet? Talk about torture. Imagine being a llama, and you're bused miles from the comforts of a pleasant petting zoo only to have some whiny bozos with issues running their bony, stinky fingers through your gorgeous fur.

> **Don't llamas spit?** I seem to remember being spit at by a llama at a petting zoo. But maybe that was my sister Les, in an especially furry hat.

Imagine a poor bunny—yes, they're using bunnies, too—forced to sit on the lap of a gender studies major griping about how studying has really cut into her social justice puppetry theater. I'd put these critters on suicide watch, because if I were an alpaca, a guinea pig, or a slow loris, I'd hurl myself into traffic before becoming a stress sponge for these pampered slackers.

And where will this end anyway? When these precious pupils graduate, how will they handle the real world? Will llamas accompany them to a job interview? Yes, that will go over well. Well, unless it's this one.

> Ironically, these animals are now more prepared for life, after enduring the stress of these students, than these students will ever be!

> This is where I show a photo of a shirtless Lorenzo Lamas.

My stress levels have already plummeted. Thanks, Lorenzo.

Where Are We Now?

As I write this, I'm obsessed with podcasts. It's like I'm going to college for the second time—trying to relearn stuff that I refused to learn the first time around when I was a legitimate undergrad and killing brain cells instead of cultivating them. I bring this up because I believe colleges are dying. Now, thanks to the internet, real knowledge is free and easily curated. Pick your deans, or your professors, and you can learn from the very best minds around the world, rather than endure places like Columbia University where fiends are indulged, and those who fight them are condemned.

With the internet, and primarily YouTube, you don't need to enroll in a Canadian college to listen to a lecture by the professor Jordan Peterson. Likewise, you don't have to fly to New York to hear Robert Wright speak, or Seattle, Washington, to track down Brett Weinstein. Curators like Joe Rogan, Dave Rubin,

Wright, Gad Saad, and Sam Harris are now fully functioning deans, finding the very best minds to educate us on the vital things in life. I know it doesn't get you a degree in anything, but at some point it will. And when it does, campuses will become nothing more than wastelands for skateboarders and old people yelling at skateboarders.

The other great thing about this new online YouTube education—it can provide intellectual sustenance in an empty world. As pop culture and media becomes more vapid, you can seek relief in the thoughtful depths of patient podcasters, cheerfully introducing you to topics as varied as any found at a university. You want to learn about stoicism? Check out Wright. You want info on psychedelics? Listen to Rogan. You want to watch a man's facial hair change over time? Watch Dave Rubin. The possibilities are endless.

And if you want to simply get better at interpreting the world through a rational lens, start off your day with Scott Adams's periscopes. They're like brain vitamins that go great with morning coffee and a shot of Bailey's.

Bottom line, you can denigrate this new world or mock the idea of an "intellectual dark web"—but in a world where attention spans are now on endangered species among anyone under thirty, podcasts might be one of the few and only lifelines available to pull people back into the universe of ideas.

CHAPTER SEVEN

THE SEXES

Leading up to the election, it seemed a foregone conclusion that 2016 would *have* to be about gender—about the ascendance of woman in the political sphere. After all, Hillary had been shoved aside for a different, more important historical first. But Hillary's nomination and subsequent loss pointed to an underlying, unspeakable truth about life: Your gender or skin color says little, in the long run, about who you are. That's the beauty of individuality: Yes, Hillary was indeed a woman, but on the whole, not the most appealing candidate. When Donald Trump—a man with a colorful history that would make any member of Guns N' Roses blush—beats you, that says something. Trump was reviled not just by the left, but by the right, middle, sideways, top, and bottom. And he still beat Hillary. The lesson: Depending on gender identity gets you only so far. You get to tick one box, true. But the average voter wants more. There are other boxes to consider, and Hillary was just too damn arrogant and entitled to even address them. Every question always returned to "But I'm a woman and he isn't!" And that was usually met with nods from TV anchors and polite applause from an audience fearing to be out of step. But before we get to that, let's talk about guns.

November 1, 2011

So, a South Carolina sheriff is urging women to get concealed weapons permits and carry a gun. Sheriff Chuck Wright said this after an arrest of a suspected rapist yesterday, telling women to pack a .45 because they wouldn't have to be accurate. Just close.

And it's true, guns do make a bigger hole than mace—and unlike rape whistles, they provide instant ventilation. Wright even suggested keeping the gun in a fanny pack, instantly making fanny packs cooler than they ever should be.

> A lot of my pistol-packing pals carry their gun in a front fanny pack. When I ask why, they show me. One famous musician friend explains: "If I am about to be mugged, they'll obviously demand my wallet. So I just say, 'Let me get it out of my fanny pack,' then I unzip the fanny pack and reach in. I never take the gun out. You don't have to— just fire through the fanny pack." I will never laugh at a fanny pack again.

Wright is right, though. Remember, women possess far less muscle mass than men. So, a gun provides the equalizer that Mother Nature forgot.

And common sense tells you if you give a rapist a choice of who to rape, an armed or an unarmed woman, who is he going to pick?

In my head a Smith & Wesson does more for empowering women than feminism ever could.

Think about it. Right now, not a single feminist group has piped up about the toxic atmosphere at the Occupy protests, where rapes and assaults go unreported, all for the greater good.

So, maybe the true feminist icon shouldn't be Gloria Steinem but Annie Oakley.

The fact is, keeping a piece is the only way to keep the peace. So, get one to match your shoes.

> That monologue might be the most often quoted one on Twitter—especially the line about Smith & Wesson doing more for empowerment than feminism. The reason is because its truth is undeniable. An unarmed feminist is powerless against a rapist, or a domestic abuser. An armed woman can blow holes in both [providing she goes to the range and becomes technically proficient]. Imagine if a group of people warned women against driving cars, because cars are dangerous, and are hard to control, especially for delicate lady hands. That's how liberals address women and guns. They're shocked by people like Dana Loesch and Katie Pavlich—tough girls who extol the virtues of firepower. It's sexism at its worst. If women can drive, why can't they pack heat?

May 11, 2012

Normally I hate days. Valentine's Day, St. Patrick's Day, Doris Day.

But Mother's Day is different, because moms serve the most important function on earth. No matter what men do—fight wars, build bridges, invent nachos—it pales to the one thing that keeps this planet percolating: giving birth.

> Terrible joke, now that I reread this. Ms. Day is probably a nice person.

Men are disposable. Women are vital. That's not opinion.

That's biology. By reproductive design, women are precious because they're carrying the cargo. Men just drop it off.

Yes, I know women have come a long way. They even drive in some states, Kimberly.

GUILFOYLE: Yes.

If all they do in life is be a great mom, that's awesome.

Now, feminists have mocked full-time motherhood as silly and old-fashioned. Maybe they're right. I mean, what do moms do really? Sure, you carry this thing inside you for nine months. And after you give birth, your body never really is the same.

And, of course, once you're a mom, all of your personal desires become secondary, as the survival of the child becomes your life's priority, which leads you to worry each day and every night whether the little one will turn out right.

How easy is that?

Maybe I hate Mother's Day.

If anything, it's an affront to all women who think full-time moms have never worked a day in their lives. Which reminds me of a good joke.

What do you call an angry feminist on Mother's Day? You don't.

That's a much better line than the first one—should have led with that, maybe. But let's ponder this line: "Yes, I know women have come a long way. They even drive in some states, Kimberly."

I wonder if I could make that kind of ironic joke on TV, now—given that we conflate ironic sarcasm with mean-spirited sincerity. Sadly most people these days couldn't take a joke if it was given to them intravenously.

May 15, 2012

So, Mother's Day took on many meanings last Sunday.

For *Newsweek*'s scribe Michelle Goldberg, it meant comparing Ann Romney to Adolf Hitler and Joseph Stalin. Roll tape, roll tapers!

MICHELLE GOLDBERG, *NEWSWEEK*: Yes, motherhood is beautiful. I found that phrase a crown of motherhood really kind of creepy, not just because of this, like, somewhat, you know— I mean, it's usually really authoritarian societies that give out like the cross for motherhood that give awards for big families. Stalin did it. Hitler did it.

Now, the hack received flak for that crap. But look, she really isn't calling Ann Romney Hitler. All she's doing is comparing Ann's beliefs with Hitler's. See the difference? Michelle learned that at Berkeley.

It's yet another toxic example of moral relativism—that our values are no better than Nazis'. But Goldberg should know. Hitler and Stalin were both leftists, just like her.

See what I did there? I pulled a Goldberg on a Goldberg! Which is why I love Anita Dunn, Obama's former communications director. At least she is open to the admiration for mass murderers. Remember this?

ANITA DUNN, FORMER WHITE HOUSE COMMUNICATIONS DIRECTOR: Mao Tse Tung and Mother Teresa, not often coupled with each other, but the two people that I turn to most.

Face the Nation, that is.

So, she gets a wow over Mao but not from Mitt, as she made her case on the "Face."

DUNN: Mitt Romney has a backward-looking attitude, particularly when it comes to women, that I think will come out.

So feminists laud a man whose great leap forward led to many million deaths, including women, but see Mitt as backward looking. I take Mitt's backward over Mao's forward any day.

So, the extremes of the women's movement now hang a ton of shame around the greatest power women have, which is motherhood. The result? Earth is now an inclusive club, and feminists are the bouncers with a message to the unborn who approach: Get a life.

I know this Romney stuff is old news, but it's pertinent—all the guff given the Romneys is—once again . . . that's how we got Trump. Fact: The media was ruthless against Romney in its effort to paint him as some clumsy, cold sexist. Remember the comments about binders full of women? He was talking about all the qualified female candidates he had for jobs, which information was kept in a binder. But the media knew that, and didn't care—and raked him over the sexist coals.

The targeted smears were so unwarranted that it could only lead to a pushback, in which finally the people also smeared by their connection to Romney had had enough. Electing Trump was a big "Screw you" to the people who trashed Romney. To translate, voting for Trump was this: "So you destroyed a decent, moral man [who let you get away with it], all for the sake of winning an election. Well, I guess we're done with men like Romney. Guys like that are just too nice to fight back. . . . So get ready for this new guy, because he's going to be your worst nightmare." In my opinion, the media's attack on Mitt Romney and his wife laid some groundwork for a groundswell of popular revolt against those who would try to smear anyone. So you could accuse Trump of sexism. It didn't matter. No one was listening. You—the media—repeatedly attacked decent men; so we're giving you the least decent man we know, and we hope to God he wins.

And let's not forget the double standard in which a media that vociferously defends women against misogynistic commentary seems to go silent when those attacks are targeting Republican or conservative women. It's pretty consistent and unforgiving: Even some liberal women in the media see no problem attacking the looks of Republican women, because their choices in life have rendered them appropriate targets. A recent example: The bitter gasbag Chelsea Handler, who mocked Sarah Huckabee Sanders's appearance, only because—well, politically she's not enough like Chelsea Handler. The good news: Sarah Huckabee Sanders is [so far] doing a great job; I'm not even sure Handler has one.

September 7, 2012

This is a Greg news alert. Liberal celebrities are chuckle buckets.

Boy, I must have been really tired or hungover, beginning a mono like that. Sigh. And yes I hate it when people write "sigh" in a book. It's like when people write "groan" or "um."

EVA LONGORIA, ACTRESS: Mitt Romney would raise taxes on middle-class families to cut his own and mine. And that's not who we are as a nation. Let me tell you why, because the Eva Longoria who worked at Wendy's flipping burgers, she needed a tax break. But the Eva Longoria who works on movie sets does not.

Yes, Eva Longoria wants you to sacrifice because she is doing the same, offering up an entire class of Americans who aren't as stinking rich as she is.

Remember, this not so *Desperate Housewife* makes millions mouthing other people's words, so it's easy for her to give away other people's money.

Sacrifice is easy when whatever the government takes still leaves you with enough cash to buy a small island. There is no difference, lifestyle-wise, between $50 million and $25 million. Even Kimberly Guilfoyle can't spend all that on shoes.

GUILFOYLE: Yes, I can.

> Yes, she can. That's why she doesn't realize some of them are missing.

But in Eva's head, a small family business is just like her. What a fake. I'd call her an actress, but that's too mean. She is just a cool kid sacrificing the uncool because they didn't get rich playing make-believe.

Then there is Kerry Washington.

KERRY WASHINGTON, ACTRESS: Today, there are people out there trying to take away rights that our mothers, our grandmothers, and our great-grandmothers fought for, rights that we fought for, our right to vote, our right to choose, our right to affordable quality education, equal pay, access to health care, and we, the people, cannot let that happen.

So, she thinks someone is taking away her right to vote?

Wait . . . maybe . . . she is in character for a role as a crusader for abused women in Afghanistan?

Where do these people live? What America do they inhabit? In the coked-up hell called Hollywood, Kansas becomes Kabul.

Finally, Scarlett Johansson claims her friends need Planned Parenthood. Wow, some friend you are. You're worth millions. Why don't you help them instead of asking me!

Look, no one is trying to take away their pills either, Scarlett.

Frankly, I don't want Hollywood to reproduce, but I'm not going to pay for that option.

Don't you see the difference, Scar Jo? Don't you get it?

If you'd like to discuss it further, I'm free for dinner. And I'll pay. I know how helpless women can be.

> Poor women. These are the standard-bearers?

No matter who the Republican is vying for the presidency, that person will be painted as evil. So even though you might think Hollywood thinks Donald Trump is the very worst creature to ever exist, they also felt that way about Mitt Romney [an obviously meek and decent man compared to Trump], and they also demonized George W before that. So, if you think that a President Rubio or a President Christie, etc., would be treated differently than the eternally triggering Trump, you're sorely mistaken. Or just mistaken. I don't know why it has to be "sorely."

Plus, by invoking such silly loaded phrases as "our right to vote" and "our access to health care," they only reveal the level of their historic ignorance. Does anyone—even in Hollywood—believe that Romney was looking to take away anyone's voting rights? Talk like that only trivializes the original battles over voting. Eva, Kerry, Scarlett, let me break it to you: You're no Jane Addams. You're not even

Gomez Addams. You're childish, overpaid, vapid creatures who would contribute more by flipping burgers. Or, at least, by not moralizing to the rest of us.

Also, why do feminists demand an intrusive, patriarchal government that provides for your birth control, but refuse that kind of relationship with individual males? They just replace one kind of dependence with another. I'd rather have a partner I could rely on than some giant bureaucracy—but what do I know. I eat Oreos in the bathtub.

January 7, 2013

Singer Marianne Faithfull just turned sixty-six. She's now alone, performing for little money. The *Daily Mail* contrasted this with her ex, the über-rich Mick Jagger.

When the media talks about rock and roll, they hailed the heroic longevity of Jagger, while forgetting those sucked into the lifestyle who cannot endure the hard living.

It's why the allure of the cool often harms women more than men. The cool life translates into pleasure without principle, which undermines female strength and power.

Dianne Feinstein said women wisely avoid strife through cooperation. Why is that? Well, as a pro-science guy, I know evolutionary science dictates that our behavior ensures survival, for reproductive immortality. That's why men fight wars. Men are expendable, women aren't.

But in China and India, it's reversed; their women are disposable. Time.com reports that the Indian census has 914 females for every 1,000 males. And China possesses as many unmarried young men as the whole population of American men.

These unbalanced sex ratios are linked to female abduction

and rape. If you look at the statistics, as the dearth of women deepens, crimes against women increase.

You don't hear much from feminists on that stuff. How come? Is it because being pro-choice isn't always pro-women? (In China, the one-child policy meant that child would be a boy.) Anyway, time is only on Mick Jagger's side because he has the bank account to pay for it. His playthings weren't so lucky.

It's something I think about a lot. What happened to all the women who partied with the rock stars, but don't have the rock star's deep pockets and connections to get them out of trouble when they're stoned, alone, and broke? Young women flock to these men and are used up like living pornography. And the media accepts it. It's the one area where the "unequal power structure" is ignored, as well as the often garish misogyny expressed in rock bands' memoirs. Musicians get a free pass for their abusive behavior, because they are "artists." Perhaps that is why they became artists in the first place. Take a minute and google the phrase "baby groupies," a phrase that described the VERY underage groupies who populated rock clubs in New York and Los Angeles in the late sixties and the seventies. Movies glamorized them, and rockers boasted about such conquests. But when you look back at it, these were teenage girls, some not even old enough to drive. One of them recently died of cancer, alone, in Nevada. We'll remember the famous names of everyone she pleasured; no one remembers her [including me—I can't remember her name].

January 24, 2013

The Pentagon is lifting its ban on women in combat. Hooray. I guess. If curbing combat roles had curbed your ability to move up the military ladder, then this shatters this camouflage glass ceiling.

So, it's a step toward total equality, but also elevated risk for a woman in combat, as her risk of death becomes the same as that of the man beside her or possibly higher. God bless her, that woman is a better man than I am.

> Clearly a joke, but does it pass muster, now? In these sensitive times?

If she wants to fight, far be it from me to say no. Chances are, she could take me. And chances are, I would enjoy it.

The only thing I ever served was a volleyball. But Senator McCain notes that women must still meet the same physical standards as men. You can't become a SEAL unless you can do what a SEAL does.

But if you lower standards, putting equality before victory, that's pointless and deadly. A win for equality must not come at the expense of the brutal, vicious killing machine that is the awesome American military.

> Do not forget it's about killing better than everyone else.

And we mustn't also deny the bigger truth, that the one thing most important to mankind is not taking a life, but actually making one. Men fought the wars so women didn't have to. Women had the bigger job—giving birth—making men like me way more expendable. That's science. One man can populate a city, but you need tons of women to do the same. Even if a woman gave birth after nine months and immediately got pregnant again, she'd make maybe forty kids over a lifetime.

Men are Doritos and women are diamonds. Denying that just to avoid mockery at cocktail parties doesn't help the war effort, unless it's a war on common sense.

It's weird how science is now considered offensive! If you bring up the differences in sexual reproduction strategies between men and women, you'd better duck quickly afterward. It's kind of interesting how the party of the left is now the party of nonscience. They dismiss the many provable elements of biology—specifically sex differences—as proof of some patriarchal construct. Seriously, it's getting tough to be a progressive, as society becomes more and more science-based. Evolution underlines the obvious, factual sex differences, which then trigger modern feminists who maintain [without any science] that there cannot be any differences between men and women. It's why they're waging war on biologists, whose work exposes the postmodern feminists' own dishonest, anti-intellectual ideology.

That's why I always implore my conservative friends to become scholars on natural selection. It puts you on the right path to a greater understanding of our human origins, and forces the left to stew in their own hypocrisy, as they deny biological realities in favor of antiscience babble—otherwise known as gender studies.

As for the military, like it or not, it discriminates. Each volunteer is graded as cost-effective. Would it cost them more to take you than it would *benefit* the team? In war, such cold reasoning is the only math that matters. If the military were grading me as cost-effective, my fat, slow middle-age ass would fall firmly in the negative.

April 9, 2014

Being a Hollywood actress is pretty cool until you say something uncool. Take Kirsten Dunst, who upset some feminists, which is easy to do.

Oxygen angers them.

In *Harper's Bazaar U.K.*, she said, quote, "The feminine has been a little undervalued. We all have to get our own jobs and make our own money, but staying at home nurturing, being the mother, cooking, it's a valuable thing my mom created, and sometimes you need your knight in shining armor. I'm sorry. You need a man to be a man and a woman to be a woman."

That's disgusting!

A top feminist blog chauvinistically dismissed Dunst as, quote, "an actress and blonde who looks good in clothes," adding, "Kirsten Dunst is not paid to write gender theory. So it shouldn't surprise anyone that she's kind of dumb about it."

> Of course, they'd feel different if she had said "gender is fluid" or "death to patriarchy" instead.

See, to them, it's dumb not to see relationships through the prism of anger, that love is really about power and ideology, that forbids traditional old-fashioned gender roles. So why not marry yourself instead?

You never need to get out of sweatpants.

Gender theory isn't a theory so much as it is a therapy, replacing loneliness with rage. Their brainwashed conclusion: If you don't get gender theory, you are a dumb chick. But if you've ever met a gender theorist, you realize they only know gender theory, which is why when they graduate, all they can do is teach you the stuff, or get you a tall latte.

> This line says it all: "Kirsten Dunst is not paid to write gender theory." As if someone should or could actually be paid to write gender theory. Sorry, if you write gender theory, you should pay us for having to read it.

July 8, 2014

Women's bodies are under assault. Victimized under the guise of evil tradition. I speak not of honor killings or lashings for adultery, but of shaving armpits. Thank heaven for feminists.

According to campus reform, ASU gender studies professor Breanne Fahs is giving extra credit to female students who stop shaving their underarms and legs and then journal on it.

On today's campus, this replaces learning. If you wish to be clean-shaven, however, you don't get credit.

Is that discrimination? Sure, but it's not like anyone cares, which is my point.

> This is so sexist. If this applied to men, I would have gotten a 5.0!

Who exactly are you rebelling against, when you advocate armpit rights to a class of feminists? What risk are you taking? A real teacher might give extra credit for stuff that challenges their worldview. Have them volunteer at the border.

> Not sure what this means, but I'm anti–armpit hair. For BOTH genders. I hate my armpit hair. I just don't see the point of it. It's really the overgrown weeds on the front yard that is your upper body. I try to trim mine regularly, and I keep the hair for a large body pillow I'm making, which I hope to sell on eBay. The bidding starts at $27.50.

Campus outrage is big over little things, and tiny over the big things. Victim of female genital mutilation Ayaan Hirsi Ali got booted from speaking at Brandeis—and not a peep. Nigerian girls are kidnapped, same thing.

Oppression galore? They just snore.

Instead, the modern professor traffics in safe, lefty dreck to elevate status in places where their beliefs go unquestioned. "I am woman, hear me roar" is now "I am woman. Read my thesis on the patriarchal assault on my armpits."

Meanwhile, millions of women are dying to come here, fleeing from real, actual oppression. But I guess it's no fun bashing a culture, if it isn't Western.

> **Weak ending. But the message is clear: Campus feminists would rather tackle stupid, made-up concerns like hairless armpit privilege than actually speak out against the actual oppression against women worldwide. It boils down to one belief: If you can't blame it on us, then blame doesn't exist.**
>
> **Right now—it's February 2018 as I write this—there is this phony kerfuffle over the idea that Doritos was planning a new kind of chip snack, based on market research, that would appeal to women. It would make less noise when crunched. Twitterverse erupted. Feminists were offended that a company would try to target women's desires in the highly competitive snack-food marketplace. Now, while this is happening, Iranian women are being imprisoned for protesting against the forced wearing of hijabs. What a contrast: As real women are fighting for real rights and risking their lives, our self-involved feminists are losing their shit over chips. Can we please do a trade? We'll take twenty of your Iranian protesters, if you just take one of our chip-hating heroines!**

August 7, 2014

Dartmouth student Taylor Woolrich says she may leave school because she can't carry a gun on campus, despite having a crazed stalker. When Woolrich was sixteen, an obsessed middle-aged creep (not me) would follow her home from work. She filed a restraining order but he kept at it, promising to visit her at school and showing up at her front door. He's in jail. Found in his car, with a noose, knife, and gloves.

To be fair, maybe he was on a scavenger hunt.

Woolrich still lives in fear, which I get. But if I were her, I would still pack heat.

Now, I get the concern about arming coeds. I went to college once . . . I think.

But there are kids that same age who carry. It's called the military. They can handle it. Stalkers are called stalkers because they don't quit, which means their target has just one recourse: boom. But this antigun push is more about the sexist notion that girls shouldn't have guns. Guns are deadly objects, but so are cars. Perhaps only men should drive.

The fact is, guns do more for female empowerment than modern feminism, which prefers government as their protector, but legal ownership gives you real power, equalizing the battle between you and evil. The confidence from learning to shoot a pistol is far superior to any gender studies course, and a stalker is less likely to stalk if you can ventilate his groin, which is why a whirring bullet is the ideal rape whistle—and the real feminist icon should be Annie Oakley, not Sandra Fluke.

Hmm . . . I felt like I said this before! (Probably in this same chapter.) That's the great thing about TV—you can repeat yourself, because chances are they missed you the first time. Now, I know many, many women who own and fire guns. Only among coastal liberals is such behavior considered exotic or detrimental [unless it's their female bodyguard, which is now considered supercool]. Think about it: Leftists think pussy hats are edgy. I beg to differ: Try firing a Bersa Thunder 380.

March 13, 2015

Doing nice things for people is evil. More specifically, doing nice things for women, if you're a man, is evil. That's the conclusion from Judith Hall, a professor in being miserable, who claims men who hold doors open for women or smile at them practice a vile behavior called benevolent sexism.

To quote Princess Poo Pants, "Benevolent sexism is like a wolf in sheep's clothing that perpetuates support for gender inequality among women."

What a mindless mix of buzz words and clichés.

The implication is that if a woman appreciates such behavior, she's too dumb to see the harm, unlike Judy, who calls it "insidious." Yes, insidious. The most overused word in today's world. It's a way of saying something is bad, even if you can't see its badness. Its very invisibility makes it insidious.

Judy's work isn't insidious. It's old. It's boring. It's wrong. For it brands a central engine of civil society—good manners—as oppressive. This at a time when we really could use more niceness in society.

Take a look at what went on at McDonald's the other day in Brooklyn. A group of girls beat the crap out of another girl while men happily look on.

So maybe it's me, but vicious, violent girls freak me out more than a smiling male.

My point: We should be applauding an inclination for civil behavior, even if it strikes you as a symptom of benevolent sexism. At least no one is losing an eye. A brawl in Brooklyn among a group of teenage girls suggests to me that doing something nice for the opposite sex is the least of our

> problems. And fear now prevents us from passing judg-
> ment on the most objectionable behavior. Also, It's weird
> how we've become so judgmental online—condemning
> any and all opinion—but express no moral outrage when it
> happens in real life, in front of our faces!

But in a world that conjures up benevolent sexism, that brutality might be a victory. Because when girls start acting like boys,
and boys stand by and cheer, they call that progress.

> This monologue illustrates how feminists lie to them-
> selves. If you asked this professor who she would rather
> share a subway ride home with around midnight—a polite
> male who held a door open for her or a pile of unruly vio-
> lent girls—she'd pick the girls. Just to, you know, remain
> politically correct. Even if, later, it results in her belongings
> being split among the gang.

April 9, 2015

In a political piece on Hillary Clinton published this week, a concerned writer states that, quote, "Some Americans, mostly women,
don't think the former secretary of state, U.S. senator from New
York, and First Lady should be called by just her first name." Because some worry that it might reinforce gender stereotypes.

Yes. Some worry. That "some" was me and only me last week
on *O'Reilly*. Roll it, Sven.

ME ON *O'REILLY*: If you call her Hillary, that's sexist, because
that's a girl's name. They should no longer refer to her by her first

name. Maybe a gender-independent thing like maybe Professor Pantsuit, something that has no gender whatsoever.

As a loudmouth pointing out flaws in leftist logic, my tactic has always been to extend liberal beliefs to the absurd until the argument can only tip in my favor.

Those comments were about Hill's supporters, who label any criticism of her as sexist. If you call her secretive, that's sexist. If you call her entitled, that's sexist. I took it a step further.

And apparently, this D.C. reporter listened and found one person to agree with me, a twenty-three-year-old named Monica. She says, "I think it's pretty unjust. I think it shows the level of inequality, inequality that still exists in the workforce. And just in general in society."

Now, I agree, calling her Hillary is degrading and demeaning, and hasn't she had enough of that? (She's married to Bill Clinton.)

So, what's the solution? What do we call her? How about her maiden name, Ms. Rodham? That's great. But wait, Rodham . . . rod, ham; it's both sexist and anti-Muslim.

> A joke so bad, it's, well, bad. Anyway, here's the secret to my shtick, from above: "My tactic has always been to extend liberal beliefs to the absurd until the argument can only tip in my favor." Basically, that's what I've been doing for twenty years. Why give something up, if it keeps working? It is working, right? Hello? Feel free to talk into the book and say, "Yes, Greg, it is."

November 1, 2016

They are shouting "female" to hide the email. In a desperate defense of Hillary, some claim the email probe is an attack on women. Berkeley professor Robin Lakoff claims it's not about emails at all. It's about men not believing women should be engaging in high-level communication. Sorry, Robin, your tragic plea is about as "high-level" as a worm's burp. Meanwhile, President Obama—remember him? He is already forecasting more sexism, even if Hillary wins.

UNIDENTIFIED FEMALE: What do you think will be the female equivalent of "You weren't born in this country"?

OBAMA, PRESIDENT OF THE UNITED STATES: I think the equivalent will be she's tired, she's moody, she's being emotional. When men are ambitious, it's just taken for granted. Well, of course, they should be ambitious. When women are ambitious, why? That theme I think will continue throughout her presidency and it's contributed to this notion that somehow she is hiding something.

> Oddly, the dual criticisms of being "emotional" and "hiding something" are exactly what the Democrats and the media use on Trump!

Dude, Mr. President, she is hiding something. Apparently, Team Hillary knew Anthony Weiner was sexting a high-schooler way back in 2011. That's pretty big. And they did nothing. I mean, Hillary is just one step removed from Weiner. She should have told Huma, "It's either him or me," but she didn't. They covered for the twerp, which is why Weiner was able to continue, and go even younger, allegedly sexting a fifteen-year-old. The lesson here is that Hillary only looks out for one woman, herself. And isn't that a real example of sexism—that a teenage girl getting sexts from a creep is ignored because the creep has connections? Call it "birds of a feather." Hillary protected Bill by shaming his victims. Here, she and Huma ignored another female victim, both scenarios driven by self-preservation and power. It just goes to show you when Hillary is concerned, it's the women, never the men, who get screwed.

What a prelude to 2017. Imagine if Hillary had walked the walk and divorced Bill. Imagine if she had vocally encouraged Huma Abedin to do the same. How far ahead of the game would she have been? What if she had come out against Harvey Weinstein, rather than conveniently playing dumb about his repulsive behavior? Then she would have tapped into the #MeToo movement before it even began.

Perhaps that's the real reason Hillary lost: Her biggest claim to fame was also her biggest lie. She maintained that she was only about "the women." But in fact, she just didn't give a crap about them. She only cared about one woman, and it's the one she sees in the mirror every day.

And it's pretty amazing that the real person who beat Hillary was Anthony Weiner. It was his laptop that forced Comey's hand to make new, ugly truths public just days prior to the election. That's the book Comey should have written—*Screwed by Weiner: The Tale of 2016*.

Where Are We Now?

As I finish this chapter, we're currently in the middle of the #MeToo movement. Actually, I'm not sure we're in the middle of it. From what I remember after reading a math book, there is no such thing as a midpoint to infinity. (BTW: If I were in a prog-rock band, I would call my first album *Midpoint to Infinity*.)

Fact is, if something never ends, the midpoint itself becomes infinite. (No, I'm not high while writing this, although it would help to be high if you are reading this.) And I don't think the #MeToo movement will ever end.

The problem is that the court currently doing a lot of the judging isn't one of law, but one of public opinion. We are now becoming what I predicted—an "allegation nation." If you're accused on Twitter, or anywhere, for that matter, you have little recourse but to withdraw into the shadows and hope that the truth comes out (and the truth could be that you're guilty of being a pig, or a callous jerk, or something less).

What's encouraging, just days ago (May 29, 2018), we all saw Harvey Weinstein do the perv walk, in cuffs outside an NYC courthouse. There is something highly gratifying about a pig getting justice, even if it took decades to get there. And so: justice doesn't just bring punishment, it also brings clarity and structure to a world where there previously was none. That world was Hollywood, a place that looked the other way, until finally everyone was looking at them.

THIS IS THE END, MY FRIENDS

So, that was my first real anthology. How'd did it go? Did you stick it out all the way through? (That sounds gross.) Was it tiresome, repetitive, annoying? Because, after all, I am tiresome, repetitive, and annoying.

It's one thing I learned from editing this book—which is a collection of things I said on TV, every day. I learned that I am repetitive. I repeat things. Also, I tend to say the same things again and again, but formulated in different ways.

It makes sense to do so . . . on television. Fact is, most people don't watch the same show every day (well, many do, actually, and I love them for it). So when I repeat myself on Thursday—saying something that I said on that previous Monday—it still might be new for a million people who didn't watch the Monday show. So, on TV, that makes sense. But in a book—you can see the repeats. Maybe that's good. At least you know what matters to me (obviously, terror is a big thing, as are tribalism and unicorns), measured by the number of times I repeat myself on those topics. Sorry about that. But I am grateful that you bought this book, and you took the time to leaf through it and put up with my barely cogent meanderings. It means the world to me that you care what I think; it resonates with you. And I hope that whatever I put on the page is something you'd like to say, but lacked the page to put it on.

Thanks for reading—and see you later. If you can't find me, just look for the short guy in a sweater yelling in your living room.

ACKNOWLEDGMENTS

Like my robes, I'll keep it short.

As always, first, I want to thank myself. Without me, this book would not be possible.

Next: I want to thank the dead, for inspiration. Many of these monos were written with the help of two inspirations—my mom, and my buddy Andrew Breitbart. Both died in the last six years. I still miss them terribly. But they're on every page, or maybe every other page.

I'd like to thank Sean O'Rourke, who helped me gather and order these monologues, making it easier to sift through. Sean, I still owe you money.

I also want to thank all the awesome folks at Fox News for giving me the platform and the opportunity to express myself in eighty-second bursts on *The Five*. I realize that I am an odd egg, someone who doesn't seem to look or act like anyone else roaming the halls.

Thanks to my editor, Natasha Simons, an original *Red Eye* fan, which helps greatly. If you're not a fan of *Red Eye*, then you don't know me!

Also thanks to Jay Mandel, a great agent with tremendous insight.

I must thank my delightful staff on *The Five*. All good people who must tirelessly put up with a "diva" like me. Yes, they think I'm a diva. But that's okay. I'll take it. As for *The Greg Gutfeld Show*, same thing—thanks to Gabby, Gene, Luigi, Joannie, Nora,

Kat, Todd, Holly, and Tom. Thanks for putting together that unique hour of TV, on TV.

Also, I would be a total dick if I didn't thank the cast of *The Five*—Kimberly Guilfoyle, Juan Williams, Jesse Watters, and Dana Perino.

Thanks to buddy Paul Mauro for his comments on the scripts. Finally, thanks to my manager and pal, Aric Webb, for listening to my rants about artificial intelligence, robots, and lucid dreaming. Thanks for putting up with me at my most obnoxious moments.

And last but not least—my wife, Elena! As usual, she puts up with my obnoxious habits, but as a troubled genius, I only expect as much.